More Praise for *My Job, My Self*

"Al Gini offers us a thoughtful and provocativ
subject of work. He has a salubrious style, so it's
—Studs Terkel, winner of the 1985 Pulitzer Prize in general nonfiction and author of *Working: People Talk About What They Do All Day and How They Feel About What They Do*

"Speaking as someone who has never had regular work, I couldn't recommend *My Job, My Self* more highly. It almost made me want to go out and get a real job!"
—Aaron Freeman, columnist, comedian, and critic

"In a decade in which work, careers, workplaces, and the meaning of work have all been stood on their head, Gini's book becomes a reflective and provocative discussion on the changes at work."
—Bradley K. Googins, Boston College, author of *Work/Family Conflicts*

"There's no more hiding after reading *My Job, My Self*! I'm a workaholic just like Al Gini and the rest of us who answer the question 'How are you?' with a remark about our workload. It's time to start living—not working—my life."
—Julie Danis, columnist for the *Chicago Tribune* and commentator on PRI's *Marketplace Radio*

"The book is a delightful combination of philosophical reflection, sociological insight, and a wealth of judicious references to popular literature. The conversational tone of the book makes you feel that Gini is talking to you personally."
—Robert C. Solomon, Quincy Lee Centennial Professor, University of Texas

"In-depth, interesting, and very readable. Everyone works and everyone has got an opinion about it. Gini's opinions are insightful and comforting as well as humorous and wise."
—John MacDonald, author of *Global Quality* and *Calling a Halt to Mindless Change*

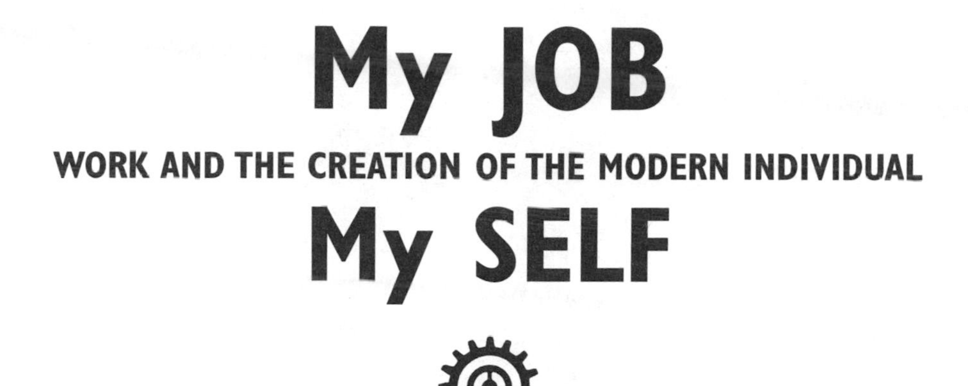

My JOB
WORK AND THE CREATION OF THE MODERN INDIVIDUAL
My SELF

Al Gini

ROUTLEDGE
New York and London

Published in 2001 by
Routledge
29 West 35th Street
New York, NY 10001

Published in Great Britain by
Routledge
11 New Fetter Lane
London EC4P 4EE

First Routledge hardback edition 2000
First Routledge paperback edition 2001

Routledge is an imprint of the Taylor & Francis group.

Printed in the United States of America on acid-free paper.

10 9 8 7 6 5 4 3 2 1

Library of Congress Cataloging-in-Publication Data

Gini, Al, 1944–
My job, my self: work and the creation of the modern individual / by Al Gini.
p. cm.
Includes bibliographical references and index.
ISBN 0-415-92635-1 (hardback) / 0-415-92636-X (paperback)
1. Job satisfaction—United States. 2. Work—United States. 3. Life Skills—United States.
I. Title
HF5549.5 J63 G55 2000
331'.01'20973—dc21 99-048225
CIP

To Allan Cox, Jim Zullo, John Dienhart, Norman Bowie, Robert Solomon, Mark Schneider, Cynthia Rudolph, and, especially, Sherry Sladek—fellow workers all!

Do your work. Do your work. This is how I
shall know you.

—Ralph Waldo Emerson

Don't confuse having a career with having a life.
They are not the same.

—Hillary Clinton

Contents

	Preface	ix
1	You Are What You Do	1
2	Work—What Is It?	13
3	Collar Color Doesn't Count	31
4	Good Work/Bad Work	43
5	Lack of Vision	59
6	All Work, But Very Little Ethics	75
7	Women in the Workplace	89
8	Squeezing Time	109
9	Workaholism, Stress, and Fatigue	121
10	The Work, Spend, and Debt Syndrome	139
11	Moral Leadership and Business Ethics	151
12	The End of Work: Is Rifkin Right?	171
13	The Failure of Work	193
14	The Future of Work	209
	Epilogue	223
	Notes	225
	Index	253

Preface

> We are so close to the world of work
> that we often can't see what it does to us.
> —Bob Black

ALMOST EVERYONE WORKS. WORK IS THE MOST common experience of adult life. Some love it, others hate it, but few of us are able to avoid it. Because we spend two-thirds of our waking life on the job, work is the way we come to know the world and are known to the world. Work becomes our mark of identity, our signature on the world. To work is *to be* and not to work is *not to be.*

I have always been fascinated by work. As a boy, I marveled at the long hours of hard labor put in by my father, grandfathers, and uncles. I was equally impressed with the skills and efforts of my mother, grandmothers, and assorted aunts in maintaining comfortable and efficient homes while also being forced to hold down full- or part-time jobs.

I come from a family of workers who immigrated to the United States in the early 1900s and who, by dint of their labor, not only survived but succeeded. My family valued and honored work. They believed in it and praised it. It was their yardstick of status and success. It was expected, demanded, an obligation of adult life. There was no shame in being out of work because you lost your job due to economic hard times. The only sin was in not wanting to work, in being lazy.

My maternal grandfather was forced out of his janitorial job in his early eighties. My father and uncle stayed on the job well into their seventies. My beloved godmother worked for the same company for thirty-eight years and would still be there if the company had not gone out of business. And my mother retired in her mid-sixties only because I begged her to do so in order to help care for my youngest child. For the men and women of my family, work was the active demonstration of their love and proof of their commitment to each other. Work was a source of pride and a badge of honor for responsibilities accepted and borne bravely.

In the old Italian neighborhood of Chicago, long before the cloistering effects of television and air-conditioning, summer nights were spent outside. While it was still light the boys played baseball in the street, the girls jumped rope on the sidewalk, and the adults, segregated by gender, would sit on the front porch steps and talk. When it got too dark to play, the younger children were sent to bed. The older kids had the option of laying claim to a porch of their own or joining the adults, but only to listen and not to be heard. More often than not I joined the adults, sometimes the women but mostly the men.

The women talked about everything. They talked about work, but usually about personalities rather than the specifics of the job. They talked about department store sales, the rising price of coffee at the A&P, what they had made for dinner, who was pregnant, who was sick, who had died, and who was about to get married. They were alternately silly and serious, and there was no limit to the range of topics they would discuss of an evening.

The men's conversation, on the other hand, was limited to two topics and two topics only—sports and work. Since most of the men were either recently arrived or first-generation citizens, the sports conversation didn't last very long. The only game they even vaguely understood was baseball, and the only players they cared about were those of Italian descent. So, what they talked about all night, *every night*, was work. They bemoaned it, complained about it, dissected and decried it. They also bragged and boasted about their work and retold complicated stories extolling their efforts, duties, and responsibilities on the job. Work was the center of their lives, and—love it or hate it—it was the only thing they really knew and understood well enough to discuss at length.

I was both fascinated and frightened by what they had to say. They taught me that there was dignity in work, a sense of fulfillment and satisfaction in earning your own way and providing for your family. They taught me that an honest man should never be too proud to do whatever was necessary—no matter how humbling or backbreaking the effort—in order to earn an honest dollar. They also taught me that although it was our duty in life, work could wear you out and break you down, and that, although all work was honorable, not every job offered honor, meaning, or even decent money. The honor was in surviving the doing, not in what was being done. Unpleasant, unsatisfying work could never be used as an excuse for not working at all. They taught me—as Abraham Lincoln's father taught him—to work hard but not necessarily to love my work. At the same time, they warned me not to do what they had to do to earn a living. They told me to go to school, get an education, find better work—work that did not break your spirit or your back, work that did not leave you empty or disappointed.

As I grew up I quickly realized that the lessons and wisdom of my neighbors and relations were not unique to the Italian-American community. The "work ethic," whether it was "Protestant," "immigrant," or anything else, was the law of the land. Work was expected. Ironically, one need only consult the wording of death notices in newspapers to fully appreciate the importance of work in our lives. Obituaries almost always list the occupation of the deceased first, and relationships last: "Joseph Doe, leading public interest lawyer, dead at 72 . . . He is survived by his wife, Jane, and his beloved children. . . ."[1] As Andre Malraux succinctly phrased it (in language that predates the dawn of political correctness): "A man is the sum of his actions, of what he had done, of what he can do. Nothing else."

Suffice to say, I heeded the warnings of my family and friends. I went to college, studied hard, and after a number of miscues and false starts stumbled onto a line of work that I had some talent for and liked. About midway in my career, and almost exactly coinciding with the first stages of "male menopause," my fascination with work and my personal satisfaction with my job, as a teacher and a writer, began to sour. In search of a self-cure, I redirected my malaise into a serious research project on the general topic of work. The more I read and the more people I interviewed about their work and observed on the job, the more I became convinced that I was a hypochondriac. Sure, there were bits and pieces of my job that I didn't always like. Yes, sometimes things got dull and a little tedious. But none of my complaints was as vociferous and hostile as the commentary of some of the people I was studying.

They complained about the "us-versus-them" mentality of the workplace. They talked about bad management policies, poor pay, and the total absence of care, commitment, and concern demonstrated among the rank and file. With striking similarity, they described their jobs as "boring," "depressing," "degrading," "enervating," and "alienating." They saw their workdays as "downtime," or "dead time," days filled with the drudgery of repetitive and seemingly meaningless tasks without any hope of remission.

On reflection, I realized I was one of the lucky ones. Despite all my job's problems, I still loved it and I still wanted to do it. It might, on occasion, wear me out or overwhelm me, but I neither resented what I did nor was in despair about having to do it. Such was obviously not the case with too many of the people that I had talked to.

This project is an attempt to understand, integrate, and develop the similarities and differences between the conventional wisdom regarding work of my parents generation, my own experiences as a worker, and the reported experiences of others. I want to understand why so many people say that they do not like their work and feel that work has, beyond the trading of labor for dollars, failed to give them what they want and need: creativity, dignity, purpose, and a strong sense of identity and self-worth.

This book is about work and what it does for us and to us. It examines the history of work and its physical, psychological, and philosophical costs and challenges. It also examines the changing nature of work and some of the gloomy predictions being offered regarding the future of work. This book is not an apologia, a ringing endorsement of work, or a diagnosis for despair. Rather, I argue that because work consumes so much of our lives, we must reinvent or, perhaps more accurately, at least recapture three primary tenets with regard to work and the person:

1. Adults need work for the same reason that children need play—in order to fulfill themselves as persons.
2. Work should produce ideas, services, and products people want and need as well as help to produce better people and a better life.
3. Work is a fundamental part of our humanity.

This book is not investigative journalism, a formal philosophical tract, or a sociologically validated economics text. It is rather an extended essay or narrative meditation on the nature and characteristics of work and how it affects our lives. I have drawn on the findings of standard scholarship, statistics, and surveys, as well as the insights of philosophy, literature, popular psychology, folklore, radio, television, and the press. I have also fully utilized the insights I have gained from innumerable private conversations, informal surveys, personal experiences, and the sometimes semiaccurate and fallible recall of memory.

One more thing: Since I have already admitted that I love my work, I have another confession to make. I am now and have always been a workaholic. Given my fascination with the topic, I'm sure you're not surprised. But I am working hard (pun intended) to control my addiction. Ironically, this project has made me appreciate and love my work even more. Nevertheless, I do not want to die at my desk with my last words being "I wish I had put in more time at the office!"

You Are What You Do

> Career and identity are inextricably bound up, indeed they are almost equivalent.
>
> —Douglas LaBier

IN THE LAST SCENE OF ARTHUR MILLER'S *DEATH of a Salesman,* Willy Loman's family and friends are standing at his graveside, saying their goodbyes, and reflecting on the character and legacy of the deceased. Willy, they suggest, was a dreamer, a schemer, a talker and teller of tall tales, a con man constantly searching for the big score. But for all of his big talk and even bigger dreams, both his mouth and his ideas were too large for his talents and abilities. Willy, they say, was a failure. But even worse, he was the kind of failure who could never admit it, either to himself or to others. And so right up to the end, Willy went on dreaming and scheming and hoping for that one big sale to come along and set him up for life.

Only one of those gathered at Willy's grave defends him. "Nobody . . . blame this man," he says. "You don't understand: Willy was a salesman. . . . A salesman has got to dream. . . . It comes with the territory."[1] It was Willy's job to smile, talk a lot, glad-hand one and all, says his defender. His job was to sell himself, sell his dream and his ideas, sell his product. It was his job that made him what he was.

The saying "it comes with the territory," from Miller's play, is now part of the lexicon. It conveys an acceptance of all the parts of a job and of doing whatever you must in order to get the job done. Perhaps Willy Loman was a failure and a fool because he didn't recognize that he had neither the temperament nor the talent for his chosen profession, but being a salesman shaped him; it drew out the best and the worst in him and made him what he was. To paraphrase Winston Churchill, first we choose and shape our work, and then it shapes us—forever.

Whether we have a good job or a bad one, whether we love it or hate it, succeed in it or fail, work is at the center of our lives and influences who we are and all that we do. Where we live, how well we live, whom we see socially, what and where we consume and purchase, how we educate our children—all of these are determined by the way in which we earn a living.

But work is not just about earning a livelihood. It is not just about getting paid, about gainful employment. Nor is it only about the use of one's mind and body to accomplish a specific task or project. Work is also one of the most significant contributing factors to one's inner life and development. Beyond mere survival, we create ourselves in our work. In his classic article "Work and the Self," Everett C. Hughes argued that work is fundamental to the development of personality. Because work preoccupies our lives and is the central focus of our time and energies, it not only provides us with an income, it literally names us, identifies us, to both ourselves and others. Hughes was convinced that even when we are dissatisfied with or dislike the work that we do, choice of occupation irrevocably "labels" us, and that we cannot understand a person unless we understand his or her work and how he or she deals with it.[2]

In the long run work can prove a boon or a burden, creative or crippling, a means to personal happiness or a prescription for despair. But no matter where we might wind up on this spectrum, *where* we work, *how* we work, *what* we do at work, and the general climate and culture of the workplace indelibly mark us for life. Work is the means by which we form our character and complete ourselves as persons. We literally create ourselves in our work. To restate the old Italian proverb *tu sei quello che mangi* (you are what you eat), in regard to work: *tu sei quello che fai* (you are the work you do). Work is a necessary and defining activity in the development of the adult personality.

According to theologian Gregory Baum, "Labor is the axis of human self-making."[3] We both establish and recognize ourselves in our work. Work allows us to find out what we can do and cannot do, how we are seen by others and how we see ourselves. In work we discover our boundaries and limits as well as our capacities for success. Work is the yardstick by which we measure ourselves against others. It is the means by which we establish our rank, role, and function within a community. Work not only conditions our lives; it is the necessary condition for life. Men have always known this, and have accepted it as part of their lot. As one forty-five-year-old machinist put it, "Being a man means being willing to put all your waking hours into working to support your family. If you ask for [too much] time off, or if you turn down overtime, it means you're lazy or you're a wimp."[4] As more and more women have entered the workplace, they too have been forced to confront this fundamental truth of adult existence: Not having a job means you're a person without salary, stuff, or status.

Assuredly other factors enter into the equation of self-identity; for example, genetic inheritance, race, gender, ethnicity, sexual orientation, religious training, and family background. But even with all of these, work remains an irreducible given, the most common experience of adult life. The lessons we learn at work help formulate who we become and what we value as individuals and as a society. Whatever the conditions of our labor, work shapes us and, unfortunately, often malforms us. But, for good or ill, work makes us human because we make something of ourselves through work, and in so doing we recognize ourselves and others in the task of working.[5] And yet, as E. F. Schumacher has indicated, despite the centrality of work in human life, the question—"What does the work do to the worker?" is seldom asked.[6] Workers and scholars alike regularly debate the benefits as well as the drawbacks of particular jobs in specific industries, but only rarely do they address the overall impact of work on the psyche and character of the worker.

The core of Karl Marx's writings is his critique of capitalism as an economic system and his attack on bourgeois society as an unjust social structure. For Marx, capitalism engenders the consolidation of capital, the concentration of power, the continuous manipulation of the market and merchandizing, the perpetuation of poverty, and the reification of society into the disproportional dominance of the "haves" over the "have-nots." A significant part of Marx's critique that is sometimes overlooked is his analysis of the specific effects of work on the character and identity of the individual worker, as is Marx's conviction that work is the primary means by which we become persons. Marx argued that the factory system alienated or disassociated workers from their work and consequently stripped work of personal meaning and purpose. He maintained that mechanized "conditions of production" (industrialization) denied workers responsibility and creativity. According to his analysis, capital investment, machinery, the industrial process, and the product became more important than people. The owners and managers of industry looked on workers not as subjects, but as objects, or as just another material factor in the production process. For Marx, when workers are regarded as objects and treated accordingly, they begin to think of themselves as objects. They lose, or perhaps never gain, the sense that they are meant to be subjects.[7]

In his earliest writings, "The German Ideology," Marx defined the individual as a worker:

> As individuals express their life, so they are. What [individuals] . . . are . . . coincides with their production, both with what they produce and with how they produce. The nature of individuals thus depends on the material conditions determining their production.[8]

For Marx, how people work and what they produce at work necessarily affect how and what they think, as well as their personal sense of self, freedom, and independence.[9] Both the process and the product of our labor help us to know who and what we are. The process of work both forms and informs us; we acquire self-definition and self-recognition through labor. In Marx's view, we need work in order to finish and refine our natures, and in work we create our individual identities as well as our collective history.

A somewhat unexpected but nevertheless important counterpart to Marx's overall thesis on work is Pope John Paul II's 1981 encyclical "Laborem Exercens" (On human work). According to John Paul, although work may be part of humanity's banishment and punishment, it is also part of a person's definition and directive in the world. According to the encyclical, the human world is not a simple given or a fixed thing. It is, rather, a "fact" continuously being produced by human labor. Work, the encyclical claims, is a good thing in the sense that it is useful and something to enjoy. It is good because it expresses and expands our dignity. Through work, one not only transforms nature, adapting it to his or her own needs, but one also achieves fulfillment as a human being and in a sense becomes "more a human being." Work is literally the "mark of man," the footprints of humanity on the sands of time.[10]

In *Civilization and Its Discontents,* Sigmund Freud wrote that the communal life of human beings has a twofold foundation: "the compulsion to work . . . and the power of love. . . ."[11] For Freud, *Eros* (love) and *Ananke* (necessity) are the true parents of civilization. *Eros* bonds us together and makes us unwilling to forgo our objects of sexual pleasure and happiness, while *ananke* compels us to toil at tasks that help us to maintain and guarantee self and community. According to Freud, both love and work cooperate in the achievement of "better control over the external world and . . . a further extension of the number of people included in the community."[12] At the very least, work gives one "a secure place in the human community."[13]

Work also helps establish the regularity of life, its basic cycles of day, week, month, and year. Without work, days and time patterns become confused.[14] Further, work organizes, routinizes, and structures our lives. It provides a safe outlet for our competitive strivings and often helps to keep us sane. More than this, as the German philosopher Martin Heidegger stated, "You are your projects."[15] Using philosophical terms, Heidegger implies that through projects (work) and their continuation into the future, a person establishes and acknowledges his or her "being" in the world. Heidegger suggests that you are what you do. Identity is largely a function of determined action or productive achievement. We are known by others and we know and define ourselves primarily by the projects we devise, by the products we create, and by the occupations we hold. A person who cannot point to an achievement does not and cannot feel like a full person. Subjective experience is simply too diffuse for self-identity. "I feel" is not as definitive as "I did." Nothing else in our lives can give us the sense of objective identity that work can.[16]

Director Elia Kazan said that the one absolute lesson he has learned in life is that "a man is what he does," and, consequently, that the secret to a good life is to make a living at what you want to do. As sociologist Douglas La Bier asserted, careers and identities are inextricably tied up; indeed, they are equivalent.[17] People are what they do, and what people do affects every aspect of who they are. The lessons we learn in our work and at the workplace become the metaphors we apply to life and the means by which we digest the world. The meter and measure of work serves as our mapping device to explain and order the geography of life. We are "typed" by our work and, in turn, we analyze and evaluate the world and others by our acquired work "types." Our work circumscribes what we know, how we know it, and how we select and categorize the things we choose to see, react to, or respond to. Work influences our use of language, our values and priority structures, our political awareness, and our repertoire of personal and professional learned skills and behaviors. As Samuel Butler wrote, "Every man's work, whether it be literature or music or pictures or architecture or anything else, is always a portrait of himself." Journalist and ethnographer Connie Fletcher, in her best-seller, *What Cops Know,* dramatically drives home this point:

> Cops know things you and I don't. It's knowledge crafted out of years spent on the street, sizing up and dealing with the volatile, cunning, confused, comic, tragic, often goofy behavior of human beings from every social, economic, and mental level, and it's knowledge won as a by-product of investigating criminal specialities such as homicide, sex crimes, property crimes, and narcotics. A cop who works traffic has peered deeper into the recesses of the human psyche than most shrinks. A cop who works homicide, or sex crimes, will tell you things Dostoyevsky only guessed at.[18]

Although different kinds of work affect different people differently, every person's "self-portrait" is both directly and indirectly influenced by the work that he or she does. Some of our job-acquired characteristics and behavioral patterns are substantial and life altering, and others are minor and relatively benign in their nature and impact. Following are a few idiosyncrasies of specific "portrait types" that may not hold up to close scrutiny, but, nevertheless, have a certain anecdotal currency that we can all recognize.

Nurses and doctors have a notorious reputation for being bad patients and even worse diagnosticians of loved ones and family members. They often immediately envision the worst-case scenario for every malady. The flip side of this example would be emergency room practitioners who witness so much trauma and gore that they are often insensitive to and seemingly uncaring or underconcerned about the more common maladies and injuries of everyday life.

Many teachers and especially college professors have acquired the well-deserved reputation of being utterly unable to offer a direct answer to a direct question. William James called this phenomenon the "Ph.D. syndrome"—the need to cite and document everything ever said on the topic under discussion. Although the ability to explain, analyze, offer examples, and disprove antecedents are all necessary elements of the craft of teaching and scholarship, too much of an answer can deaden the curiosity and interest of even the brightest of students.

Accountants and librarians share a reputation for being excessively detail-oriented and having a compulsion for organization that borders on being anal retentive. For both professions, order, exactness, and accuracy are the core virtues for high job performance. Unfortunately, these characteristics, when too zealously applied, can prove counterproductive in both professional and personal spheres.

It is said of psychiatrists and psychologists that their work lives are often so abstract, so cerebral, and deal so much with abnormality that they often lose the ability to be spontaneous and nonanalytical with individuals who are not their clients. This stereotype is perhaps best captured in the old chestnut about the two professors of psychology who happen to pass each other in the hall on the way to their offices. As they pass, one says, "Good morning!" The other responds, "How are you?" And as each is entering his respective office, he is thinking, "Hmm . . . I wonder what he really meant by that?"

Finally, there is the profile that is sometimes associated with those who earn their living by the sweat and strain of their hands and bodies. Tradespeople, artisans, and construction laborers are workers whose jobs require specific intellectual and technical skills as well as physical ability. Strength, dexterity, and endurance are requisites of the job, and these types of workers often measure themselves and others in terms of their raw physical prowess. (This profile is, of course, commonly assumed to be one of the reasons that women are not represented proportionally in these fields.) For many of these workers their reputation on the job and their personal sense of who they are is directly connected to their demonstration of physical prowess. These are blue-collar folks who take pride in their toughness and think themselves physically and morally superior to those whose work does not require them to wear steel-toed boots.

Recently, I attended a family wedding and the first person I saw was my Uncle Frank. "Hey, college kid," he said to me as he shook my hand in a vicelike grip and peppered my shoulder with a series of heavy blows. "How you been?" Uncle Frank is in his mid-seventies but his punches still hurt, as did his annoying habit of calling me "college kid." I had just turned fifty-three. "Uncle Frank," I said, massaging my shoulder, "you look great. Where did you get the tan? Have you been playing a lot of golf?" "Naw," he said, "you know I hate golf. I had a couple of jobs this month." "Jobs? But you've been retired for ten years!" "Yeah, but they were easy jobs," said Uncle Frank. "A couple of driveways, some concrete steps, a few sidewalks. It was a piece of cake." "Uncle Frank," I said, "this doesn't make sense. Is something wrong? Do you need money"? "No! No!" said Uncle Frank. "It's nothing like that." "Then why?" I persisted. "Why did you take these jobs?" He smiled, grabbed me roughly and drew me to him. "Because," he said with a wink, "I wanted to see if I could still do it, college kid. *Capice?* I just wanted to see if I could still do it."

Samuel Butler's notion that "every man's work . . . is always a portrait of himself" is a part of what psychiatrists and psychologists refer to as "ego boundaries," by which they mean the clear perspectives that well-balanced people have on the limits and outlines of their identities. They possess a clear sense of integrity and continuity, and do not suffer from "boundary diffusion." For most of us the primary source of ego boundaries is our work. In work we come both to know ourselves and to orient ourselves to the external world. Work establishes a "coherent web of expectations" of the rhythm, direction, and definition of our lives,[19] which allows us to feel contained within precise outlines: "I'm a doctor" versus "I'm a cardiovascular surgeon"; "I'm a lawyer" versus "I'm a litigator in my firm's antitrust division"; "I'm in advertising" versus "I'm the artistic director for Leo Burnett"; "I'm an educator" versus "I'm a professor of physics at MIT"; "I'm a carpenter" versus "I'm a cabinetmaker." The more precise and descriptive we can be about ourselves, the greater our sense of self-definition. Nothing is so uniquely personal, so active a representation of individuals as their skills and works.[20] According to sociologist Robert Kahn in his study *Work and Health,* occupation and identity are closely intertwined:

> When people ask that most self-identifying of questions—Who am I?—they answer in terms of their occupation: toolmaker, press

> operator, typist, doctor, construction worker, teacher. Even people who are not working identify themselves by their former work or their present wish for it, describing themselves as retired or unemployed. And work that is not paid lacks significance, much as we might wish it otherwise. Many people who are usefully occupied, but not paid, respond to questions in ways that deprecate both their activities and themselves. A woman who takes care of a home and several small children and is engaged in a wide range of community activities may answer with that tired and inaccurate phrase, "just a housewife." A retired man equally busy with an assortment of projects, is likely to say, "Oh, I'm retired; I don't do anything."[21]

Psychiatrist Leonard Fagin believes that our personalities are intimately bound up with our work. Work is our calling card to the rest of the world. Men and women alike use their work to identify themselves to others.[22] Picture yourself silently circulating at a cocktail party and eavesdropping on how people introduce themselves to one another. I guarantee that you are not going to hear anything like the following: "Hi, I'm Bob, and I'm an Episcopalian"; "Hello, I'm Patty. I'm active in the Democratic Party"; "Good evening, I'm Peter and I'm the proud father of three kids"; "Howdy, I'm Susan, and I support Habitat for Humanity." It just doesn't happen that way. Workers describe themselves first by "name, rank, and serial number," that is, by name, occupation, and title. It is only later, if at all, that they might divulge what they like, what they value, and how their lives are structured outside of work. Because of their traditional role as breadwinners, men may be especially tied to this form of identity.

Robert Bly, poet and founder of the "men's movement," maintains that most men are more obsessed with work than any other thing in their lives. Having a job is a man's primary job, suggests Bly. It is the one cultural imperative men cannot shirk if they are to have any status in the human community and especially in the enclave of men. Sadly, even if their work is joyless, or uninteresting and leaves them no time to be with their families, men will still talk passionately about it, because it establishes both their basic sense of masculinity and their specific status in the "pecking order" of other males. Like it or not, Bly concludes, men have been conditioned to believe that the baseline of their masculinity is determined by the work that they do.[23]

Perhaps the easiest way to prove the point that we (men and women alike) are all affected, labeled, and formed by the work we do is to consider its converse. Imagine the now too common scenario of a forty-eight-year-old employee who has been "reengineered," "downsized," or "five-plus-fived" out of a job. With the anchor of adulthood ripped away, with few prospects in sight, but with bills to be paid, mortgages to be met, and children to be educated, the "terminatee" is often reduced to adolescent torpor, and is forced to ask the questions: Who am I now? What have I accomplished? What can I do? Who will I become? Joseph Epstein calls being out of work "the surest path to self-loathing." People out of work, said Rollo May, "quickly become strangers to themselves." And without work, Albert Camus said, "all life goes rotten."

Part of the "psychopathology" of work, says Leonard Fagin, are the personality and behavioral disorders that can occur when a person loses his or her job. Fagin argues that unemployment can constitute a severe mental and emotional crisis. If work influences identity formation, the continuity of self, time orientation, and interpersonal relationships, the sudden loss of work, conversely, disorients or disassociates our sense of self, time, and space, and our connections to and relationships with others. If work is our calling card, then when it is withdrawn, for whatever reasons, that loss affects how we see ourselves and the world, and how we relate to others. Work, Fagin argues, not only identifies us, but it also identifies what we are not, and thus determines all of our role boundaries, and group and class identities. Unemployment changes both the quality and clarity of our private interpersonal relationships and our social and professional network of relationships as well.[24] To be denied work is to be denied far more than the things that work can buy. It is to be denied a basic and primary organizing principle in life—the ability to define and respect ourselves as persons.[25] The relationship between work, self-identity, and mental health is nicely summarized by historian Elliot Jacques:

> Working for a living is one of the basic activities in a man's life. By forcing him to come to grips with his environment, with his livelihood at stake, it confronts him with the actuality of his personal capacity—to exercise judgement, to achieve concrete and specific results. It gives him a continuous account of his correspondence, between outside reality and the inner perception of that reality, as

> well as an account of the accuracy of his appraisal of himself. . . . In short, a man's work does not satisfy his material needs alone. In a very deep sense, it gives him a measure of his sanity.[26]

E. F. Schumacher believes that work is part of the "university of life." Life is a school, a training ground, and in work we become something more than what we are. We need work, we are formed by work, and the quality of our lives is directly dependent on the quality of the work we do.[27] Mirroring Schumacher, philosopher Adina Schwartz maintains that mental health requires work. In theory, Schwartz argues, it is at work that people learn skills, practice and perfect a craft, rationally choose actions to suit their goals, take responsibility for their decisions, and learn and grow from observing the consequences of their choices. In framing, adjusting, pursuing, and accomplishing their work tasks, individuals grow in initiative, intelligence, and autonomy. Individuals are then able to translate these learned work skills to other dimensions of their life. For Schwartz there is a direct relationship between the quality of life on the job and off it. The mix of the substantive complexity of the job, individual innate intelligence and talent, and the degree of discretion and freedom allowed in work have a direct bearing on who we are and who we will become both as workers and in our private lives.[28]

The effects of work on our lives and personalities are both immediate and long-term. Analogous to psychiatrist Robert J. Lifton's understanding of "delayed stress" or "post-stress syndrome among soldiers who have engaged in combat," many of the lessons we learn on a particular job remain with us forever, consciously or subconsciously, as part of our catalog of learned experiences. Some of these experiences, according to Lifton, inform us and direct us positively, and some can haunt us and have a negative impact years later. Every job creates its own experiences, its own standards, its own pace, and its own self-contained *weltanschauung* (worldview). Every job, depending on the intensity, depth, and duration of the individual's involvement, leaves its mark. Lifton asserts that no soldier walks away from combat untouched by the experience. The same can be said of most jobs, even those far less traumatic than soldiering.[29]

As stated in this book's preface, adults need work for the same reason that children need play—in order to fulfill themselves as persons. Unfortunately this thesis applies even to those of us who spend our lives laboring at "bad jobs," jobs that Studs Terkel refers to as "too small for our spirit" and "not big enough" for us as people. These jobs are devoid of prestige, are physically exhausting or mindlessly repetitive, demeaning, degrading, and trivial in nature. Even these kinds of jobs, however—though we are often loath to admit it—provide us with a handle on reality, access to services and goods, and a badge of identity. Self-proclaimed philosopher for the proletariat Bob Black agrees that occupation and identity are inextricably linked. "You are what you do," said Black. The problem is, "if you do boring, stupid, monotonous work, chances are you'll end up boring, stupid, and monotonous."[30]

Because work looms so large in our lives I believe that most of us don't reflect on its significance. Work is, well . . . work, a necessary activity that is required to sustain and justify the hours between sleeping, eating, and attempting to enjoy ourselves. However, work cannot be easily separated from the rest of our lives. The point is, according to neuropsychologist Walter Tubbs, if we are not satisfied with our work, if it does not give us what we want and need, then—even if this discontent doesn't spill over into our social and family lives—we are, at the very least, unhappy in well over half of our daily existence.[31] In the words of Thomas Aquinas, "There can be no joy of life without joy of work." Perhaps because we live in a society that values the fruits of our labor and not the labor itself, we have forgotten or never really appreciated the fact that the business of work is not simply to produce goods, but also to help produce people.

René Descartes was wrong. It isn't *Cogito, ergo sum* (I think, therefore I am), but rather *Labora, ergo sum* (I work, therefore I am). We need work, and as adults we find identity in and are identified by the work we do. Our work tells us who we are. If this is true, then we must be very careful about what we choose to do for a living, for what we do is what we become. At its worst, work is a burden and a necessity. At its best, work can be an act of personal freedom and self-realization. But either way, work is a necessary and defining ingredient in our lives.

2

Work—What Is It?

> You can't eat for eight hours a day, nor drink for eight hours a day—all you can do for eight hours is work. Which is the reason man makes himself and everybody so miserable and unhappy!
>
> —William Faulkner

IN PERHAPS THE MOST POETIC PHRASING I HAVE ever come across on the topic of work, Pope Pius XI said, "Man is born to labor, as a bird to fly."[1] More parochially, sociologist Peter Berger wrote "to be human and to work appear as inextricably intertwined notions."[2] The first sounds like a gift and a blessing; the other more like a report and a curse. The truth of the matter, I think, lies somewhere in between.

For most of us, working is an entirely nondiscretionary activity, an inescapable fact of existence. In its worst light, work is seen as something evil, a punishment, the grindingly inevitable burden of toil bestowed, along with mortality, upon the human condition. At best, work looms so large and problematic in our lives that we either take it for granted or we actively suppress its full significance.

In fact, none of us is neutral and completely silent on the topic of work. Everyone has an opinion. The reason is simple. *Work, food,* and *sex* are the most commonly shared behavioral activities of adult life. While the latter two are subject to aesthetic taste and availability, and therefore constitute a discretionary choice, work, for 99 percent of us, is an entirely nondiscretionary matter. Most of us must work. What other option do we have?

As adults there is nothing that more preoccupies our lives than work. From the ages of approximately eighteen to seventy we will spend our lives working. We will not spend as much time sleeping, enjoying our families, eating, or recreating and resting as much as we will working. Whether we love our work or hate it, succeed in it or fail, achieve fame or infamy through it, like Sisyphus we are all condemned to push and chase that thing we call our job, our career, our work all of our days. "Even those of us who desperately don't want to work," wrote Ogden Nash, "must work in order to earn enough money so that they won't have to work anymore." So, work we must. And maybe if we're lucky, as Voltaire pointed out, our work will keep us from the jaws of three great evils—boredom, vice, and poverty. But only maybe.

Because work, like time, is so much a part of our lived experience, a universally acceptable definition of work is difficult to formulate. Matthew Fox, in *The Reinvention of Work*, offers us a rather profound interpretation of our labor:

> Work comes from inside out; work is the expression of our soul, our inner being. It is unique to the individual, it is creative. Work [is also] an expression of the Spirit at work in the world through us. Work is that which puts us in touch with others, not so much at the level of personal interaction, but at the level of service in the community.[3]

The curmudgeonly philosopher Bertrand Russell defined it this way:

> Work is of two kinds: first, altering the position of matter at or near the earth's surface relative to other matter; second, telling other people to do so. This first kind is unpleasant and ill-paid; the second is pleasant and highly paid.[4]

While both of these observations correlate with the respective comments of Pope Pius XI and Peter Berger, neither of them offers us sufficient insight into the phenomenon. Both definitions are loaded and carry with them a whole series of subjective presuppositions about the nature of work. What is needed is a more commonsense look at what we mean by the word *work* itself.

In its most general and benign sense work can be defined as any activity we need or want to do in order to achieve the basic requirements of life or to maintain a certain lifestyle. Essayist Terry Sullivan argues that the central feature of any and all forms of work is compulsion or desire.

Work is something we either have to do or want to do. Some forms of work can combine both of these core ingredients, and others possess only one of them. For example, many people would say that work is something, anything, they do for money, because, at a very basic level, they need money. Hence, when they are paid to do something, they generally feel permitted to call that work. This correlation of trading labor for dollars as a defining principle of work holds true for college professors, cement finishers, senators, and hit men alike. But, says Sullivan, what of the remark, "I have a lot of work to do around the house this weekend"? It's a perfectly sensible thing to say, and virtually everyone understands what is being implied—"I have chores to perform, which I do not wish to perform and probably won't enjoy, but which I'm compelled by necessity to do."[5] Clearly, household chores are work, even though nobody is going to pay us to do them. The operative principle, in both of these cases is compulsion—either in the requirements of the task at hand or the necessity to make money.

But, says Sullivan, what can we say about the sentence "I love my work"? Can we still call something work when we get paid to do something we enjoy? Something we would do anyway, whether or not we were compelled or paid to do it? Of course we can. The problem is, since most of don't enjoy that for which we are paid, we confuse all unwelcome or duty-bound tasks with work and call them work. Conversely, we confuse all things for which people are paid with unwelcome tasks.[6]

And yet, clearly, when an utterly unknown and as yet unpublished writer gleefully announces, "I'm totally absorbed in the novel I'm working on," we surely understand what is being said. The would be author is happily working at something she enjoys, and will probably continue to work on it, even though she might not expect to be paid for her efforts. If work is what we are compelled to do for money or because it must be done, then, according to Sullivan, the writer's work can also be defined as that which she is compelled to do for another reason, such as desire or the feeling that it must be done. Is it not perfectly sensible that writers or artists must do their work to achieve a sense of well-being, just as others must clean the garage because they haven't anywhere else to park the car, and that others must go to work because they have no other means of paying the mortgage on the house?

Work, then, is that which we are compelled to do by some intrinsic or extrinsic force—the need for money, for self-expression, for accomplishment. The question of which of these compulsions is greatest, and who has which, is another issue entirely. Work remains what we have to do. Only if we're lucky will it be pleasant, pay well, and make us happy. The degree to which we can find this combination is the degree to which work, any work, is satisfying.[7]

According to Joseph Epstein, "The most fortunate people of all are those rare few for whom the line between work and play gets rubbed out and for whom work is pleasure and pleasure is work."[8] Both contemporary experience and the lessons of history reinforce Epstein's point. Work has always carried with it a certain coercive quality. Personal pleasure, satisfaction, and happiness are not terms readily associated with the phenomenon of work. Indeed, folk wisdom has it that the main problem with work is that so few people are able to avoid it. Perhaps the late *Chicago Tribune* columnist Mike Royko comes closest to the spirit of the "common man's" feeling about work when his alter ego in the column, Slats, says:

> Why do you think the lottery is so popular? Do you think anybody would play if the super payoff was a job on the night shift in a meatpacking plant? People play it so if they win they can be rich and idle. . . . like I told you years ago—if work is so good, how come they have to pay us to do it?[9]

According to some anthropologists, in primitive subsistence societies there was no distinction made between working and not working. To be awake was to be working. A person was born, worked, and died. To work was the law of life. Frank Tannenbaum, in *A Philosophy of Labor,* updates and reaffirms this thesis for the contemporary American workforce:

> We have become a nation of employees. We are dependent upon others for our means of livelihood, and most people have become completely dependent upon wages. If they lose their jobs they lose every resource, except for the relief supplied by the various forms of social security. Such dependence of the mass of the people upon others for all of their income is something new in the world. For our generation, the substance of life is in another man's hands.[10]

The bottom line for all of us is that we must work in order to survive, certainly to survive with a modicum of security and comfort.

I take it to be the case, however, that the common laments against work are not simply based on the fact that most of us are part of the captive workforce and must accept work as inevitable. The real issue is, as over a hundred studies in the last twenty-five years have demonstrated, not work itself but the job. Workers regularly depict their jobs as being physically exhausting, boring, psychologically diminishing, or, worse, personally humiliating and unimportant. Studs Terkel's *Working* has become the modern bible for those who feel that work is by definition degrading, debilitating, and dehumanizing. True believers in this thesis can open Terkel's text at random to find documented proof that work is one, if not the major, cause of "economic unfreedom," "physical debasement," "personal alienation," and "social ennui." The opening lines of *Working* compellingly capture Terkel's point of view:

> This book, being about work is, by its very nature, about violence—to the spirit as well as to the body. It is about ulcers as well as accidents, about shouting matches as well as fist fights, about nervous breakdowns as well as kicking the dog around. It is above all (or beneath all) about daily humiliations. To survive the day is triumph enough for the walking wounded among the great many of us.[11]

The poor reputation that work has earned in popular mythology has a long and convoluted history. The image of the "negative necessity" of work seems to have its partial origins in the various etymologies of the word itself. In classical Greek the word for labor, *ponos,* means "sorrow." In modern Greek its derivative, *ponei,* connotes pain and hurt. In Latin the word *labor* means "extreme effort associated with pain." According to Hannah Arendt, *labor* has the same etymological root as *labare* (to stumble under a burden), signifying "trouble, distress, difficulty." The French word *travailles* replaced the older term *labourer* and connotes "a heavy burdensome task." It likewise is of Latin origin and it originally denoted the *tripalium,* a three-pronged instrument of torture used by the Roman legionnaires, hence the suggestion of "sorrow and pain." In medieval German the word *arbeit* (to labor) can also be translated to signify "tribulation, persecution, adversity, or bad times."[12]

Matthew Fox points out how the word *job* also conforms to this negative imagery. The Middle English word *gobbe*, from which *job* is derived, means "lump," and the now obsolete word *jobbe* meant "piece." Samuel Johnson, in his eighteenth-century dictionary, defined *job* as "petty, piddling work; a piece of chance work." At the turn of the twentieth century, in the garment district of New York City, the term *jobwork* used to mean "piecework," the lowest calling and most poorly paid tasks in the industry.[13] Finally, the word *occupation* emerges from the Latin *occupare*, which connotes the adversarial posture of "seizing hold of or grappling with a task."

Another way to highlight antiquity's etymological association of work with pain or irksomeness is to examine a few words that are associated with its converse meaning: leisure, amateur, and diversion. The root of the word *leisure* comes from the Latin *licere*, which means "to be permitted," suggesting that leisure is about unstructured, free time. The Oxford English Dictionary defines leisure as "time which one can spend as one pleases." Witold Rybczynski, in his extended essay on leisure and how we spend our nonwork time, *Waiting for the Weekend*, pointed out that according to C. K. Chesterton, *leisure* is used to describe three different things: "The first is being allowed to do something. The second is being allowed to do anything. And the third (and perhaps the most rare and precious) is being allowed to do nothing." The first, Chesterton acknowledged, was the most common form of leisure—the ability to do something other than work. The second—the liberty to fashion exactly what one wanted out of one's leisure time—tended to be restricted to creative types and those of sufficient financial means. The third was Chesterton's favorite and for him the truest form of leisure: idleness, "the noble habit of doing nothing."[14]

According to psychiatrist Leonard Fagin, control is the crucial psychological distinction between work and leisure. The feeling, if not the reality, of greater control over one's activity characterizes leisure; leisure implies doing what one wants to do with one's free or nonwork time. Fagin argues that although work does not imply a total loss of autonomy and control, one's activities at work are never totally arbitrary and without purpose. Rather, they are structured, goal-oriented, and, more often than not, supervised and monitored. At the very least, says Fagin, in work one temporarily hands over control to other agencies. Ostensibly, control is sacrificed in exchange for financial gain, which offers the possibility of control over one's nonwork time. Conventional wisdom is clear on the matter: Leisure is our time; work belongs to another.[15]

The word *amateur* comes from the Latin *amare,* which means "to love" and connotes "doing something that you love," "doing something without obligation," "doing something as a dilettante or in a nonprofessional capacity." In English the word *diversion* suggests "the ability to do something else," "to be otherwise engaged." Diversion literally means "to turn aside, as from a course or purpose," and it comes from the Latin *divetire,* "to turn in the opposite direction." Diversion also means "distraction from business cares as in recreation, entertainment, amusement." In modern Italian the word *divertise* is commonly used to denote "doing something different, a diversion from one's usual activity." It is also used as a synonym for vacation, *vacanza,* meaning "to temporarily suspend an activity," from the Latin *vacare,* "to be empty, nonoccupied."

If, as Aristotle suggested, the converse proves the point, then, etymologically speaking, the point is clear. The terms *leisure, amateur,* and *diversion* connote downtime, choice, freedom, personal discretion, and activity an individual engages in for his or her own purposes. The term *work,* on the other hand, always connotes forced time, required time, an encumbrance, an obligation, imposed busyness.

The common perception of work as a "negative and ignoble" activity can also be traced to other ancient sources. The Bible tells us that originally there was no work to be done in the Garden of Eden; toil was described as a curse imposed by God to symbolize humankind's banishment. After the Fall, work became a necessary activity. Genesis graphically expresses the curse that sin brought with it: "Cursed is the ground because of you; in toil you shall eat of it all the days of your life. . . . In the sweat of your face you shall eat bread till you return to the ground, for out of it you were taken."[16] As John Milton put it, "man's first disobedience" resulted in the curse of work.

One interpretation of the Jewish tradition perceives work as "painful drudgery" to which we are condemned by sin. It is accepted as an expiation through which one can atone for sin and prepare for the arrival of the Messiah. Work is a "heavy yoke" that is "hard to bear," and Ecclesiastes can be heard to sigh, "The labor of man does not satisfy the soul."[17] Early Christianity, like Judaism, regarded work as a punishment from God, as a result of original sin, but also as a means of redemption if one shared the goods of one's labor with those in greater need. Thus work, as a means of charity, was a source of grace. Yet work is never exalted as anything in itself, but only as an instrument of purification, charity, or atonement.

To the ancient Greeks, whose physical labor was in large part done by slaves, work brutalized the mind and made men unfit for the practice of the gentlemanly virtues. The Greeks regarded work as a curse, a drudgery, and an activity to be conducted with a heavy heart. Plutarch, in his chapter on Pericles, remarks that no well-born man would want to be the craftsman Phidias, because while a gentleman enjoys the contemplation of the sculptor's masterpieces, he himself would never consider using a hammer and chisel and being covered with dust, sweat, and grime.[18] The Greeks felt that work enslaved the worker, chained him to the will of others, and corrupted his soul. Work by its very nature inhibited the use of reason and thereby impeded the search for the ultimate ends of life. Work was accepted not as an end in itself but as a means by which some might be freed to pursue higher goals. Aristotle declared that just as the goal of war was peace, so the object of work was leisure. Leisure meant activity pursued free of compulsion or desire for gain, free for contemplation of philosophical truths. Aristotle saw physical work as a burden that he had no duty to bear. He never worked, accepting the slavery of others because it freed him for leisure.[19]

By the thirteenth century, work was considered a necessity of nature. According to Thomas Aquinas, each of us must use our innate talents in the service of both ourselves and others, an obligation Aquinas termed stewardship. In fulfilling the duty of work, we acquire skill, fulfill our obligations of charity, and pay homage to our creator. With the scholastic synthesis, work became a natural right and duty, the sole legitimate basis for society, the foundation for property and profit, as well as the means for personal salvation. Nonetheless, the work of this life was still thought to be of little consequence compared to the spiritual work of preparing to face God. By itself, work had no purpose, for only the contemplation of God could redeem life.[20]

Work both as a private activity and as a way of life began to take on a less onerous role during the Renaissance and the Reformation. It was during this period that work, no matter how high or low the actual task, began to develop a positive ethos of its own, at least at the theoretical level. Most historians attribute the origin of the work ethic to Martin

Luther. According to Luther, one was summoned by God to a secular "calling," which today we would call a profession or a career.[21] Luther stressed that all callings were necessary to life; no one calling was to be recognized as more necessary or blessed than another, and, therefore, all callings had equal worth in the sight of God. For Luther, work was a form of serving God: "There is just one best way to serve God—to do most perfectly the work of one's profession." Thus the only way to live acceptably before God was through devotion to one's calling. However, God demanded more than occasional good works. He demanded a methodical life of good works in a unified pattern of work and worship.[22]

With John Calvin in the sixteenth century, we find Luther's ideas extended, systematized, and institutionalized. Work was the will of God, and even ceaseless "dumb toil" sufficed to please him. Calvin preached the "predestination of the elect." He believed that the elect could be recognized by certain outward signs, which included self-denial and devotion to duty, and that God caused the elect to prosper. "To prosper" or "to succeed" meant to enjoy not only wealth and happiness on earth, but eternal salvation. Success was the symbol of "selective salvation." Calvin managed, no matter how indirectly, to provide a rationale that linked work and the divine with material success and comfort.

In *The Protestant Ethic and the Spirit of Capitalism,* Max Weber observed that the rise of Protestantism and the rise of capitalism generally coincided in England and throughout most European countries. Weber's explanation was that many basic Protestant ideas encouraged capitalistic activities. For example, the Reformation taught that each person would be individually judged by God, and that judgment would be based on one's whole life's work or "calling." The reformers also taught that the fruits of one's "calling"—money—should not be spent frivolously or unnecessarily. According to Weber, these ideas led to a life of hard work, self-discipline, asceticism, and concern with achievement. This ethic helped advance the rise of the private entrepreneur in that it led to the accumulation of money that could not be spent on luxuries, but that could and should be put into one's own business.[23]

Labor analyst Michael Cherrington maintains that the work ethic typically embraces one or more of the following beliefs:

1. People have a moral religious obligation to fill their lives with heavy physical toil. For some, this means that hard work, effort,

and drudgery are to be valued for their own sake; physical pleasures and enjoyments are to be shunned; and an ascetic existence of methodical rigor is the only acceptable way to live.
2. Men and women are expected to spend long hours at work, with little or no time for personal recreation and leisure.
3. A worker should have a dependable attendance record, with low absenteeism and tardiness.
4. Workers should take pride in their work and do their jobs well.
5. Workers should be highly productive and produce a large quantity of goods or services.
6. Employees should have feelings of commitment and loyalty to their profession, their company, and their work group.
7. Workers should be achievement-oriented and constantly strive for promotions and advancement. High-status jobs with prestige and the respect of others are important indicators of a "good" person.
8. People should acquire wealth through honest labor and retain it through thrift and wise investments. Frugality is desirable; extravagance and waste should be avoided.[24]

For Weber the work ethic means a commitment to work beyond its utility in providing a living. It is "a conviction that work is a worthwhile activity in its own right, not merely . . . the means to a material comfort or wealth."[25] No matter what the outcome, work is a good thing in itself, and it is a demonstration of one's piety, duty, and devotion.

The direct theological descendants of the Reformation, and of John Calvin in particular, were the Puritans who migrated to New England. Citing the parable of the talents (Matthew 25), Calvin urged the Puritans to prosper: "You may labor to be rich for God, though not for the flesh or sin."[26] The gospel of work in America was also preached from many other pulpits. William Penn constantly reminded the Quakers that "diligence is a virtue useful and laudable among men. . . . Frugality is a virtue too, and not of little use in life. . . . It is proverbial, 'A Penney sav'd is a Penny got.'"[27]

Perhaps the real solidification of the work ethic in America occurred with its practical translation and secularization by Benjamin Franklin. In his various publications, Franklin taught that wealth was the result of virtue and the proper display of character. In his *Autobiography,* he defines the ethic of work in his list of ideal traits: "Temperance, Silence, Order, Resolution, Frugality, Industry, Sincerity, Justice, Moderation, Cleanliness, Tranquility, Chastity, Humility."[28] With Franklin, the work ethic shifted from a direct form of worshiping God to an indirect way of rendering service to God by developing one's character and doing good to others.[29] Unlike the Puritans, Franklin's craftsman no longer worked for God's glory, but for himself. He maintained that "God helps those who help themselves." Nevertheless, hard work remained the only standard for private success and social usefulness.

By the nineteenth century the Protestant ethic in America had changed its name at least three times, but its essential focus had not changed at all. Whether it was called the Protestant ethic, the Puritan ethic, the work ethic, or the immigrant ethic, hard work was seen as good in and of itself, the only ticket to survival and the possibility of success.

According to the noted labor historian Daniel Rodgers, the central premise of the work ethic is that work forms the core of the moral life. "Work made men useful in a world of economic scarcity. It staved off the doubts and temptations that preyed on idleness; it opened the way to deserved wealth and status; it allowed one to put the impress of mind and skill on the material world."[30] In many ways the work ethic posited one's very right to existence; one achieved worth through work.

During the nineteenth century we see the first stirrings of dissatisfaction with this ethic. These came not from churches, employers, or even workers themselves, but from artists. The popularity of Charles Dickens's novels and of plays such as Gerhart Hauptmann's 1893 drama about cottage industries, *The Weavers*, foreshadowed a discontent that would manifest itself in the mid-twentieth century. Until that time the moral preeminence of work stood essentially unchallenged as an accepted social value.

C. Wright Mills pointed out that "the gospel of work has been central to the historic tradition of America, to its image of itself, and to the images the rest of the world have of America."[31] There can be little question that this reverence for work, along with an abundance of natural resources and human capital, was an important determinant of America's material success. Moreover, because of this need for a pool of diligent laborers, every agent of authority and education proclaimed the merits of work. From Luther to Franklin to Horatio Alger, workers received a steady diet of exhortation and incantation from press, pulpit, and primer. All work was worthwhile and laudable; work done well would inevitably bring reward, while avoiding work would lead to degradation and ruin.[32]

Daniel Yankelovich, in *New Rules: Searching for Self-Fulfillment in a World Turned Upside Down,* contends that in post–World War II culture the Protestant work ethic was reformulated into something more akin to the nuclear family "giving-getting compact:"

> I give hard work, loyalty and steadfastness. I swallow my frustration and suppress my impulse to do what I would enjoy, and do what is expected of me instead. I do not put myself first; I put the needs of others ahead of my own. I give a lot but what I get in return is worth it. I receive an ever growing standard of living, and my family life with a devoted spouse and decent kids. Our children will take care of us in our old age if we really need it, which thank goodness we will not. I have a nice home, a good job, the respect of my friends and neighbors, a sense of accomplishment at having made something of my life. Last but not least, as an American I am proud to be a citizen of the finest country in the world.[33]

For Yankelovich, no matter what the source or accuracy of this compact, it is difficult to exaggerate how important it has been in supporting the goals of American society in the postwar period. It lies at the very heart of what we mean by the American Dream. Right or wrong, the giving-getting compact has helped to sustain and direct the efforts of millions over the years.

In the mid-1980s our collective understanding of the work ethic began to change yet again. Although, as a virtue, work remains ensconced in the constellation of values that includes apple pie, motherhood, and the flag, the aging of the baby boomers and the maturation of their children, Generation X, has changed our focus on the centrality and meaning of work in our lives.

According to an article in the *Chicago Tribune Magazine,* members of the postwar generations who entered the workforce since the 1960s are significantly less satisfied with their jobs than were the workers of their parents' and grandparents' generations. Only one in four workers between the ages of eighteen and forty-nine report being completely satisfied with their jobs, as compared with nearly double (43 percent) the number of older workers.[34] A recent Roper Organization survey indicated that when workers were asked to compare the importance of work and leisure in their lives, only 36 percent put work first, while 41 percent of those surveyed opted for leisure as the most important thing in their lives.[35]

Former president of the United Auto Workers' Union Douglas Fraser readily acknowledges that people's attitudes toward work have changed radically. "The new generations," says Fraser, "are more interested in time off the job than their fathers and grandfathers were. . . . They have other values [in mind]—living a fuller life with their family, having more time for recreation, more time to socialize."[36] Landon Jones, in his landmark book on the baby-boom generation, *Great Expectations,* argues that while previous generations ardently believed in the work ethic and its precepts of concerted effort, self-sacrifice, delayed gratification, and loyalty, many of todays workers have no intention of denying their "real selves" because of a job.

To any observer of the business scene, the underlying reason for this "pursuit of self over the job" is neither mysterious nor particularly complicated. In an age of companies downsizing, right-sizing, and, with alarming regularity, simply going out of business, the payback for hard work, self-sacrifice, and loyalty have become both practically and morally moot. When our GI fathers and grandfathers came back from World War II, finished college or acquired a trade, and entered the workforce, it was expected that hard work and loyalty would automatically pay off in the admittedly paternalistic, but nonetheless rock-solid, employer covenant "Keep your nose clean, give us your time, your talent, and your commitment, and we'll give you a decent salary, a stable career, and the promise of long-term security." In the not so long ago "good old days," there was a solid reason for being a "company man"; it usually meant you had a job for life.

Everything is different now. Possessing a trade or a college degree can no longer guarantee a starting position, let alone lifelong job tenure in one's chosen field. Lawyers can't find work. Finance majors and CPAs wind up in sales. Doctors, in ever-increasing numbers, are picking up MBAs and giving up medicine. Tool and dye makers are being computerized out of their jobs. Dedicated teachers are getting fired mid-career. In a prediction that sounds more menacing than hopeful, former Secretary of Labor Robert Reich projected that due to continuing technological innovation and changes in the global economy, in the near future a normal worker can expect to have as many as three to five separate careers and seven to fifteen different jobs in his or her lifetime. Given this general scenario, is it any wonder that the Protestant work ethic is on the wane and that neither employers nor employees readily offer or expect eternal, absolute loyalty and commitment from each other?

In place of the traditional work ethic has arisen what some critics have referred to as the personal work ethic and the "ethics of sequential loyalty." The new personal work ethic maintains that work is good, or at least that work is necessary, but that individuals should primarily work for themselves and not the company. That is, individuals should and must work hard if they want to succeed and achieve status and recognition. But the focus of this dedication and hard work is primarily self-serving and not centered on a commitment to the values and goals of the company.[37] As one "new worker" recently told me, "If the company does well by my efforts, fine and good, but my motivation is personal and purely selfish. I want to do a good job because I want to make a decent living. They're in it for the money, and so am I."

Sequential loyalty, like the personal work ethic, has as its first principle commitment to self and not to a place. One is loyal first to one's skill or profession and only secondarily to one's immediate place of employment. Again, as another "new worker" pointed out to me: "I put in my time, do my job, read the trades, network as much as possible and keep my résumé up to date. You have to. I could lose my job tomorrow, but I can't afford to lose my skills, my profession, my career, my future." Sequential loyalty is by definition limited and transitory. It is based on a quid pro quo relationship: unlike unrequited love, it must be offered and received before it can be returned, and it persists only as long as it proves to be mutually beneficial.

Not surprisingly, our traditional understanding of the Protestant work ethic persists with most of its ideological purity intact in the hearts, minds, and labor of recent immigrants to our shores. These new immigrants, like the generations of immigrants that preceded them, are the true keepers of the flame of the traditional work ethic. During the nineteenth century the greatest mass movement in human history occurred. More than thirty million Europeans left their homelands to settle in

America. This pattern of European immigration continued well into the twentieth century. As recently as 1940, 70 percent of all immigrants came from Europe. But by 1992 the pattern of immigration had changed both in terms of numbers and countries of origin. Presently the United States legally admits 700,000 to 900,000 new immigrants each year and absorbs an additional 300,000 illegal immigrants. However, only 15 percent of recent immigrants now come from Europe. Forty-four percent of all new immigrants come from Latin America and the Caribbean, and 37 percent come from Asia. But no matter what their country of origin, these new immigrants share a number of common links with the tidal wave of immigrants who came before them. First, the primary motive for most newcomers is and was economic—"Ubi panis ibi patria" ("Where there is bread there is country"). This may be, at bottom, the motto of all immigrants. Second, as a group, immigrants are self-selected self-starters. They are, if not born optimists, men and women who had the courage to pursue their dreams. Finally, immigrants seem to share a belief in the redemption and rewards of hard work. Their faith is the traditional faith of our Puritan forefathers: "Get a job, work hard, do well and things will necessarily be better than they were before." They work hard because they believe their efforts will secure a better future for themselves and, perhaps more important, for their children.[38]

The work ethic in all its various formulations contains elements of both myth and reality. The myth is in the sense that nineteenth-century philosopher George Sorel used the word, that is, that the truth of the myth is relatively unimportant as long as it furthers the end in view.[39] The reality is that some people do get ahead through hard work. In general, it must be remembered that the work ethic is a product of an era of scarcity and deprivation, when one either worked or starved. It made the negative aspects of work bearable by giving work a moral quality. It is also important to keep in mind that tracing the idea of work through history is difficult, and that the record is inconsistently one-sided. As Barbara Tuchman pointed out in *A Distant Mirror,* the history of an ancient society is usually limited to the record-keeping of the nobility and the intelligentsia. Few records are to be found depicting what the lower classes actually thought or felt about any momentous occurrence of their age, much less about the day-to-day experiences of work. We do, however, have the philosophical speculations of Aristotle, Aquinas, Calvin, and Jonathan Edwards. It is possible, therefore, that the proposition of the "nobility of work" is not a working-class concept but a middle-class one.[40]

In saying this, however, I do not wish to embrace the negatively cynical point of view that has labeled the Protestant work ethic as nothing more than ideological subterfuge geared to maximizing the workers' efforts, thereby increasing the owners' pool of capital and profits. An irate labor lawyer once told me, "The work ethic is nothing but management bullshit, designed to get the last ounce of energy out of their workforce! Duty? Commitment? Finding dignity in doing a job well? What dignity can be found in a job task that ends with the phrase, 'Would you like fries with your order, sir?'" Instead I believe that, historically, the Protestant work ethic has more often than not been used to mask the drudgery and necessity of work. Part of the overall effect of the work ethic myth was to acclimate the individual worker to the inevitable. It glorified and legitimized work and gave it a teleological orientation—a sense of purpose or design—that helped both to sustain individual effort and to ameliorate its temporal brutishness. At the very worst, Bertrand Russell may have been correct when he said, "The work ethic . . . is a device to trick people into accepting a life without leisure."[41]

According to labor and cultural historian Herbert Gutman, until quite recently few historians questioned the supposed ease with which most past Americans affirmed the Protestant work ethic. He points out, however, that many prominent Americans have made clear that the work ethic was not as deeply ingrained in our nation's social fabric as some today would have us think. Alexander Hamilton and Benjamin Franklin worried about the absence of such virtues within the working classes. When Hamilton proposed his scheme to industrialize the young republic, an intimate commented, "Unless God should send us saints for workmen and angels to conduct them, there is the greatest reason to fear for the success of the plan." Franklin too had such fears. He condemned relief for the poor in 1768 and lamented the absence among English workers of regular work habits. "Saint Monday," he said, "is as duly kept of our working peoples as Sunday; the only difference is that instead of employing their time cheaply at church they are wasting it expensively at the ale house." Franklin believed that if poorhouses were shut down,

"Saint Monday and Saint Tuesday" would "soon cease to be holidays."[42] In effect Hamilton and Franklin were lamenting the absence of a code of work values. They were advocating the imposition of some sort of myth or belief that could instill a productive focus in the working habits of an emerging nation. Obviously, they were more than a little successful in their endeavors.

For all of its glorification, and no matter how many honorifics we attach to it, work remains, in the eye of the common laborer, a task to be endured. As trade unionist Gus Tyler has stated, "There are at least two work ethics: that of the overseer and that of the overseen." He claims that workers are not opposed to the work ethic in any literal sense. "But work *per se* as an ethical imperative gets little, if any, attention because to union people work is such a necessity that it is almost unnecessary to construct a system of values, with theologic overtones, to justify labor. If American unionists have an ethic, it is probably best summed up in the old slogan: 'a fair day's pay for a fair day's work.'"[43] From the unionist point of view, therefore, the proper and only response to Max Weber's question "Do we work to live or live to work?" is "We work to live."

Recent appraisals of work and the worker by such scholars as Daniel Bell, Clark Kerr, Robert Strauss, Juliet Schor, and Daniel Yankelovich have confirmed the suspicion long held by most workers—dull, hard work is not necessarily ennobling and does not produce cultural heroes and role models. Working hard is a basic dimension of human existence; it is a duty. From this point of view, working is obligatory and, while it may at times well warrant a red, or at least a gray, badge of courage, it is basically a requirement of existence and only a means to an end. As a character in an Elmore Leonard detective mystery put it, "If work was a good thing, the rich would have it all and not let you do it."[44]

No matter what its historical origins, theological purpose, or economic intent, the Protestant work ethic, says Joseph Epstein, exists today almost solely as a pejorative phrase.[45] According to social critic Michael Harrington, whatever value it may have had, the Protestant work ethic has devolved to the notion that "a man establishes his worth in the eyes of his neighbor and his God . . . by doing drudgery and engaging in savings." [46] Too much of the work of life remains uninteresting, unenjoyable, and without obvious purpose and distinction. For too many of us, work remains the "curse of Adam," and to be relieved of it would be counted a boon and a blessing. Perhaps Sigmund Freud summed up the issue best:

> As a path to happiness, work is not highly prized by men. They do not strive after it as they do other possibilities of satisfaction. The great majority of people only work under the stress of necessity, and this natural human aversion to work raises most difficult questions.[47]

3

Collar Color Doesn't Count

> We don't consider manual work as a curse. . . . We consider it as a high human function, as a basis of human life, the most dignified thing in the life of a human being. . . . Men ought to be proud of it.
> —David Ben-Gurion

POPES, POETS, PSYCHIATRISTS, PHILOSOPHERS, and pundits all agree: Only the human race works, and work is the mark of humankind. Work forms and shapes our private lives and character as well as our collective history and physical accomplishments. None of us is completely neutral about work. Work is always a four-letter word, and, for all of us, our work is the primary means by which we are perceived, evaluated, and accorded social status. In excess of 129 million people constitute the American workforce. This vast army of workers labors at approximately 25,000 different full-time occupations. Although many of these occupations share similar income ranges, education, living standards, and lifestyles, class designation has conventionally been based on job description.

The traditional and most commonly used indices of determining class and status have been the distinctions made between blue-collar and white-collar workers. In the 1970s, with the sudden and continuing influx of women into the workforce, the term *pink-collar worker* had a short-lived currency in the literature. This classification was quickly dropped for a number of practical as well as philosophical reasons. To begin with, the term lumped all women into one category without regard to specific job descriptions or the usual distinctions that can be inferred from the stereotypes of blue and white-collar workers. Second, the term *pink-collar* suggested that women were transitory participants in the workplace—part-time or short-time workers, minority, underskilled participants who would not long remain on the job—rather than representing, as they presently do, 46 percent of the workforce. Finally, and not so surprisingly in an age of political correctness, the term was dropped because men and women alike found it not only inaccurate, but gender-biased.

The term *blue-collar* has always carried with it a certain negative, lowbrow connotation. As a group, blue-collar workers are thought of as physical laborers, earning their living primarily by means of their hands, their bodies, and their sweat. They are the farmers, masons, baggage handlers, assembly-line workers, and tradespeople of the world. As my grandfather, whose entire working life alternated between being a construction worker, a factory laborer, and a janitor, once told me, "A blue-collar guy is one who's got callouses on his hands and stinks so bad at the end of the day that he's got to change his clothes before he can get on the bus to go home at night. Guys who never have to change, and stay in the same clothes at night that they come to work in, they're either a salesman, a boss, or the owner."

As with all stereotypes, exceptions can easily be found. The general category of blue-collar worker also includes such uniformed jobs as skycaps, train conductors, bellhops, chefs, bartenders, maids, hairstylists, ticket vendors, and ushers. Nevertheless, the stereotype contains some truth. Blue-collar jobs are seen as physically taxing, often dangerous, tedious, and, for the most part, mindlessly repetitive. A popular song of the mid-1950s, "Sixteen Tons," by Tennessee Ernie Ford, neatly captures the spirit of the stereotype for blue-collar workers. "Sixteen Tons," about coal mining and coal miners, glorifies the efforts and determination of the miners and criticizes both their working conditions and the enormity of their workloads. The song chorus ends with the refrain: "Muscle and blood, skin and bone, a mind that's weak and a back that's strong."

White-collar jobs, on the other hand, do not have physical labor as a primary or regular ingredient. *White*-collar work does not soil one's clothes or cause one to perspire profusely, which is the reason for its metaphorical name. The color blue, by contrast, is more practical for jobs outside an office. White-collar jobs are supposedly professional jobs, office jobs, clerical jobs, management-type jobs that require brains rather than brawn and that demand a certain level of education and training. Stereotypically, white-collar jobs involve information, people contact, reasoned dialogue, and, today, of course, computer literacy.

White-collar workers have traditionally been accorded higher social status and a greater contentment rating than their blue-collar counterparts. Salaries aside for the moment, a white-collar job has been thought to be more engaging, more challenging, more complicated, and more creative than manual labor. A brief examination of the etymological origins of the basic job title of "clerk" helps to further explain the supposed social superiority of white-collar workers. The word *clerk* is derived from the Latin *clerics(us),* meaning "priest" or "ordained one." In medieval times it also connoted a person who was able to read, write, and calculate, because most, but not all, priests were required to know and study scripture and theology. Hence, clerics were distinguished from the general laity, which included both the nobility and the peasant populations, by virtue of their superior priestly functions and "clerical" abilities. Overall, it has long been maintained that white-collar workers' lives were physically easier and intellectually more satisfying than their blue-collar counterparts. As Dave Barry, nationally syndicated columnist and humorist, put it in a recent interview about writing and being a writer: "It sure beats the hell out of working a real job. The computer has made my life a snap. I have got the only job I know where I don't have to leave the house or even get dressed to earn a living."[1]

At the turn of the century white-collar workers constituted less than 20 percent of the workforce. In 1979, according to *U.S. News & World Report*, for the first time in our history, half of all American workers held white-collar jobs.[2] Harvard sociologist Daniel Bell claims that the rapid emergence of the white-collar class of workers coincides with our progression from an industrial-based economy to a postindustrial society. In the heyday of the industrial revolution, during the nineteenth century, we moved from a tool-based to a machine-based system of production. But these machines, which produced the modern benefits of an economy of scale, had to be maintained and supported by a vast army of industrial workers. The machines, for all their might, required intensive and constant human labor. Necessity and availability made the assembly-line job the model of what we understood to be typical urban work. According to Bell, it was only after the boom and bust of the 1920s, the slow rebuilding of the 1930s, the war economy of the 1940s, and the consumer goods explosion of the 1950s that we finally moved from a product-driven economy to an economy based on human services and knowledge.[3] Although this postindustrial economy also requires an army of workers to sustain it, the job descriptions and requirements of this labor force are quite different. Craftsmanship and physical strength are no longer the qualifications being sought; rather, the transference of information, the manipulation of data, and people-management skills have become the requisite skills for employment.

Jeremy Rifkin, economist and futurist, agrees with Daniel Bell's assessment that we live in a world that has been transformed by at least two major industrial revolutions. The first industrial revolution saw steam power help to mine ore, produce textiles, and manufacture a wide range of products formerly produced by hand. In the second industrial revolution, oil replaced coal and electricity as the new energy source to run our motors, light our cities, and provide us with instant communications. In the second industrial revolution, raw power and machines combined to replace more and more of the human tasks in the economic process.

Today, notes Rifkin, we are in the midst of yet another major industrial revolution that even further diminishes the need for manual laborers. The third industrial revolution, claims Rifkin, is being fueled and propelled by the continuous advances being made by the technology of the "information age." Sophisticated computers, robotics, telecommunications, and other cutting-edge technologies are changing the landscape of the workplace with regard to both the kinds of work that we do and the kinds of workers needed.[4] Although the old distinctions between white- and blue-collar workers will persist, the new technology of the information age is rapidly reducing the number of workers needed to maintain our economic base.

The new white-collar, or knowledge, workers will, in a short time, be represented by only the top 20 percent of the present white-collar workforce. The future of blue-collar work is in even greater peril, with less than 17 percent of the present workforce expected to be needed in the near future and continuing projected reductions of 5 percent per decade for the next two decades.[5] Soon white-collar, knowledge workers will be the new model of the typical urban worker and will represent the absolute majority of the working population. The problem of the future, according to Rifkin, will not be whether you are a blue- or white-collar worker, but, rather, whether you have a job at all.

Although they are a long-standing part of our cultural lexicon, the distinctions drawn between blue- and white-collar workers are neither accurate nor informative. These "portraits" of the labor force no longer help us to determine class, social status, affluence, or job satisfaction. Today, only a few of the characteristics of these stereotypes hold up to prolonged analysis.

To begin with, many professionals (individuals whose jobs require specialized training) bristle at being lumped, no matter how high in the pecking order, into the general category of white-collar workers. Lawyers, physicians, dentists, nurses, college professors, teachers, librarians, members of the clergy, social workers, musicians, police officers, and career military personal often do not see themselves as *workers*. Instead, they define what they do as a service, a social function, a stewardship, and in some cases a contribution or a gift to the community. They see their role, their occupation, as a calling, a lifestyle, a commitment to something or someone other than themselves. Typically, they believe in what they do, enjoy doing it, and are sensitive to the way in which their work affects others. Although many professionals earn high salaries, some claim that their primary motivations are the work itself and service to others. Interestingly, in a survey that asked a group of randomly selected professionals: "What would you do with the extra two hours a day if you had a twenty-six-hour day?" two out of three college professors and one out of four lawyers said they would use the extra time in some aspect of their profession. On the other hand, when nonprofessional workers were asked the same question, only one out of twenty reported that they would use the extra time in work-related activity.[6]

As an alternative to this outdated method of categorization, Tony Mazzochi offers a more meaningful perspective. Mazzochi, former vice president of the Oil, Chemical and Atomic Workers Union and labor advisor in the Clinton Administration, argues that the distinctions drawn between blue- and white-collar workers are artificial, arbitrary, and sociologically misleading. Like Samuel Gomphers and John Lewis before him, Mazzochi argues that within a capitalistic economy the only distinction of any real importance in the workplace is the line drawn between bosses or owners and labor. Although many blue- and white-collar individuals have achieved many of the benefits of middle-class existence, most workers remain economically entrenched in the lower class. For example, says Mazzochi, 1994 Census Bureau statistics suggest that 20 percent of workers in full-time jobs earn a wage under the poverty level of $13,500 for a family of four. And even many workers who have white-collar, professional jobs are forced to live perilously close to the financial edge. As a single working mother put it, "I have struggled for many years and it does not get better. . . . I am only one paycheck away from being homeless."[7]

Given these realities, Mazzochi suggests reviving the historical and now little used term "working class." The working class includes anyone who works for a paycheck, on a fixed or hourly basis, is not a member of management (but may have some minor supervisory responsibilities), and does not own a business. Members of the working class lack the resources of either large personal savings or family wealth, and while they may own their own homes, they do not own income-producing real estate. They must work for others because they have no other means of support and are dependent on a regular salary to maintain themselves. Being a member of the working class has nothing to do with your level of education, the amount you earn, or whether your job is blue- or white-collar. The working class includes both unskilled laborers and highly skilled professionals who are not self-employed. If you get a paycheck, whatever your job, title, or collar color, then you are a member of the working class.[8]

Another twist on the collar colors found in the workplace is offered by Ralph Whitehead, journalist and political demographer at the University of Massachusetts. Like Mazzochi, Whitehead doesn't feel that the categories of blue- and white-collar accurately reflect the realities of the modern workforce. Somewhere in between the professional and laboring ranks, says Whitehead, the postindustrialist economy has produced a new cadre of "rinso-blue" workers, which Whitehead calls the "new-collar class." New-collar workers are baby-boom kids all grown up and with a job. They are over 22 million strong, are now between thirty-three to fifty-two years of age and earn between $25,000 and $45,000 a year. About 55 percent of them have some higher education, but most of them find that their college education has little direct application to their current jobs. These new-collar workers are the yeoman successors of the traditional blue-collar class who didn't aspire to be young, upwardly mobile professionals (Yuppies, or to be more accurate, given their age, Muppies—middle-aged, urban professionals) or tradesmen, but rather entered that nether region of modern economic life known as the service sector.[9]

The category of new collar contains a wide variety of jobs. New-collar workers service and maintain computers; manage fast-food restaurants and retail shops; telemarket; teach at preschools and day-care centers; drive limos, work as travel agents, executive assistants, truck dispatchers, warehouse managers, dental hygienists, insurance adjusters, and real-estate appraisers, to name just a few examples. Most of these jobs do not conform to the standard models of blue- and white-collar occupations; instead, they are often a combination of both. For example, managing a McDonald's requires supervisory and organizational skills, but it also requires the ability to run the fry-machine when the staff is shorthanded. Computer and copy-machine technicians may show up at an office wearing a suit and carrying a briefcase, but the briefcase is full of tools. The technician's primary task is that of a repairperson, but in the new economy it also requires understanding computers and sophisticated electronics.

According to Whitehead, this recently recognized new-collar class of workers is not just an empty academic exercise in sociological labeling. New-collar workers represent 13 to 18 percent of the electorate, with annual spending patterns in excess of $400 billion. Individually, these workers may lack power and position, but collectively they represent one-third of the baby-boom generation, and their potential influence and impact on the nation is immense. Social scientists, therefore, want to understand them better. Advertisers and merchandisers are trying to tap into their lifestyles, their dreams, and their pocketbooks. Politicians have targeted them as the new "crucial swing bloc" that can decide the outcome of future elections at both the local and national levels. Holding positions somewhere between the professional and laboring ranks, the new-collar worker is a segment of the population that must now be reckoned with.

Another factor that has traditionally influenced our understanding of the differences between blue- and white-collar workers has been money. It was long assumed that blue-collar workers as a group made less money than white-collar workers as a group. It was, of course, understood that some blue-collar workers earned more than some white-collar workers, for example, a specialized tradesman versus a low-level clerk. Overall, however, white-collar workers were assumed to be financially better off than blue-collar workers, and this pay differential was a primary means of determining class status and lifestyle. This equation was never entirely accurate and, perhaps, is even less so now. Recently the Census Bureau released a series of statistics that categorizes class by incomes—specifically, combined household income—without consideration of either the types or the number of workers per household. At the very least, this practice of "class designation by dollars" partially reinforces Tony Mazzochi's argument that regardless of collar color, most of us are part of the working class.

According to the Census Bureau, 53 million households in America, with incomes of $25,000 to $100,000 a year, now constitute the middle class. These households represent 53.8 percent of all income-producing households, with 40.3 percent of other households earning less money and only 5.8 percent earning more. Within the spectrum of middle-class households, 14.7 percent earn $25,000 to $35,000; 16.3 percent earn $35,000 to $50,000; 16.1 percent earn $50,000 to $75,000; and 6.7 percent earn $75,000 to $99,000. Of those households below the cut-off for middle-class status, 16.9 percent earn $15,000 to $25,000, and 23.4 percent earn less than $15,000.[10]

Both the Census Bureau survey and a related story in *Newsweek* magazine celebrate the fact that so many working households (nearly three out of five) have achieved middle-class rankings. However, neither of them reflect on the 40.3 percent who earn less than $25,000 a year or comment on the shocking statistic that 23.4 percent of all working households earn only poverty wages ($13,500) or slightly more. Nor do either of them question the equity of only 5.8 percent of working households earning $100,000 or more a year (and, I hasten to add, just how much "more" is not specified).

Equally troubling is the broad range among those households categorized as being middle-class. At the higher end of the range the report's statistics seem fair, but the lower threshold figures for middle-class status are open to criticism and debate. Does $30,000 per year really qualify a household for middle-class status? It depends on a number of variables: How many people live in the household? How many of them are working? Full- or part-time? Is the household located in a rural or urban setting?

After taxes, an urban household of four to six individuals, with two of them working full-time, and a combined income of $30,000, would not necessarily be able to operate financially in or possess the mindset usually associated with middle-class existence. If, as William McCready, director of the Cultural Pluralism Research Center at the University of Chicago, suggests, being middle-class has traditionally meant being a property owner and having some degree of financial security, I doubt that the individuals in the last scenario would qualify.[11] Even an urban family of four with household earnings of $50,000, but with a mortgage to pay, children to educate, and cars to maintain might have a hard time maintaining their middle class-status and expectations. Certainly, such a household need not be pitied or thought of as poverty stricken. However, while they have options and are comfortable, they can hardly be considered affluent or free of financial worries.

There are a number of other crucial factors that the Census Bureau statistics don't tell us. To begin with, what makes up a household's total income? How many people must work to qualify for middle-class status? Assuming a traditional family structure, does the husband work full-time? Does the wife work full-time? Are the Social Security checks of a live-in mother-in-law computed into total monies earned? Are child-support payments for children from a previous marriage part of the household total? Assuming that two adults are working and that grandma and the kids receive monthly checks, such a household may add up to a middle-class living wage, even though no one of the parts involved would qualify.

The most important implication of the statistics generated by the Census Bureau is that we can no longer lump all white-collar workers into the middle class and all blue-collar workers into the lower class. If a $25,000 salary is the benchmark for middle-class status, then more people qualify than ever before, and, conversely, many jobs traditionally regarded as middle-class no longer qualify. For example, many "common" and most "elite" laborers can now be categorized as middle-class. In a casual survey I conducted of local, urban, nonunion, independent tradespeople who either work by themselves or with a crew of fewer than four, the following household incomes were reported. Assuming a forty-hour week and steady work throughout the year, small-appliance repairpersons reported earnings of between $15 and $17 per hour, or an annual income of at least $31,200. Finish carpenters said they charged $24 to $30 per hour, or $49,120 annually. Plumbers, electricians, and mechanics (a group I term elite laborers) demand $35 to $50 per hour, or a $72,800 annual wage.

On the other hand, many white-collar jobs that traditionally conferred middle-class status to their holders no longer meet the minimum financial threshold. In a number of interviews with human resource officers, employment agency personnel, and college job-placement departments, I learned that bank tellers and general office workers earn only $7.00 to $10.00 per hour, or $14,560 to $20,800 per year; experienced retail sales clerks and nonlegal secretaries earn $8.00 to $12.00 per hour, or a maximum salary of $24,960 per year; experienced word processors can expect to make $7.45 to $10.92 per hour, $15,500 to $22,750 per year; and telemarketing representatives are likely to earn $8.29 to $10.22 per hour, or $17,250 to $21,250. In these same interviews I also learned that the beginning salaries for most college graduates, including primary and high school teachers and those who majored in business or have a degree in accounting, is between $23,500 and $28,500 per year. The starting salary for a clinical social worker with a master's degree is approximately $19,500 annually, or $9.38 per hour. Moreover, because most social workers are employed by fiscally strapped community health programs, it often takes seven or more years before they achieve a $25,000 annual salary, or $12.02 per hour.

The final factor by which we have traditionally defined the differences between blue- and white-collar workers is job satisfaction. As I indicated earlier, it was simply taken for granted that white-collar workers enjoyed greater job satisfaction than did their blue-collar colleagues. The perpetuation of this belief was due in no small measure to the cries and laments of blue-collar workers themselves.

Since the mid-1950s, hordes of sociologists and industrial psychologists have descended upon the workplace (primarily, but not exclusively on the shop floor) in a frantic attempt to measure and analyze how workers relate to work, what they feel about work, and how work affects their private lives, personal values, and general world view. The results of these various surveys and studies have, for the most part, been strikingly similar. While the services and products they produce might be worthwhile, needed and desired, blue-collar workers report widespread dissatisfaction with their work. In what has come to be known as "blue-collar blues," blue-collar workers decried the uninteresting, unchallenging, nonstimulating, noncreative nature of the work they are forced to do. They claimed they felt trapped, bored, and humiliated by their work. As one worker related to Studs Terkel: "I think most of us are looking for a calling, not a job. Most of us . . . have jobs that are too small for our spirit. Jobs not big enough for people."[12]

In an important article, Stanley Seashore and J. Thad Barnowe argue that blue-collar workers by no means have a monopoly on job dissatisfaction.[13] They suggest that "vulnerability to 'blue-collar blues' is endemic to the whole workforce" and only slightly more exaggerated and recognized in blue-collar workers. White-collar workers also have their blues. The lament of uninteresting, unchallenging, uncreative work is no longer heard exclusively from the blue-collar worker. Managers and laborers, office workers and mechanics alike can now be heard to lament their nonexpansive occupations. After all, in terms of repetitive behavior, job inflexibility, and sheer boredom, data entry at a computer terminal doesn't differ much from operating a drill press or tightening down the same four bolts on an assembly line. However, Seashore and Barnowe are quick to point out that this does not mean that the "hierarchical gap" between managers and workers no longer exists. While managers remain generally more satisfied than clerical, hourly, and piecework employees, the distinctions and specific issues that once clearly separated management from all other types of employees are becoming blurred.[14] Whether you are a boss or just a common working stiff, every job has its problems. Just because you stay clean all day long working in an office doesn't mean you are any better off than an assembly-line worker. At the level of hassle, harassment, and headaches, a job is a job is a job.

Blue-collar, white-collar, new-collar—it doesn't matter. Collar designation doesn't count. Collar color no longer constitutes, in itself, the necessary and sufficient conditions required to categorize the workforce in terms of social class and salary levels. Bad jobs and poor pay can no longer be automatically associated with blue-collar workers, and good jobs with decent pay are no longer the exclusive domain of white-collar workers. Federal salary statistics have shown that our once handy social barometer of collar color designation now tells us nothing whatsoever—if it ever really did—about a worker's sense of self and job satisfaction. To determine job satisfaction we must look at specifics of the workplace beyond salary to take account of the attributes, talents, and potential of the worker. In other words, we must look at all aspects of the workplace—the process, the product, and the person.

Good Work/Bad Work

> A good job not only has to pay well, it also has to offer hope.
>
> —James Baldwin

WE WORK BECAUSE WE MUST. FEAR AND NEED make work a requirement of life. But we also work hoping to find self-expression, recognition, creativity, camaraderie, satisfaction, and meaning. Work fulfills a dual function in the development of the human psyche and character. It is both a response to the necessities of existence and the means by which we come to know who we are and how and where we belong. As Michael Maccoby, director of Harvard's Program on Technology, Public Policy, and Human Development has said:

> Work ties us to a real world that tells us whether or not our ideas and visions make sense; it demands that we discipline our talents and master our impulses. To realize our potentialities, we must focus them in a way that relates us to the human community. We need to feel needed. And to feel needed, we must be evaluated by others in whatever coinage, tangible or not, culture employs. Our sense of dignity and self-worth depends on being recognized by others through our work. Without work, we deteriorate. We need to work![1]

If work is the main activity by which we define and assess ourselves and others, then the type of work we do and the satisfaction we derive from it tells us a great deal about the quality of our lives. Abraham Maslow asserts that self-esteem and job satisfaction are fundamentally interconnected. He argued that "healthy and stable self-esteem (the feelings of pride, influence, importance, etc.) rests on good, worthy work."[2] People who feel needed, useful, satisfied in their work become important to themselves and more satisfied in other aspects of their lives. Maslow claimed that the only truly happy people he had ever known were individuals who were "working well [self-satisfaction] at something they consider[ed] important."

Self-worth and self-satisfaction are the direct results of having a worthy task to perform. Conversely, to be trapped in some mindless, robotized form of work is an absolute prescription for failure. Maslow claims that it is impossible for anyone to develop a strong sense of self and feelings of personal satisfaction with their lives if they work, for example, "in some chewing gum factory [presumably doing some repetitive job on the assembly line], or a phony advertising firm [pitching irrelevant and inane products], or in some factory that turned out shoddy furniture." Real achievement is the essential condition for both job satisfaction and self-esteem. Doing an idiotic job very well is not a real achievement because it does not contribute to self-worth and personal accomplishment. At the level of self-esteem and self-satisfaction Maslow's bottom line is simple: "What is not worth doing is not worth doing well!"

Unfortunately, both conventional wisdom and sociological surveys tell us that a significant portion of the workforce feels trapped in jobs that lack the possibly of "real achievement," "feelings of satisfaction," and the opportunity for the development of a "healthy and stable sense of self." For these individuals work remains an obstacle to endure instead of an opportunity to expand one's life. Clearly, the only satisfaction to be found in some jobs lies in the necessity of getting it done when no other alternatives are available. Survival, not satisfaction, becomes the goal. As a "survivor" of the Depression once told me: "Job satisfaction? What, are you kidding? Sometimes you gotta be satisfied just because you got a job!"

When a chewing-gum factory in New Jersey closed in the late 1970s, the workers most distressed were those who packed the cartons for shipping. Most of these workers were first-generation immigrants from Central Europe, and many had been at the plant for more than twenty years. The workers had shared lunches, celebrated birthdays, and supported each other in times of crisis. They found comfort and collegiality in what they did and who they were with.[3] These workers were probably not "self-actualized" by their work, according to Maslow's definition, but they were able to achieve a modicum of satisfaction and contentment in what they were doing.

In raising the topic of job satisfaction and what constitutes good work, we are, of course, venturing into well charted but highly contested territory. On one hand, we have the investigations and statistical surveys of the social scientists, and on the other, the insights of conventional wisdom and philosophical analysis. Neither camp is particularly willing to cede ground to the other.

Alex C. Michalos, editor of the *Journal of Business Ethics*, argues that human happiness and satisfaction are too elusive and subjective to be captured in the "clichés of common sense" or in the "wisdom of sages."[4] Michalos points out that philosophers don't even agree with each other. Some have claimed that happiness comes from living a virtuous life, while others claim that it comes from doing what you want and getting away with it. Some have said happiness comes from knowing the truth; others say it comes from believing in comfortable illusions. Some say it comes from making others happy; other say it comes only when we are primarily interested in our own well-being. Altogether, Michalos cites more than two dozen contradictory prescriptions for happiness and leaves us with a clear conclusion: We cannot rely on philosophers or conventional clichés. We need controlled investigations to distinguish the true from the obvious, the real from the apparent. The truth of the matter probably lies somewhere in between.

Life and labor are intertwined. Work is part of the human condition. We must work to survive as individuals and as a group. The history and progress of humankind can be measured by our combined efforts. Most of us possess a great deal of firsthand experience and knowledge about work. Therefore, I believe, the insights of all workers, be they servants or sages, are at least fundamentally true, and must be accorded serious consideration.

In the 1970s and 1980s thousands of surveys were conducted regarding the satisfaction or happiness of the worker on the job. The combined results of these surveys are edifying. These various studies concluded that job satisfaction increases with job enrichment, when workers participate in decision-making, with workers' perception of personal development through work, when workers are able to set their own work goals, and with flextime, and that it decreases with role ambiguity, with role conflict, and with high job turnover rates. Finally, the job satisfaction of working women was higher than the satisfaction that nonworking women got from doing housework.[5] The results of these and other surveys offer us an invaluable prescription for what the worker needs and the qualities necessary for a good workplace.

Nevertheless, job satisfaction is hard to define because of the number of variables involved. Clinical psychologist John Shack is convinced that job satisfaction is ultimately dependent upon the "doer" and what is being "done." The most important factor is the fit, the personality typology, of the worker for the job.[6] Personality typology, as first described by Carl Jung, is the sorting of personality types according to temperament and talent, and it can be applied to the workplace. According to Shack, this approach assumes that personality tendencies influence how individuals relate to general environmental stimuli as well as to particular work functions and demands. For example, if we can understand that someone makes decisions slowly because of a psychological processing style that requires lengthy periods of reflection, that person should not be looked upon as less intelligent than others if he or she takes longer to reach a decision. If someone is forgetful and disorganized as part of an introverted thinking style, they should not be blamed for conforming to their personality-type, especially under stressful circumstances. When job requirements are matched with a person's personality type and habitual behavior patterns, greater predictability and productivity prevail.

Shack argues that although talent and temperament do not define one's destiny, one's abilities directly influence what one is suited for as well as one's success on the job. The reality is that our biological types, as well as factors in our environments, place natural limits on our human potential. It is the "goodness of fit" between the "type of person" and the "demands of the workplace" that leads to work satisfaction. Part of the overall problem of job satisfaction, from both the employee and the employer's point of view, is getting the right type of talented people in the right type of job. Better matching of people to the job does not guarantee mutual satisfaction, but it is clear that people who are mismatched to their job tasks rarely, if ever, achieve satisfaction. Training and technique can allow an individual to achieve a modicum of success on the job, but success or accomplishment alone do not always result in personal satisfaction. Regardless of a job's status, individuals must be suited to the tasks of the job for satisfaction to be even possible.[7]

I once worked for about a year as a medical orderly in a major inner-city hospital emergency room. The injuries I saw varied widely. Some of the patients had just fallen or cut themselves while cooking. Others came in shot or stabbed or badly mangled from an automobile crash. They were white and black, men and women, young and old, and all of them were scared and in pain. I never developed thick enough skin for the job. Their wounds, their tears, their fears all got to me.

Each of the orderlies was assigned to a team. The teams were made up of two orderlies, four nurses, and a doctor. The doctor on the team I was regularly assigned to was one of the coolest, calmest people I had ever met. No matter how many people hit the door with cuts to be stitched, arms to be set, arteries to be stanched, he never panicked. He simply took care of the person in front of him with kindness and efficiency.

One morning toward the end of my tenure at the hospital, I told him how much I admired his work. He replied, "That is all just the result of good training and who I am." He said he had always had focus and that it was easy for him to get lost in particulars. He liked details, and when his father insisted that he go to medical school, he found he liked it because he found the details fascinating. The only thing he didn't like was dealing with people, with patients; so he decided to specialize in emergency-room care, which required less interaction with patients than other specialties. You only had to deal with the problem in front of you and then send the patient on to somebody else. "I simply learned to make a game out of it," he admitted. His patients were like puzzles to him, problems to solve. He concluded our conversation by saying, "I'm good at what I do, but I don't particularly like it."

In *The Will to Believe,* William James suggests that finding satisfaction in any aspect of life is dependent on a number of variables completely outside of the control of individuals, but in the end, it also depends on "the liver."[8] Although the meter and measure of work affects the character of what we do and how we think, none of us comes to work as a neutral entity without insights, interests, and predilections. While who we become is part of what we do, who we become also remains circumscribed by who we have the potential to be. Individuals whose talents and temperaments are suited to their particular job have a better chance of being a more satisfied person and a more productive employee.

In trying to match types to tasks there is, of course, the problem of job prestige and social status. There are a lot of jobs that people simply don't want to be connected to even though they may be well suited to them. Although I don't want to be an apologist for the necessity of "nasty" jobs, I think Albert Schweitzer was correct when he stated, "A man can do only what he can do. But if he does that each day he can sleep at night and do it again the next day." "Know thyself," as Socrates stated, and you will have a greater chance for professional happiness. According to John Shack, the wrong person in the wrong job affects not only the quality of the job performance, but the psychological well-being of the worker as well. In the end, job satisfaction is a delicate balancing act between the work, the worker, and the workplace.

However we choose to calculate the elusive goal of job satisfaction, one thing is certain: A substantial and ever-increasing portion of the workforce is not satisfied or happy with their work. More and more workers report that although their job absorbs and consumes their time and energy, it doesn't give them what they need. In 1974 national pollster Daniel Yankelovich claimed that only one out of every five American men felt that his work filled his psychological as well as economic needs.[9] In 1979 a survey of men and women, published by the University of Michigan, reported that worker dissatisfaction was at its highest point in over a decade: 60 percent of the workers surveyed wanted new jobs; 39 percent thought they were underpaid; 36 percent said they had unused skills; 36 percent felt overqualified for their jobs; and 55 percent wanted more time off.[10]

In 1987 in a nationwide survey, one out of four American workers claimed they were unhappy with their jobs. Another study in 1987 indicated that one-third of the middle managers interviewed wished they worked someplace else.[11] In 1991, Donald L. Kanter and Philip Mirvis surveyed 1,115 working Americans and found that 72 percent of the workers surveyed said they were dissatisfied with their jobs.[12] In a 1992 survey of 3,581 managers, 33 percent of those surveyed answered "no" to the question "All things considered, are you happy with your present job?"[13] In a 1994 survey, of 2,000 workers polled, one out of four reported being dissatisfied with their jobs, indicating that more than twenty-seven million American workers are unhappy at work.[14]

In 1995, career consultant Tom Welch rather pessimistically claimed that only 15 percent of us like our work and are able to find happiness in doing our jobs. Welch believes that 85 percent of the workforce has negative feelings, ranging from mild dissatisfaction to deep dislike toward their jobs. According to Welch, in a survey of retirees, 80 percent of those who were asked "What do you most regret in your life?" chose the response "Staying in a job or a career I did not like."[15]

In 1997 *GQ* Magazine commissioned an in-depth, nationwide survey on men's attitudes and expectations regarding work. Not surprisingly, 55.1 percent claimed that job satisfaction and work enrichment were their most important career goals. Only 25.3 percent said that they were more concerned with being a good provider and that job satisfaction was irrelevant. Fewer than 19 percent said making enough money in order to enjoy their time off was more important than job satisfaction. Personal and professional satisfaction were so important to those surveyed that 65 percent of them said they would seriously consider working fewer hours or accepting lower pay if it meant they could do what they really wanted to at work. However, although the men's avowed goal was personal career satisfaction, the reality of their jobs fell far short of their expectations. Although 58.4 percent said that they were working in a job or a field they wanted to continue with in the future, 48.7 percent claimed that their day-to-day work was neither interesting nor satisfying. Of those surveyed, 47.7 percent said their work was not creative, 46.3 percent said it lacked challenge, and 42.8 percent said that their jobs did not allow them the opportunity to learn new things.[16]

In effect, what many workers are now saying is that work is not enjoyable or satisfying in itself. More and more workers feel that their jobs lack any meaning and value beyond the utilitarian function of providing them with a paycheck. They feel caught in bad jobs, or, to use E. F. Schumacher's term, they feel caught in "bad work." According to Schumacher, bad work is

> mechanical, artificial, divorced from nature, utilizing only the smallest part of man's potential capabilities; it sentences the great majority of workers to spending their working lives in a way which contains no worthy challenge, no stimulus to self perfection, no chance of development, no element of Beauty, Truth, or Goodness.[17]

For Schumacher one of the darkest aspects of contemporary work life is the appalling number of men and women who are condemned to work that has no connection with their inner lives, no spiritual meaning for them whatever. Bad work offers no opportunity for the individual to become more than he or she already is, no sense of beauty and delight, and no sense of well-being in knowing that a job is contributing to oneself and others.

Work, for too many, is perceived as "downtime," something that must be done but that does not add to who they are. In the early 1970s *Life* magazine did a story on a twenty-five-year-old male auto worker at General Motors. His job was a simple one: As a car came down the line he inserted the right front window into the door frame of the car. Someone else would later connect it to the window assembly. Because times were good for the company, he performed this same task eight to ten hours a day, Monday through Friday, and, often put in six to eight hours of overtime on Saturday. This "lineman" had been doing this task for four years. The money and the benefits were good, and in ten years or so, he'd have enough seniority for a better job on the line. The problem was finding a way to stick it out till then.

Each day he worked on the line alone. His closest coworker was on the other side of the car putting in the left front window, but the din of the line made it impossible for them to talk. Except for three ten-minute breaks and a forty-five-minute lunch, he did his job alone and without human contact. He said the trick of getting through the day was to get into "downtime" and not to think about anything else but the job. You had to get into a rhythm and become a robot. Daydreaming or not paying attention was too dangerous. You could put the wrong window in and have to stop the line, or you could break a window and get cut. Like Ben Hamper, blue-collar journalist and author of *Rivethead*, who was simultaneously working down the road at the GM truck assembly plant, our lineman quickly learned that the cardinal rule for survival and sanity was to never, never look at the clock. Looking at the clock made what Raymond Carver called "the sluggishness of swampy time" pass even more slowly. It made, said Hamper, "the monotony gnaw away at you." It made you nervous, jumpy. It made you make mistakes. Worktime was downtime, and downtime let you shut everything else off and get through the day.

Like this lineman, and Ben Hamper, too many workers feel that the goal their jobs is survival rather than productivity and personal growth.

Too many workers believe their jobs have nothing to do with their inner sense of self, at least not in a positive sense. Too often, they're right. Too often, frustration at work finds expression in addiction, depression, withdrawal, or violence. The interviews in Studs Terkel's book *Working* hammer the point home that for many of us work is a purely alien occupation, one that we try to distance ourselves from whenever possible. As one worker put it, "Unless a guy's a nut, he never thinks about or talks about it. Maybe about baseball or about getting drunk the other night or he got laid or didn't get laid. I'd say one out of a hundred actually gets excited about work."[18]

Schumacher asserts that bad work alienates the worker both from himself and from his work. An alienated worker is one who engages in activities that are not rewarding in themselves, that might be demanding in some respects but permit little or no originality, latitude, discretion, or sense of fulfillment. In this regard Schumacher echoes one of Karl Marx's earlier descriptions of alienation:

> What constitutes the alienation of laboring? That working is external to the worker, that it is not part of his nature and that, consequently, he does not fulfill himself in his work, but denies himself, has a feeling of misery rather than well-being, does not develop freely his mental and physical energies but is physically exhausted and mentally debased. . . . Its alien character is clearly shown by the fact that as soon as there is no physical or other compulsion it is avoided like a plague.[19]

Schumacher and Marx contend that most workers in routine jobs perform adequately even though their tasks are not stimulating. Even when work is not intrinsically rewarding, pay and job security offer a modicum of satisfaction. The subtleties of this satisfaction are illustrated by an interview that sociologist George Strauss had with a worker in a fairly routine blue-collar job. The worker told Strauss, "I got a pretty good job." When Strauss asked, "What makes it such a good job?" the worker responded somewhat quizzically:

> Don't get me wrong. I didn't say it is a *good* job. It's an O.K. job—about as good a job as a guy like me might expect. The foreman

leaves me alone and it pays well. But I would never call it a good job. It doesn't amount to much, but it's not bad.[20]

Strauss calls this attitude "worker apathy." The worker's expectations are low, but he accepts the situation because of the pay or because it's the best he can get. The worker may be unhappy, but his unhappiness is manageable and does not lead to troublesome on-the-job behavior.

Sociologist Robert Kahn suggests that for most workers the only choice is between no work or a job burdened with negative qualities. In these circumstances, individuals choose work, and they then pronounce themselves moderately satisfied with what they do.[21] Some workers adjust to their job by viewing work in purely instrumental terms or as a means to other ends. Strauss indicates that a significant number of workers elect to take on high-paying but boring jobs in order to support their real interests.[22] This is the kind of compromise that many people feel they must make.

In his encyclical "On Human Work," Pope John Paul II stated that in work not only should "matter gain in nobility," but individuals should not experience "a lowering of [their] nobility" in the work being done.[23] This statement is similar to one by Schumacher regarding good work. "Good work," according to Schumacher, "ennobles the product as it ennobles the producer." Schumacher believes that good work is part of the "university of life." It is one of the joys of life and is a requirement for our mature development, but meaningless work is detrimental to our well-being.[24] Schumacher's message is analogous to the ancient Greek definition of happiness: Good work is the use of all of one's powers to achieve excellence.

Practically speaking, good work means meaningful work, the nature of which is neither esoteric nor mysterious. W. H. Auden believed only three things are necessary for meaningful work: The person must be fit for it, must not do too much of it, and must achieve some sense of success in doing it.[25] According to demographer and pollster Daniel Yankelovich, for most people meaningful work is work in which they become involved and to which they are committed, work that challenges and increases their capabilities, and work that allows them to participate in decision-making.[26] Sociologist Robert Kahn calls meaningful work "humanistic work" and defines the humanization of work as the process of making work more appropriate for an adult to perform:

> 1) Work should not damage, degrade, humiliate, exhaust, stultify, or persistently bore the worker; 2) It should interest and satisfy him; 3) It should utilize many of the valued skills and abilities he already possesses and provide opportunity for him to acquire others; 4) It should enhance, or at least leave unimpaired, his interest and ability to perform other major life roles—as husband or wife, parent, citizen and friend, and 5) It should fulfill the instrumental purpose of getting a living, in terms acceptable to him.[27]

According to *Work in America,* the 1973 task force report to the Secretary of Health, Education and Welfare: "When it is said that work should be 'meaningful,' what is meant is that it should contribute to self-esteem, to a sense of fulfillment through the mastering of one's environment, and to sense that one is valued by society."[28]

In sum, a meaningful job is one that the employee enjoys and excels in, often feeling in control of the work activity. It is a job that fits the individual worker's talents and personality. It is a job in which the incentive to work is not fear or compulsion but rather a search for fulfillment. Most important, as ethicist Patricia Werhane has pointed out, meaningful jobs require that one has information about one's work; without it, job decisions cannot be intelligently made. According to Werhane, since work enjoyment can develop only from involvement in business decisions, meaningful employment requires some form of participation in the decision-making process.[29]

Business ethicist Norman E. Bowie argues that while making a profit is an important and necessary condition for any business, the main purpose of all businesses and corporations should be to provide meaningful work for their employees:

> I take it as a psychological truth that all human beings need to be engaged in rewarding work where rewarding work is defined as work that is useful, challenging and respectful of individual autonomy. Moreover, providing meaningful work is more important than the producing of goods and services. It seems obvious that a

> person can be deprived of nearly any product or even most products industry produces without suffering severe psychological harm. But if a person is denied meaningful work the psychological harm is very great. That is why I argue that it is morally . . . important for business to focus on the employee.[30]

Employees cannot and should not be treated as so many means to an employer's end. Human labor should never be treated solely in accordance with the economic laws of profit maximization. Employees should not be treated like mere equipment in the production process, and any system that fails to recognize the distinction between human beings and other nonhuman factors of production is morally deficient. Like Thomas Peters and Robert Waterman, the authors of the classic bestseller *In Search of Excellence,* Bowie suggests that work must be both a means to an end and an end in itself. Therefore, the central focus of the workplace must be "How do people work best?" and not "How can work best use people?"

Bowie maintains that in focusing on the employee and providing meaningful work, businesses will exhibit morality. Moreover, as a direct result of their commitment to their employees, businesses are more likely to produce quality goods and services for their customers and generate greater profits for themselves. In other words, "In doing good they are also likely to do well."[31]

Bowie's fellow business ethicist Joanne B. Ciulla disagrees with much of Bowie's argumentation but agrees in principle with his conclusion that corporations have a moral responsibility to redesign jobs and create meaningful work. Where jobs cannot be made more interesting, Ciulla believes companies need to think of ways to accommodate employees so that their jobs do not hinder their need to lead a satisfying life outside of the workplace. At bottom, morality requires that corporations offer meaningful work because all individuals have a right to a meaningful life.[32] As Albert Camus wrote in his allegorical essay on the human condition, *The Myth of Sisyphus*:

> The Gods had condemned Sisyphus to ceaselessly rolling a rock to the top of a mountain, where the stone would fall back of its own weight. They had thought with some reason that there is no more dreadful punishment than futile and hopeless labor.[33]

This need for good or meaningful work is also seen in workers' physical health. It is well established that work stress can lead to physical illness, heart disease, ulcers, as well as alcoholism or drug addiction. The impact of routine or boring work, however, is less clear and more difficult to measure. Many people who do routine work report having happy and uncomplicated home lives, but the percentage who do not is high, and statistical studies indicate a direct correlation between routine, low-skilled work and off-the-job dissatisfaction. These studies imply, as philosopher Adina Schwartz has argued, that interesting work is a requirement of mental health.[34] One such study is Arthur Kornhauser's classic text *Mental Health of the Industrial Worker*, in which he states:

> Factory employment, especially in routine production tasks, does give evidence of extinguishing workers' ambition, initiative, and purposeful direction towards life goals. . . . The unsatisfactory mental health of working people consists in no small measure of their dwarfed desires and deadened initiative, reduction of their goals and restriction of their efforts to a point where life is relatively empty and only half meaningful.[35]

Kornhauser's study of the Detroit automobile worker concludes that mental health at work, like job satisfaction, varies according to status. "Mental health is poorer among factory workers as we move from skilled, responsible, varied types of work to jobs lower in those respects."[36] Kornhauser also concluded that mental health was poor among those workers who felt that they had no chance to use their abilities. It was suggested that low-grade work caused lowered self-esteem, discouragement, futility, and feelings of failure and inferiority, in direct contrast to the sense of personal growth and self-fulfillment resulting from more varied, responsible, challenging undertakings that afford opportunity to develop and use one's ideas and skills.

A somewhat different argument that nevertheless reinforces the position that people want and need good work can be found in the theory of clinical psychologist Fredrick Herzberg, one of the pioneer researchers in the allied fields of "meaningful work" and "satisfaction in the workplace."[37] Herzberg's research led him to conclude that job satisfaction and dissatisfaction are not simply opposite points on a continuum but actually two separate dimensions. Herzberg believed that motivation is composed of two factors: first, extrinsic factors, or those issues and activities that prevent dissatisfaction but do not propel workers to grow; and second, intrinsic factors, or those elements that directly motivate workers to grow and excel. Extrinsic factors, such as company policy, incompetent supervision, or unsatisfactory working conditions, often lead to dissatisfaction. This dissatisfaction may be reduced by such "hygienic measures" as higher pay, increased fringe benefits, better working conditions, human relations training for supervisors, or improved company policies. However, such measures will not make workers satisfied. For true satisfaction to be obtained, intrinsic factors such as achievement, accomplishment, responsibility, and challenging work must be provided. Satisfaction, then, is a function of the content of work, while dissatisfaction is based in the environment or the context of work. For Herzberg, only satisfaction can lead to increased productivity. The presence of dissatisfaction may cause low morale or absenteeism, but its elimination will not raise motivation or productivity. Therefore, while traditional hygienic, extrinsic improvements may make the work environment more tolerable, they will not necessarily raise motivation or productivity. The latter depends on enriching jobs to make them more interesting and important.[38]

In the end, all workers want the same thing—a good job! According to Robert Kahn, this holy grail has a universal definition:

> A good job is one in which the work is interesting, I have a chance to develop my own special abilities, and I can see the results of my work. It is a job where I have enough information, enough help and equipment, and enough authority to get the job done. It is a job where the supervisor is competent and my responsibilities are clearly defined. The people I work with are friendly, and helpful, the pay is good, and so is the job security.[39]

Regrettably, however, only a few of us have jobs wherein the details of our daily work are meaningful, work that the worker is proud of, is in control of, is able to make a living at and learn from.[40]

Good work is the ideal, but, clearly, good work is hard to find. Perhaps the only realistic compromise available to most of us is to focus on whatever is good in our work. The conclusion, nevertheless, remains

Marx's dictum: "As individuals express their life, so they are."[41] As individuals we must find work that is good for us; as a society we must create work that is good for individuals. Educator and essayist Joseph Epstein nicely summarizes these thorny issues of good work and the well-balanced personality:

> I sometimes think that the world is divided between those who work so they can live and those who live chiefly so they can work. I make this sound more black-and-white, either-or, one-way-or-the-other than it truly is. But the fact is, in my experience, some of the most forlorn people I know are those who haven't found their work: people of artistic temperament who have no art to practice, leaders without followers, serious men and women with nothing serious to do. On the other side, people who have found their work can seem, while at work, creatures of great dignity, even beauty. "A man blowing a trumpet successfully is a rousing spectacle," noted the Welsh writer Rhys Davies in one of his short stories. And so, too, is a man or woman working at anything he or she loves.[42]

Lack of Vision

Work without meaning is deadly.
—Matthew Fox

IF WORK SHAPES AND DEFINES PEOPLE, THEN forms of work are needed that will help rather than impede self-realization: jobs that offer meaning as well as money; jobs that impart dignity to the product and the person; jobs that *connect* workers and their lives; jobs wherein "the doing is as important as what gets done, the making as valuable as the made."[1] Jobs that meet workers' three kinds of needs: body, mind, and spirit.[2] But jobs such as these are hard to find. According to theologian Matthew Fox, too many of us cry out, "Our jobs are too small! . . . Our work is not revelatory." For too many of us, work contains no mystery, no deep passion, no real truth. It is drudgery without meaning, sweat without purpose, duty without play, toil without learning. Worst of all, our work lacks dignity and hope for the future. And when our work lacks dignity and hope, so do we.[3]

E. F. Schumacher holds that the process of production seeks, no matter what it promises in regard to the "empowerment" and "enfranchisement" of the workforce, "efficiency." Except in the most superficial manner, work is not adapted to the needs of the worker, but, rather, the worker must adapt to the needs of the work. The needs of the work stunt the worker and reduce the work to "nothing but a more or less unpleasant necessity." Although the modern workplace goes to great lengths to protect workers' bodies, little or no attention is paid to the potential damage to their psyches and spirits.[4]

Lost in the "equation" of the workplace are the needs and aspirations of the worker. Work becomes most relevant for the worker when it is, as Studs Terkel put it, "about a search . . . for daily meaning as well as daily bread, for recognition as well as cash, for astonishment rather than torpor; in short, for a sort of life rather than a Monday through Friday sort of dying."[5] Classical wisdom defines the core of human nature, at least partially, as *homo faber:* man the doer, man the worker. As *homo faber* humankind deserves good work, and the requirements for good work are not fulfilled by money and job security alone.

According to Schumacher, work should fulfill three basic functions, each of which is central to human life. First, work should provide the goods and services needed for existence. Second, work should allow us a chance to utilize and develop our talents and abilities. Third, work should create community through collaboration with others.[6]

Most of us get only the first of Schumacher's three basic functions. For too many of us, in any type of job, "work is regarded as little more than a means to making money."[7] Too many of us merely trade our labor for dollars and then busy ourselves with trying to better our private lives. Satisfaction has been reduced to finding a job that pays enough so that we can afford to pursue the life we desire *off* the job. Too many of us feel trapped by our jobs. We feel, in the words of the thirteenth-century German mystic Meister Eckhart, stuck in "work without a why" or a vision.[8]

One of the underlying reasons for this failure of meaning and vision in our work is that so few of us participate in the whole purpose, including the final product, of our work. The root of this disassociation lies in the centerpiece of modern industrial capitalism—Adam Smith's division of labor. In *The Wealth of Nations,* Smith reported on visiting a small pin factory employing only ten people, each of whom was doing just one or two of the eighteen specialized tasks involved in making a pin.

> One man draws out the wire, another straightens it, a third cuts it, a fourth points it, a fifth grinds it at the top for receiving the head; to make the head requires two or three distinct operations; to put it on is a peculiar business, to whiten the pins is another; it is even a trade by itself to put them into the paper. . . . Those ten persons could make among them upwards to forty-eight thousand pins a day. . . . But if they all worked separately and independently . . . they certainly could not each of them have made twenty, perhaps not one pin a day. . . .

> This great increase of the quantity of work . . . is owing to three different circumstances; first, to the increase of dexterity in every particular workman; secondly, to the saving of the time which is commonly lost in passing from one species of work to another; and lastly, to the investment in a great number of machines which facilitate and abridge labor, and enable one man to do the work of many.[9]

Smith believed the "division of labor," as reflected in the pin factory, would create efficiency and wealth for both nations and individuals. All laborers' income would be increased when production rose, and it would indeed rise because "the whole attention of [workers'] minds is directed toward [a] single object."[10]

More than a hundred years and an entire industrial revolution later, Frederick Winslow Taylor expanded on Smith's concept of the division of labor. Taylor, a machinist and engineer who worked in the early twentieth century, applied the scientific method to the workplace. He believed the productivity of any job could be improved by breaking down the components of a task, motion by motion, finding the best way to perform each motion, and then redesigning the job so that each motion could be done as efficiently as possible. According to management professor Robert A. Russell, Taylor's contribution to the efficient management of production can be summarized in four basic ideas.

1. The development of laws and scientific principles for work tasks to replace old-fashioned or traditional methods.
2. The scientific selection and training of workers.
3. The bringing together of science and the trained worker by offering better treatment and an opportunity for the expression of employee needs.
4. The division of work into two equal sections, one section for the worker and one section for management, the total effort requiring a cooperation between the two parties.[11]

Taylor saw his theories as benevolent. He was seeking "the one best way" to do a job by uniting the needs of the job, the ability of the workers, and an outcome that produced profit for all. In his landmark book *Scientific Management,* Taylor argued that the objective of every job is "to secure the maximum prosperity for the employer, coupled with the maximum prosperity of each employee." Both must be served for progress to be made.

What grew out of Taylor's work are the now-infamous "time-and-motion" studies which sliced and diced every job into overly simplified specific tasks to streamline workers' movements and thereby increase their output. It was hoped that workers would benefit, not from the meaningfulness of their tasks, but from the increased pay based on the greater efficiency of their labor. Although Frank and Lillian Gilbreth, husband-and-wife industrial psychologists, were successful in applying time-and-motion studies to the needs of handicapped workers, Taylor's efforts to "humanize" the workplace generally came to be viewed as an attempt to manipulate laborers in the same way engineers manipulate machines.

According to Michael Hammer and James Champy, the reigning gurus of corporate reengineering, the legacy of Smith's prototypical pin factory and Taylor's scientific management still serve as a model for the modern workplace.

> Today's airlines, steel mills, accounting firms, and computer chip makers have been built around Smith's central idea—the division or specialization of labor and the consequent fragmentation of work. The larger the organization, the more specialized is the worker and the more separate steps into which the work is fragmented. This rule applies not only to manufacturing jobs. Insurance companies, for instance, typically assign separate clerks to process each line of a standardized form. They then pass the form to another clerk, who processes the next line. These workers never complete a job; they just perform piecemeal tasks.[12]

Sadly, such a model of work, in the words of Schumacher, ennobles neither the product nor the producer. The process of our work affects who we are and how we view the world, and surely Smith's and Taylor's contributions to the workplace produce workers who—as Smith himself suggests—are both numb and dumb to what they do and why they do it.

Although Smith praised the pin factory arrangements in *The Wealth of Nations*, in another section called "The Education of Youth," Smith makes clear that he fully understood the dehumanizing effects of the "mode of production" on the worker.

> In the progress of the division of labor, the employment of the far greater part of those who live by labor, that is, of the great body of the people, comes to be confined to a few simple operations, frequently to one or two. But the understanding of the greater part of men are necessarily formed by their ordinary employments. The man whose whole life is spent in performing a few simple operations has no occasion to exert his understanding. . . . He naturally loses, therefore, the habit of such exertion, and generally becomes as stupid and ignorant as it is possible for a human creature to become. The stupor of his mind renders him not only incapable of relishing or bearing a part in any rational conversation, but of conceiving any generous, noble, or tender sentiment and consequently of forming any just judgement concerning many even of the ordinary duties of private life. . . . It corrupts even the activity of the body, and renders him incapable of exerting his strength with vigor and perseverance, in any other employment than that to which he has been bred.[13]

If work is human living, human being, human becoming—what can we realistically become when we do work such as this?

Partially underlying and explaining Smith's and Taylor's perspectives both historically and ideologically, is the Newtonian model of the world and its philosophy of human nature. Sir Isaac Newton's principal metaphor for the universe was a machine. Like a machine, reality is made up of parts, and the way these parts interact maintains the world as we know it. Like a machine, all of nature is controlled by eternal mathematical laws, and God, the supreme engineer and mathematician, created these laws and set them in motion. Humankind can apply scientific reasoning to learn these laws and then to predict and partially control the mechanics of the universe. In Newton's machinelike worldview, human beings are replaceable, interchangable cogs in the system. Any of us can do any job as long as we conform to the system and abide by the rules. In Newton's cosmology the world is a machine, and humankind is a part of the machine. An individual can be retooled, reprogrammed, or reconfigured to fit the needs of the system.

Cultural historian Theodore Roszak believes that the Newtonian model remains the operational ideal in the worlds of business and commerce today, and that, as individuals, we are servants of its dictates.

> Industrialism demands massification for its extra-ordinary power over nature: mass production, mass media, mass marketing. Our complex global economy is built upon millions of small, private acts of psychological surrender, the willingness (and necessity) of people to acquiesce in playing their assigned parts as cogs in the great social machine that encompasses all other machines. They must shape themselves to be prefabricated identities that make efficient coordination possible.[15]

Roszak suggests that good work may not be possible because there is no exit from the demands of industrialism and the mechanistic view of nature. Our only purpose is to produce. Desire, larger purpose, love, attraction—these are not necessary components of work. The machine does not honor or value beauty—only utility and efficiency.[16]

Let us be very clear about the problem at hand. The issue is not work per se. Work has always been the center of life. To live is to work. We accept it as a necessary fact; but at the same time we see it as external, imposed, and unnatural. We rebel against boring brutality, its staggering emptiness. As one working stiff put it: "I work to take care of my family and so I don't stop to ask whether I like my work or not."[16] Perhaps poet-farmer Wendell Berry best framed the problem when he said: "All work contains drudgery; the issue is whether it holds meaning or not."[17]

Survey after popular survey reports that people, when given a choice, want to work. In 1955 two sociologists, Nancy Morse and Robert Weiss of the University of Michigan's Survey Research Center, published the results of a study of more than four hundred men. They asked, "If by chance you inherited enough money to live comfortably without working, do you think you would work anyway?" Eighty percent of all respondents replied positively, but the percentages were slightly higher for professional and lower white-collar workers (86 percent) than for blue-collar workers (76 percent).[18]

At regular intervals this survey was expanded (by both increasing the numbers surveyed and including women) and repeated by various research organizations. The results of these follow-up surveys essentially reaffirmed the original survey results: The percentage of those choosing to work ranged from 67.4 percent (1969, University of Michigan), 71.5 percent (1977, University of Michigan), 73 percent (1974, Yandelovich), to 75 percent (1978, University of Michigan).[19]

In 1983 researchers at the University of Kentucky polled 7,281 adults nationwide on the same topic. Seventy-four percent of the men and 64 percent of the women surveyed said they would continue to work. While married men were more inclined than married women to keep working, single men and single women were equally likely to stick with it. Younger, better educated respondents with more prestigious jobs were more likely to want to stay employed than older individuals and less educated respondents, but the majority of all groups still reported that they would stay at work.[20]

In 1987 *The Meaning of Work,* a survey of 15,000 persons in eight nations, reported the following results. Eighty-six percent said they would continue to work even if they had enough money to live comfortably for the rest of their lives without working.[21] In the combined samples of all nations, when asked which was the most important among five life factors (family, work, community, religion, and leisure), 39.5 percent placed family as most important, while 26.5 percent placed work. A 1997 survey by *GQ* magazine reported that 55.1 percent of the men interviewed were satisfied with their jobs and 58.4 percent looked at their jobs as a career choice in a field they would like to continue with in the future.[22]

Of course, besides these surveys of hypothetical behavior, we can now analyze the actual choices of recent multimillion-dollar lottery winners. Although many of these lucky individuals see their winnings as liberty from labor forever, a surprising number of them claim, at least at their initial press conferences, that they are going to keep their jobs, or at least keep working. These winner-laborers report that, although they plan to live "better," they either like their jobs, don't know what else to do with themselves, or just don't want to do anything else with their lives.

There is a big difference between attitudes toward specific jobs and attitudes toward working. According to the 1973 report *Work in America*, one of the most reliable indicators of job dissatisfaction is the response to the question "What type of work would you try to get into if you could start all over again?" Significantly, of a cross-section of white-collar workers surveyed, only 43 percent said they would choose the same work that they were doing, and only 24 percent of blue-collar workers reported that they would choose the same kind of work if given another chance.[23] Three University of Michigan surveys also indicate that although many people maintain a high motivation to work, fewer and fewer people want to stay with the work that they do.[24]

"If you were free to go into any type of job you wanted, what would your choice be?"

	1969	**1973**	**1977**
The job he or she now has:	48.2%	43.7%	38.1%
Retire and not work at all:	6.4%	4.6%	1.9%
Prefer some other job to the job he or she has now:	44.4%	51.7%	60.0%

Although these statistics are somewhat dated and I have not been able to find these particular surveys replicated recently, I believe their findings remain valid: People want to work but they don't like their jobs. In the *GQ* survey, although 55.1 percent responded as being satisfied with their jobs, 65 percent of those surveyed said they'd consider working fewer hours or accepting lower pay if it meant they could do what they really want to earn a living. Seventy-three percent said they would like to quit their jobs and run their own business, and 40.9 percent of them viewed their jobs as nothing more than a means to earn money or as a steppingstone to another job. These statistics certainly reinforce the thesis that of people are willing to work, but not necessarily at the jobs they presently hold.[25]

Furthermore, since 1990 I have been conducting an informal survey of my male friends and associates about their attitudes regarding their careers and work in general. (I intentionally limited my survey to men because, for the most part, the women in my age group, born in the 1940s, either did not begin their careers until their families were started or interrupted their work life to start their families.) All of the 150 men I have questioned were over forty-five years of age and had been working a minimum of twenty years. Seventy-five percent of them were college-educated. Eighty percent considered themselves professionals (i.e., having a career rather than just a job), and 85 percent of them have been working in the same field their entire work lives. Ninety percent of them were Caucasians, and all of them considered themselves "comfortably middle-class." Although all of them had good or positive things to say about their work, to one degree or another they shared three complaints: exhaustion, burnout, and disillusionment/disappointment.

Their complaints of exhaustion seemed to be directly connected to their age and the particular difficulties of their various jobs. All reported being tired and lacking in energy to one degree or another. Even those who said that they loved their work lamented that they no longer had the stamina they once had. As one of the men said, "I can still keep up with anybody and do my job, but when I get home at night, I'm through. I want to eat, watch a little TV, and get to bed before ten P.M.; otherwise, I can't function the next day."

Burnout also seems to be connected to age and time rather than to desire and commitment to one's work. Complaints of burnout centered on "doing too much of the job too long," losing "edge," or losing "focus." As a longtime high-school teacher put it, "I have been at it for thirty-two years. That's five classes a day, nine months a year, not counting summer school. Don't get me wrong—I think education is important, and I love kids . . . but enough is enough. I just don't have it anymore, and it's beginning to show. I'm beginning to hate Septembers. Hate freshman. Hate Intro to Latin. Sometimes I think that if I have to repeat the phrase *America est pulchra, America est pater noster* (America is beautiful, America is my home country/fatherland) too many more times, I'll go nuts! Think about it, nobody can do a matinee and two supper shows seven days a week and stay sharp. Nobody!"

Exhaustion and burnout are perhaps inevitable in any job. Fatigue is, after all, simply the natural result of labor. However, my survey group's third and most telling complaint of disillusionment/disappointment speaks directly to the issue at hand: We want to work but don't always like the work we do.

Fifty-five percent of the men I interviewed said that they were unhappy with their chosen work and would rather have done something else with their lives. A criminal defense attorney said he loved the law but regretted the branch of law he had chosen. "Too many times," he said, "I got people off, even though I knew they were guilty. The game is about evidence, not justice, and I played the game well and got paid well for doing it. So I kept doing it, but I wish I hadn't." A successful salesman was even harsher in his assessment of his career. "Besides the money, what have I accomplished? What have I done that matters? What have I contributed to anybody outside of my company's bottom line? To top it off, most of the time I was bored to death with what I was doing!"

While comments such as these can be written off as the jaded grumblings of middle-aged men, at the core of their complaints are a series of issues common to the group. Most of the men felt that although they had worked hard, their efforts left no real imprint on the world. Many felt that although their jobs had given them a good life in safe suburban enclaves, their work gave them very little else of lasting social value. Echoing the thesis of Barbara Ehrenreich's *Fear of Falling,* these men felt they had struggled to achieve middle-class existence for themselves and dutifully passed it on to their children—but nothing more.[26]

Surprisingly, when asked what they wanted to do instead, few men were able to say exactly. However, when asked to list the qualities they hoped to find in their dream job, they agreed almost unanimously regarding two key ingredients: stimulation and an active contribution to the well-being of others. Like psychologist Otto Rank, they wanted work that allowed them to "leave behind a gift."[27] Even though many of these men had achieved status and financial security, they felt that at best their successes were Pyrrhic victories. It's not always nastiness that makes a job unappealing; sometimes it's a gnawing sense of emptiness.

Forensic psychiatrist Park Deitz claims in his TV documentary, *Murder 9 to 5,* that 10 percent of the American public suffers from clinical depression and that one of the major factors contributing to this growing social malaise is the way many workers feel about their jobs. This pervasive discontent and depression most commonly expresses itself in high rates of absenteeism, poor job performance, industrial sabotage, substance abuse, and being socially withdrawn while on the job. Increasingly, however, it is being expressed in violence and mayhem directed at fellow workers.

In a ten-day period in March and April 1994, a blitz of violent behavior occurred on the job nationwide. In one instance a disgruntled Federal Express pilot attacked three fellow pilots in the cockpit of an in-flight DC-10 with a hammer, seriously injuring them and almost causing the plane to crash. In a suburb of Chicago, a purchasing agent of a small plant stabbed his boss to death over a disagreement regarding office procedures. And, in a fiber-optics laboratory in North Carolina, a technician who quit in a dispute with his female supervisor came back to the plant, pulled out a semiautomatic pistol and fired at random. When he was through, two were injured and three were dead, including the assailant, who had shot himself.[28]

According to the National Institute for Occupational Safety and Health, in the late 1980s and early 1990s, post offices around America were the most common scenes of high-profile shootings and murders.[29] The general scenarios of most of these shootings were strangely similar. One day, without warning or apparent motivation, a postal worker reports to work, takes out a gun, and shoots fellow workers and customers alike, with no regard for intended victims and unlucky bystanders. After the melee, the shooters turn the gun on themselves in about half of the cases, while others either calmly leave the scene to return home and await the arrival of the police or directly surrender themselves to the authorities.

Incidents such as these have both horrified the general public as well as served as rich fodder for grizzly humor. For example: Question: "Do you know why the post office has installed bullet-proof glass at all the clerks windows? Answer: To protect the customers from the employees!" And the phrase "going postal" has now achieved slang status and means "going ballistic," "losing control," and "acting out violently." There was even, for a short time, a computer shoot-em-up game called Postal!

More than a thousand people are now murdered on the job every year—32 percent more than the annual average in the 1980s. Murder has become the number-one cause of death for women in the workplace, and for men it is the third leading cause (after machine-related mishaps and driving accidents). While many workplace murders occur during robbery attempts, increasingly these victims die because angry spouses and lovers track them down at work or because disgruntled coworkers or customers want to settle a score.[30] A 1993 survey conducted by North western National Life Insurance suggests that more than 2 million employees suffer physical attacks on the job each year and more than 6 million are threatened in some way. These threats and attacks "run the gamut from anonymous love letters on secretaries' desks, to feces smeared on men's room walls, to death threats sent to CEOs' homes, to workers talking mass murder and specifying which guns they'll use on which supervisors." Joseph Kinney, executive director of the National

Safe Workplace Institute in Chicago, reports that "violence directed against employers or former employers is the fastest-growing category of workplace violence."[31] (A 1996 report from the National Institute for Occupational Safety and Health concluded that on the average, 20 American workers are slain and 18,000 are assaulted on the job each year. However, these statistics refer to injuries inflicted by the public, not by fellow workers, so they list the most violence-prone jobs as: taxicab driver or chauffeur; sheriff or bailiff; police detective; gas station worker; and security guard.)[32]

Most experts in the field believe that the rising tide of workplace violence is being fed by a number of different but converging factors. Some blame the downsizing and continual waves of layoffs of the last ten years for creating a climate of fear, uncertainty, and dispensability in the minds of many workers. Others claim that the growing salary gap between the shop floor and the executive suite is a major factor in the violence equation. And many believe that, at a more basic level, for workers who feel trapped, overworked, and overwhelmed by their jobs, violence often becomes a logical, if not necessarily rational, response to an unacceptable situation. Although not all worker discontent finds its outlet in violence, the rising incidence of violence is an undeniable indication of growing worker dissatisfaction and desperation.

The equation remains a simple one: Jobs that lack dignity cannot offer dignity to the worker. To paraphrase humorist Garrison Keillor, because so few of us experience the pleasure as well as the necessity of work, work devolves into drudgery. In any form, drudgery can erode and destroy our sense of purpose about the work we are doing. It can make us lose sight of how our work makes a contribution to or is connected to the work and needs of others. Lacking purpose, we endure rather than enjoy our work. According to a 1997 Wilson Learning Corporation report, 80 percent of employees today are "inactive," or minimally involved in or committed to their jobs, "just doing their jobs but unwilling to expend their energy."[33]

All work is a struggle. It cannot always be enjoyable. All work contains some element of drudgery, but if work is the evidence of our existence, the means by which we establish identity, then work should not be something we are simply forced to endure. Work should not only maintain our lives, but add to them as well. The issue is not then the drudgery of work, but whether our work holds meaning for us.

Matthew Fox argues that we need a new philosophy or a new vision of work—a vision of work that allows us to distinguish the drudgery and meaning of work; a view that sees work as both a necessity and a privilege; a position that acknowledges and responds to the human need to work. Using the language of theology, Fox contends that modern capitalism has resulted in a lack of an eschatological overview of work. Beyond the immediate benefits derived from our individual labor, we have no goal, no hope in any future greater purpose of our work and its possible contribution to humankind. We must change the way we define, create, and compensate work, and, finally, we must learn "why and for whom we do our work."[34]

According to Fox, as a society we remain emotionally and intellectually tied to the Newtonian model of the machinelike universe. As workers and individual parts of the economic machine, our primary responsibility is to perform a function. But in merely performing and functioning we do not see ourselves as part of the whole, part of a community. Since each of us, as a part, is replaceable, we feel in competition rather than in community with others. We see work as isolated, utilitarian, and impersonal. We operate, in Hobbes's terms, "each of us against the other" and are thereby limited in our ability to see life and work as organic and interrelated. Our concerns for the success of the business or task we are contributing to is limited to how that success will affect our personal needs. We see in the "unpleasant necessity" of work no larger purpose beyond our own parochial well-being. Our work offers us no glimpse of our natural inclination to stewardship and community.[35]

Fox suggests that the Newtonian model is quite compatible with Adam Smith's theory of the "invisible hand" of the marketplace. Smith believed that, given the interconnected nature of life and the marketplace, each of us acting on our own in pursuit of our self-interests will naturally and quite inadvertently advance the interests and well-being of others. Unfortunately, as Fox points out, Smith's faith in the benefits of the invisible hand theory was misplaced. The theory is now used to justify isolated individual responsibility, private entrepreneurship, and rugged individualism.

George Gilder, conservative economist and former White House speechwriter, suggests that communities are nothing more than collections of similarly minded individual self-seekers. Consequently, the tension between an individual and a community is delicate and complicated. Communities are both a necessity for and an impediment to individual well-being and achievement. While we need others, their presence, their needs, and their rights constrain and limit us. The requirements of community must be overcome in order to achieve success. Although morality requires us to abide by certain minimal standards of fair play, we must constantly operate in an adversarial relationship against others to succeed. For Gilder, communities cannot produce both wealth and well-being. The invisible hand mechanism as described by Smith, which indirectly creates "the greatest possible good for the greatest possible number," can only be produced by individual entrepreneurs. According to Gilder, the true catalyst propelling the laissez-faire economic system is the "trickle-down effect" of wealth produced by risk-taking, hardworking, rugged individuals.[36]

Unfortunately, Fox laments, in praising the hard work and achievement of the individual, we reinforce the rights of the self over those of the community and perpetuate the belief that success is always a competitive, zero-sum game. True work, Fox argues, must not only provide for our needs, but also place us within a community of others. We need a vision of work that takes into consideration other needs and issues beyond the self.

> Work is about the future. Therefore it is about fulfilling dreams, achieving promises, and entering into mysteries greater than ourselves and greater than our own work. This makes work eschatological. Good work is about hope. It brings hope and awakens others to hope.[37]

Fox maintains that there is something fundamentally human at the core of our dissatisfaction and displeasure with work. If work touches all of life, then living in depth, living with meaning and purpose, must include a sense of contributing to the greater community. The meaning of work cannot be reduced to finding a job that pays well enough. Meaningful work puts us in touch with others, at the level not so much of intimacy, but of interaction and service to the community. Work that does not at least minimally fulfill all of these requirements is reduced to "joyless striving."[38]

Michael Lerner, in *The Politics of Meaning,* persuasively argues that community is not a backdrop to our lives or an impediment. Community is a natural and necessary part of the human condition. We are not a herd of animals who exist only in proximity to each other; we are, in Aristotle's words, "social animals" who are dependent upon others for our physical and psychological well-being. Except for dying there is almost nothing we do alone. Even our personal sense of individual identity and uniqueness is something we, at least in part, arrive at by measuring ourselves against others. To be human is to exist in the context of others.

Unfortunately, says communitarian spokesman Amitai Etzioni, in Western society we have made a fetish of individual rights over the rights of the community. We have forgotten that although the individual is sacred, the community is a necessary precondition for individual existence. The community is much more than just "a mass movement of individual seekers," and happiness is not just "one more purchase away." We have forgotten that the community is a commonwealth and that the quality of our collective life speaks volumes about the quality of our individual lives. Psychiatrist and philosopher Victor Frankl argues that at the center of each man's "stubborn search for meaning" is the need to feel that our lives, our efforts, make a difference to others, and to be denied this recognition is to be diminished in our humanity. Because so few of us feel we are part of a larger purpose, we lose ourselves in the pay-off, the paycheck, and are driven solely by the goal of pecuniary well-being. The primary meaning of our labor is reduced to what it allows us to get or buy. We no longer work to create or contribute but only to consume.

Work can bring out the divine as well as the demonic in us, raise us to creative heights, or drown us in despair.[39] It all depends on the doer, what is being done, and why he is doing it. All work should afford us the opportunity to contribute to the collective whole. Bad work is repetitive, nonexpansive, and does not significantly contribute to the worker, the product, or the community. It alienates the worker from herself and others. Its main byproducts are anger, despair, and outrage. Good work, on the other hand, is human and authentic. It makes a contribution to the worker, the product, and the community. It creates satisfaction and the strength to endure the necessary struggle to work. Reflecting the ideas of Karl Marx and Pope John Paul II, Fox contends that good work recognizes that life is not just a simple fact, but an artifact continuously being created by us. Just as our individual jobs form our private lives, so too do the fruits of our common labors shape our collective lives. In work we are the cocreators of both our personal lives and all of human destiny. As workers we are not only citizens of the world, but creators of the world.[40]

Like Fox, I believe we need a vision of work that does not separate our lives from our livelihood, our personal values from our work values, our personal needs from the needs of the community. We need a value system in which "money is never sufficient reason for work; nor does money ever justify the immoral consequences of our work."[41] We should strive to embrace the subtleties of John Adams's famous admonition:

> I must study politics and war, that my sons have the liberty to study mathematics and philosophy. My sons ought to study mathematics and philosophy, geography, natural history, and naval architecture, in order to give their children the right to study painting, poetry, music, architecture, statuary, tapestry and porcelain.[42]

The educational model being suggested here is the medical one: *Learn* one, *do* one, *teach* one—and so pass it on.

All Work, But Very Little Ethics

> To say a man holds a job is to mistake the fact. The job holds the man.
>
> — James Gould Cozzens

AT THE END OF THE NINETEENTH CENTURY THE major goal of the American labor movement was simple and distinct: "Eight hours for work, eight hours for rest, and eight hours for what we will." For brief periods in the twentieth century, for some workers in specific industries, this goal was achieved. But the forty-hour standard workweek is either a long-forgotten memory or a still-sought-after dream for most Americans. As a nation we are working more now than ever. According to Harvard economist Juliet B. Schor, technological progress and industrialization have produced more rather than less work and the "unexpected decline of leisure."

Research into the history of work shows a surprising array statistics regarding the amount of time individuals and societies have dedicated to work. The lives of so-called primitive peoples, are commonly thought to be dominated by the incessant need to work. In fact, Schor demonstrates, primitive or subsistence peoples do very little work. For example, the Kapauku of Papua never work two days in a row and the Kung Bushmen never work longer than six hours a day, two and a half days a week. Australian Aborigines and Sandwich Islanders, when they work, never work more than four hours a day.[1]

The work profiles of the Mediterranean basin and early western Europeans reflected this pattern of minimal work. The ancient Egyptians limited work to about 70 days a year, or, on average, once every six days.[2] Nonwork time in ancient Greece and Rome was also plentiful. The Athenians celebrated 50 to 60 annual multiday festivals a year, and in some Greek city-states, such as Tarentum, this figure was more than three times higher. In the old Roman calendar, 109 of 355 days were designated "unlawful for judicial and political business."[3] By the mid-fourth century, the number of public festival days reached 175, which meant that the average Roman worker spent fewer than a third of his waking hours at work.[4] (These figures are for free men and do not reflect the efforts of slave laborers. Factoring in slave work-hours would clearly alter the average working day of free people and slaves alike.)

In medieval times, the Church coopted and converted many of the old Roman rituals and holidays into Christian holy days and feast days. Between the holy days of Sunday, Christmas, Easter, specific saints' days and feasts, the celebrations of weddings and wakes, as well as seasonal and political festivals, leisure time in medieval England took up probably one-third of the year. In the *ancient régime* of France there were 180 guaranteed work-free days a year, and in Spain holidays and holy days totaled more than five months per year. Throughout Europe, it is estimated that, except for harvest time, peasants worked fewer than 20 hours a week.[5]

The lives of ordinary people in the Middle Ages or ancient Greece and Rome, as Schor described, may not have been easy, pleasant, or particularly abundant, but they were leisurely. Depending upon climate, growing seasons, food supply, caloric intake, social custom, political traditions, and Church edicts, the rhythms of life and time did not revolve around, nor were they measured by, work. Workers in these societies worked hard, often at back-breaking tasks, but contrary to conventional wisdom, they did not toil from sun-up to sun-down, 365 days a year. It wasn't until the full flowering of the market system and the industrial revolution in the eighteenth and nineteenth centuries that work took on a Draconian, routinized schedule and began to absorb the vast majority of our waking hours. In the words of anthropologist Marshall Sahlins, it was the market system that handed down to human beings the sentence of "life at hard labor."[6]

The European and American industrial revolution of the eighteenth and nineteenth centuries was undoubtedly the period of the longest and most arduous work schedules in the history of humankind. Although one of the enduring myths of the capitalist system is that it will reduce the need to work, this claim certainly did not apply to capitalism in its incubation period. According to Schor, before the eighteenth and nineteenth centuries labor patterns were seasonal and intermittent, but the advent of capitalism immediately resulted in steady employment for 52 weeks a year, and seventy- to eighty-hour six-day workweeks immediately became the norm. At their peak, then, working hours under capitalism were 200 to 300 percent longer than in medieval times.[7]

Charles Dickens's fictional renderings of the birth of the industrial age are not far from the truth of the matter. In such novels as *Oliver Twist, David Copperfield, Bleak House*, and *Hard Times,* all written around the mid-nineteenth century, Dickens painted a picture of dark, dingy, coal-polluted English cities crowded with a surplus population of laborers. Because of their desperation for work, these men and women were at the mercy of unscrupulous employers and the technological limitations of the day. Men, women, and children alike worked stupefying hours in sweatshops and factories fueled more by human power than horsepower. Their working conditions were horrific and unsafe, and their pay was low, with few or no benefits. At night, exhausted from fourteen-hour days, they returned to wretched living conditions only slightly less squalid and unsafe than their work environment. Dickens suggests that the only thing that got these workers up each morning and kept them going was the utter absence of any kind of a social safety net, their lack of personal savings, and the gnawing fear of being replaced by the teeming numbers of unemployed waiting just outside the factory gates.

In America, the squalor and crowded conditions of New York City closely mirrored those of London. In each of the five boroughs of New York, pockets of sweatshops and factory buildings were jammed with laborers working long hours, at a maddening pace, in dark, badly ventilated spaces, for pennies an hour. The shops and factories of the garment industry, mostly located in southern Manhattan, were perhaps the most notorious abusers of their workforce. In these shops a workforce of mostly women and young girls were oftentimes locked into their places of employment and kept at their tedious tasks of cutting and sewing for up to sixteen hours a day without a break. This type of all-too-common practice led to the infamous Triangle Shirtwaist Factory tragedy on March 25, 1911, when an eighteen-minute flash fire took the lives of 145 employees who were trapped in the workplace because there was only one exit door and no fire escapes.

In spite of their abuses and their utter disregard for the safety of their employees, these factories and shops survived and in fact flourished, in part, because they were fed by the constant influx of immigrants who landed at Ellis Island. These new arrivals to our shores often wound up in an unending cycle of work, exhaustion, and grinding poverty.

North of the densely packed boroughs of New York City lay the rolling green hills of Massachusetts, New Hampshire, and Vermont—and more sites of industrial labor abuses. The textile industry of New England was notorious for its standards regarding its labor force. Generally recruiting teenage girls and young women from surrounding small towns and rural areas, the mills treated their employees more like indentured servants than paid laborers. The lives of these women were completely determined by the dictates of "the company." Rules and regulations for every aspect of their lives—work hours, living arrangements, meals and rest times, bed checks, acceptable forms of recreation, mandatory church attendance, and courting procedures—were rigorously enforced. As labor theorist David Ewing has suggested, in the nineteenth century the concept of "employee rights" meant little more than the right of employees to put up with the dictatorial demands of an employer if they hoped to find and keep a job.[8]

Judith Rossner's historically based novel *Emmeline* offers us a compelling and well-researched depiction of what it was like to work in the "satanic" mills of New England. Set in Lowell, Massachusetts, in 1839, *Emmeline* is the story of Emmy Mosher, who, before her fourteenth birthday, was sent from her farm home to work in a cotton mill to support her family. The mills advertised board and protection, honest work for decent pay, and a "good time all the whilst they're doing it." Once there, however, Emmy could contribute little to her family's welfare; two dollars a week dwindled to 55 cents after room and board. The book offers a realistic portrait of mill workers' living and working conditions. The boardinghouse is spartan but sufficient, but the effects of work are more insidious. She is not brutalized by her shop overseer or in constant physical danger while on the job, in contrast to many of her contemporaries in urban factory settings, but the real brutality of the mills lay in how they overworked their employees. The workday often began at five A.M., and ended at seven P.M., six days a week. The long days and repetitive work affected employees physically. Their legs grew stiff, arches became permanently swollen, toes turned numb, and their necks and shoulders throbbed with constant pain.

The greatest damage, however, was psychological. Earning just enough to get by but never enough to get free, Emmy and her coworkers soon lost hope but were nevertheless forced to toil on in exhaustion and debt. Survival became the only sustainable approach to life. Stoicism, rather than happiness, was one's only real goal. In the words of one of Emmy's more experienced and insightful supervisors, "Try not to think about it at all—that's the best way. Do as well as you are able, and think as little as you are able."[9]

Arguably, the most vivid images that many of us have of the physical and psychological brutalities associated with full-blown, unregulated industrialism are drawn from Upton Sinclair's muckraking exposé, *The Jungle*. Set in 1900 to 1904 in the stockyards district of Chicago, or "Packingtown," *The Jungle* is an admitted "propaganda novel." Sinclair set out to shock and mobilize an uninformed and compliant public by graphically depicting the living and working conditions of the men, women, and children forced to labor for the "barons of the beef trust." *The Jungle* attempts to highlight the issues of oligarchial control, a captive immigrant labor pool, wage slavery, child labor abuses, unsafe working conditions, unsanitary food production, government corruption, and, in Sinclair's interpretation, the inevitable degeneration of individuals into alcoholism, prostitution, and crime as a direct result of the debilitating effects of poverty and the loss of hope.

Motivated by his socialist beliefs and his profound conviction that unbridled capitalism inevitably resulted in the enslavement of the workforce, Sinclair created a fictional landscape that had its origin in solid facts. He told the story of men working from dawn to dusk at an inhuman pace on the "killing bed" floors of the slaughterhouses for 17.5 cents an hour. He wrote of women who stood or sat at long tables twelve to sixteen hours a day trimming meat, making sausages, or painting cans for 9 to 10 cents an hour. He shocked his readers when he wrote of children working long hours at a series of disgusting and dangerous jobs at the rate of 5 cents an hour.

In perhaps the most arresting scene in the novel, Sinclair writes of the common practice of having children walk the planks that were suspended over large vats of cooking meats that would be made into bologna. Their job was to walk back and forth over these vats and continuously stir the simmering gruel with long, boardlike spoons. Sinclair suggested that on occasion, due to the rising heat or the exhaustion of their long workdays a child would slip and fall into the vats, and when and if it was realized that a child was missing, no attempt was made to retrieve the body or stop the cooking process and empty the vats. The production of bologna went on unabated, and a new child was assigned to walk the planks.

From Sinclair's perspective perhaps the single greatest social injustice that befell those who worked for the "beef trust" was the individual worker's utter lack of security regarding his or her job, and the trusts' intentional policy of employee abuse and replacement. Sinclair argued that the jobs in the stockyards were designed to be performed by unskilled laborers. Only strength and speed separated the highest-paying from the lowest-paying jobs. Workers could hold their jobs only insofar as they could perform them. Injury, illness, or absenteeism for any reason resulted in termination. By maintaining this policy, the owners were able to control labor and liability costs and maintain production quotas through a continuous turnover of fresh and healthy workers.

Upton Sinclair wanted to entirely restructure American society and economics. He intended to advance and establish socialism in America as the only realistic alternative to the wage slavery of the working class that is enforced by capitalism. He believed that the working class could achieve dignity, freedom, and justice only through the public ownership of the means of production. The result of *The Jungle* instead was the raising of public and congressional awareness about the unsanitary conditions of packing houses and meat production. Six months after the publication of *The Jungle*, in January 1906, the Pure Food and Drug Bill and the Beef Inspection Bill became law. Some scholars believe that *The Jungle* also contributed to the passage of the Interstate Child Labor Act of 1916 and the Fair Labor Standards Act of 1938. But, perhaps, the most enduring legacy of *The Jungle* is Sinclair's portrayal of what any workplace can degenerate into when workers are seen only as another means and cost of production. "[U]nder such circumstances," wrote Sinclair, "immorality was exactly as inevitable, and as prevalent, as it was under the system of chattel slavery."[10]

Sinclair's argument, which was supported by many labor economists who did not share his socalist agenda, was that the exploitation of labor through maintaining low pay and steadily lengthening hours, was inherent in the structure of nineteenth-century capitalist industrialism.[11] The union movement wanted many of the same changes that Sinclair proposed, but they sought to reform rather than abandon both capitalism and industrialism. The union movement for an eight-hour workday began in earnest around the time of the Civil War. It meant both to curtail the continuous extension of working hours and to overcome the exploitation of subsistence wages. The movement encountered stiff resistance from the leaders of both commerce and Congress and took more than fifty years to achieve.

At a time when religious faith played an important role in many facets of citizens' lives, the barons of industry cited scripture as their rationale for long days and long workweeks. Popular verses were "By the sweat of your face you shall eat bread" (Genesis 3:19); "Anyone unwilling to work should not eat" (2 Thessalonians 3:10); "A slack hand causes poverty, but the hand of the diligent makes rich" (Proverbs 10:4); "Whatever your task, put yourselves into it, as done for the Lord and not for your masters" (Colossians 3:23). Scripture even was cited to establish industry's beneficence: "Six days you shall labor and do all your work; but the seventh day is a Sabbath to the Lord your God, in it you shall not do any manner of work" (Exodus 20:9–10).

These early capitalists also evoked our Puritan past and our pioneering forefathers. Paraphrasing Jonathan Edwards, they exhorted the working masses to be "dutiful Christian soldiers" and "diligent in their toil" so that America's success will be seen as a "beacon on a hill" and a living testimony to our national character and superiority. John D. Rockefeller's famous (or perhaps infamous) metaphor of "the American Beauty rose" was used to explain and justify the toil and burden of work as the price that had to be paid for collective success and individual progress.

In the late 1880s the rhetoric of the captains of industry turned more political, advocating antilabor and anti-immigrant positions. The catalyst for business's growing conservatism was the Chicago Haymarket Square bombing on May 4, 1886. The day before, police had shot and clubbed a number of independent trade unionists who had been striking for the installment of an eight-hour day. In response, a group of anarchists called a meeting in Haymarket Square on May 4 to protest the police brutality. At the end of the speeches, an estimated two hundred policemen arrived and ordered the crowd to disband. At the same time a bomb exploded, immediately killing one policemen and fatally wounding several others. The police opened fire on the crowd and killed and wounded many civilian protesters and even accidentally shot other officers.

The national reaction of outrage and horror was directed at the unions. In the resulting hysteria, employers were particularly vehement in denouncing most union activities, especially the demand for shorter working hours, as un-American and a threat to national financial prosperity. In Chicago, eight men were arrested, some of whom were recent immigrants with alleged connections to the international labor movement. Those held responsible for the explosion were vilified as "vipers" and "foreign traitors."[12] These individuals were convicted on what has since been seen as flimsy and inconclusive evidence; four of them were executed and the others imprisoned.[13]

Another factor that intensified the viciousness of business owners' antiunion rhetoric was the infiltration into the American labor movement of ideas from the European Catholic labor movement and the 1891 publication of Pope Leo XIII's encyclical "Rerum Novarum" (On the condition of the working class).

Leo XIII argued that the international social questions of justice and charity were being overrun by the economic imperatives of the industrial age. Human labor, Leo wrote, cannot be measured only by its economic outcome. The purpose of human work is the well-being of the worker, and not the value of the work produced. Since all wealth and capital are created by labor, labor is innately superior to both. Furthermore, both labor and capital have equal rights to the benefits achieved through their economic interdependence.[14]

Leo XIII believed "the wealth of nations originates from no other source than the labor of workers," and the efforts of labor must be seen as the final purpose of capital. As would popes coming many decades after him, he expressed concern that we had forgotten that the fundamental right of every human being is to get from the earth that which is necessary for life. Because people have both a need and a right to work, we must recognize the "dignity of work" as well as the "dignity of the worker." Honoring the "priority of labor" over capital is the first step in establishing a "social morality." The Church, therefore, as guardian of human dignity, must call attention to the rights of those who work and condemn situations in which those rights are violated.[15]

Predictably, the American business leadership did not embrace Leo XIII's message as a basis for their economic activity.[16] On the contrary, they saw in the encyclical seeds of such terrors as socialism, international Catholicism, and a direct threat to the "rugged individualism" and entrepreneurial spirit in America. They maintained that American capitalism was Christian insofar as it produced "the greatest good for the greater number," but they cautioned that no economic system can guarantee "equal benefits and outcome for all."

The "theology" of the marketplace that most closely represented management's view on social justice was that of Herbert Spencer and his theory of Social Darwinism. Spencer, an English social scientist, applied Charles Darwin's theory of biological evolution to social and economic life; and consequently, according to historian Samuel Eliot Morison, "raised *laissez-faire* to a dogma among American businessmen."[17] For Spencer the social question was a simple one. As in biology, success in business was predicated on "survival of the fittest," an idea that appealed to those already at the top of their fields.

In Spencer's theory "predatory capitalism" was neither an aberration nor excessive, but an exact mirror of the "laws of the jungle." In both life and economics, the weak fall by the wayside and the strong push forward. "The greatest perfection and the most complete happiness," wrote Spencer, "was the result of continuous evolutionary struggle, and any attempts to alter the situation would inevitably impede progress."[18] Spencer believed that the American economy was governed by a "national aristocracy" that had risen to the top by playing by the "natural rules."[19] Because of this Spencer suggested that "Americans may reasonably look forward to a time when they will have produced a civilization grander than any the world has known."[20]

Social Darwinism suited the barons of industry because it gave them a rationale for their actions. Whatever abuses they committed were just an unfortunate byproduct of the competition connected with progress. Against such a backdrop, organized labor's demands for reform languished but did not die.

After years of persistent struggle, the almost universal policy of long hours and six-day workweeks began to change in the early twentieth century.[21] As Juliet Schor has suggested, although the forty-hour week was held up as the ideal, its reality was but a short-lived "blip" in the demographics and history of the American workforce. In 1830 the average workday was more than twelve hours long, but by 1910 a growing number of people worked as little as nine hours a day.[22] Although some changes were a direct response to union demands, the motives of many employers were self-serving: Machines needed to be rested, repaired, and retooled to guarantee maximum productivity. Periodic shut-downs and shorter working days often had more to do with the needs of the machines than those of the personnel. Henry Ford, founder of the Ford Motor Company and a staunch antiunionist, exemplified this less than altruistic motivation.

In 1914 Ford employed important innovations that would change industrial production and labor relations for decades to come. He applied the general principles of Frederick Winslow Taylor to his auto plant in Highland Park, Michigan, by installing a moving conveyor belt. The belt brought the work to the worker and theoretically increased efficiency and productivity, but workers did not respond well to the redundancy, lack of autonomy, and the rapid pace of the conveyor belt system. Consequently, Ford faced rising rates of absenteeism, tardiness, and worker turnover.[23] As a corrective he initiated two new policies designed to improve the well-being of individual workers, and of course of the Ford Motor Works. First, Ford reduced the daily shift in the plant from nine hours to eight; second, he increased the pay to five dollars a day.[24] These changes made jobs at Ford more desired than those in other plants, where the going rate was about two dollars a day. If this policy did not exactly breed loyalty, unwavering commitment, and a sense of empowerment (terms not then current in management literature), it did breed feelings of gratitude, a sense of stick-to-it-ive-ness, and increased efficiency. In 1926 Ford added yet another carrot to his employees' benefit package: He announced that his factories would be closed all day Saturday.

Though Ford's voluntary reforms were praised by the union movement and held up as a model for other industries, Ford's motivation had as much to do with the worker as consumer as with the worker as producer. His rationale was that an increase in pay and leisure would stimulate an increase in consumer spending including automobile sales.[25] Like his German contemporary Ferdinand Porsche, inventor of the Volkswagen, Ford set out to produce a "people's car"—a car that the average worker earning an average paycheck could afford and have time to use for weekend outings and pleasure trips. In increasing the pay and leisure time of his own workforce, Ford established the standard he hoped other industries would follow. More than just an inventor, Ford was a shrewd businessman who understood the central ingredient of the capitalist economic system: continuous production and consumption. In initiating his supposedly prolabor policies, Ford was, in effect, priming his own pump.

The large-scale inauguration of the eight-hour workday and the two-day weekend in offices and factories across America was generated not by altruism, activism, or prosperity, but paradoxically, by the Great Depression. The rationale was clear. Shorter hours were a remedy for unemployment; people would work less, but more people would have jobs. It was hoped that the capitalistic equilibrium between production and consumption could be maintained. The New Deal and the Fair Labor Standards Act of 1938 mandated a maximum forty-hour week, but historical necessity intervened during World War II, when wartime production requirements caused the workday to be lengthened to ten hours, including Saturdays if necessary.[26]

As the end of World War II America entered its "golden years." We were universally recognized as the leader of the Western Alliance, as the chief military power in the world, and the world's predominant industrial giant. Real opportunity was at hand, but it was at this time that long hours became part of the fabric of our collective working lives. Having survived the long, lean years of the Depression and the war, the nation was hungry for the deferred benefits of "normalcy": homes, cars, services, gadgets, and gizmos of all kinds. So began the postwar trajectory of increased hours on the job in order to acquire money and stuff.

By 1948, the Bureau of Labor Statistics estimated that 13 percent of Americans with full-time jobs worked more than forty-nine hours per week. Forty hours quickly became the baseline rather than the optimum amount people put in on the job.[27] Although the hours in a workweek in 1949 were not much different than they had been at the turn of the century, the length of the week was altered dramatically. After World War II, people were unwilling to work a six- or even five-and-a-half day week. Thus, the five-day workweek and the two-day weekend became a fixture of American life.[28]

Presently, most, but certainly not all, of the 129 million Americans working full-time have 126 days off a year: 52 weekends; 11 to 12 public holidays and personal days; two weeks of vacation.[29] Looked at this way, this schedule seems manageable, but not if one computes the hours per week that people put in on the job. The statistic that everyone is now using on talk shows, in radio and television commentaries, and in popular essays and scholarly articles is that blue- and white-collar workers are putting in an average of 47–49 hours per week on the job, not including commuting. Moreover, a series of statistics reflect and exceed anecdotal accounts of time on the job. According to writer Arlie Russell Hochschild, both men and women average slightly more than 47 hours per week.[30] Charles Handy noted in 1994 that the typical American works 47 hours per week, for an annual total of 2,330 hours, and in 2014 the average American worker will put in 3,000 hours per year on the job.[31] *Newsweek* reports that 85 percent of us work more than 45 hours a week.[32] Juliet Schor estimates that annual hours on the job, across all industries and occupations, have been increasing over the last twenty years, so that the average employee is now on the job an additional 163 hours, or the equivalent of an extra month, per year. In 1990, one-fourth of all full-time workers spent 49 or more hours on the job each week. Of these, almost half were at work 60 hours or more.[33]

In 1995, a researcher at Penn State University claimed that lawyers and physicians regularly put in 50- to 60-hour workweeks, and that college professors average a 54-hour workweek.[34] Thomas Geoghegan, labor lawyer and syndicated columnist, estimates that middle-management types and senior executives endure a 55- to 65-hour week, and that 11 percent of all workers report working more than 65 hours per week.[35]

In an informal poll of my graduate students in the Institute of Human Resources and Industrial Relations at Loyola University in Chicago, over 80 percent of those surveyed during a seven-year period reported doing the work of 1.25 jobs to 1.5 jobs at their various places of employment. They said that because of downsizing and restructuring, the staff size had dropped but the workload had not. Making matters worse, the *Statistical Abstract of the United States, 1996,* claims that more than 6 percent of the workforce has a second full-time job.[36] The 1995 Labor Department publication "Working Women Count" claims that a growing number of people (especially women) hold down a series of part-time jobs that exceed 50 hours a week but barely earn a living wage.[37] If some of these figures and projections are accurate, by the year 2010 the average workweek will exceed 58 hours.

It must be remembered that these figures reflect only hours on the job and do not represent the other aspects of our day, such as getting to and from the job as well as household and family responsibilities. A 1993 survey conducted by the Families and Work Institute of New York concluded that both spouses in a double-income household with kids put in 15 hours a day on work, commuting, chores, and children.[38] These figures, based on a Monday through Friday schedule, mean that both spouses have already logged 75 hours before the weekend. Moreover, although Sundays in many households are still reserved for family outings and social events, Saturdays are often just another workday. "Honey-do lists" are drawn up, chores are assigned, projects are attended to, and kids are schlepped to music lessons and the mall. So much for the union cry of "eight hours for work, eight hours for rest, and eight hours for what we will."

It is both palpably and statistically clear to most of us that we are working harder and longer than ever before. And more than just the extra time we are putting in on the job, the intensity and stresses associated with our work seem to be accelerating. We cram more and more into each day, and yet we feel that we never have enough time to do all that must be done.

7

Women in the Workplace

> What's all this talk about women wanting a career? I've always had a career, or at least a job. And I didn't have any choice about it either!
>
> —Josephine Sally Palmeri

NOT ONLY ARE WE WORKING MORE, MORE OF US are working than ever before. The single most important event in the American labor market in the twentieth century has been the unprecedented entry of large numbers of women into the workforce.

> When the history of the last quarter of the 20th century is written scholars may well conclude that the nation's most important social development has been the rise to positions of power and influence of its most vigorous majority: American women. So many women have flocked to the labor force . . . that more Americans are now employed than ever before. This is no less than a revolutionary change, one that has created profound shifts not only in the family and the workplace but also in basic U.S. economic policy making.[1]

When Freud cited work and love as the foundations of human behavior, he might as well have used the words work and family. These are the two major institutions on which any society is based. Work and family are the two primary pillars of human existence, and every society in every age must grapple with the delicate mechanisms and relationships that influence and support these two fundamental phenomena.[2] As we step onto Bill Clinton's proverbial "bridge to the twenty-first century," the sheer numbers of women who have entered the workforce threaten to irreparably alter both the quality and quantity of our work and family lives. And, like it or not, we must be prepared to adapt or modify some of our most sacred social ideals and stereotypes about work and the family.

Cultural critic Barbara Ehrenreich once commented that in the 1960s the stereotypical liberated women was a braless radical, hoarse from denouncing the twin evils of capitalism and patriarchy.[3] Today's stereotype is more often a blue-suited executive carrying an attaché case and engaging in leveraged buyouts—before transmogrifying into a perfect mother, gourmet cook, and seductive lover in the evenings. Neither stereotype is or ever was perfectly true, but they can tell us a great deal about what many women and men would like to believe. What is true, according to newspaper columnist Carol Kleiman, is that the official organizational policy of most workplaces continues to operate as if white men constituted the majority of the workforce and most women are still at home managing the multiple roles of homemaking and child-rearing. As a result, both male and female employees must cope with the mounting stress of balancing work and family demands.[4] Workplaces need to accept and accommodate the inescapable demographic fact that since the mid-1980s, women and minority males make up the majority of the workforce.[5]

Women have always been part of the workforce and working mothers are not simply a "new demographic phenomenon of the later-half of the 20th century."[6] Stephanie Coontz has documented that women's active participation in the workforce has always been dependent on need, circumstance, and, to a very large extent, "cultural permission," which has varied over the years. A classic example is "Rosie the Riveter" the icon of American women during World War II. When the GI Joe husbands, brothers, and sons of "Rosie" marched off to war, "Rosie" marched into factories across America and took on complicated new jobs, gained new skills, and produced both the necessary domestic goods and the military hardware needed to win the war, doing her bit to once again "make the world safe for democracy." When the war was won and our GIs came home, many of the women were happy to leave the workplace to the men. Others were reluctant to give up their newly won responsibilities, independence, and income, and expressed a desire to continue working. Management, however, went to extraordinary lengths to purge women from high-paying and nontraditional jobs. The women who wanted or needed to work were not expelled from the labor force, but were downgraded to lower-paid, "female" jobs. Nevertheless, according to Coontz:

> Even at the end of the purge, there were more women working than before the war, and by 1952 there were two million more wives at work than at the peak of wartime production. The jobs available to these women, however, lacked the pay and the challenges that had made war time work so satisfying, encouraging women to define themselves in terms of home and family even when they were working.[7]

During the war, working as "Rosie the Riveter" was a badge of honor, a mark of distinction, a woman's patriotic duty. After the war, however, "cultural permission" once again shifted. *Esquire* magazine called working wives a "menace," and *Life* termed married women's employment a "disease." Being a full-time wife and mother was lauded as a woman's true vocation, the only job that could provide a woman with a "sense of fulfillment, of happiness, of complete pervading contentment."[8]

Sixty years ago, the notion of an unfulfilled homemaker was for most—but certainly not all—women unheard of. Prior to World War II, the maintenance of a house and, often, a large family was a full-time occupation and acknowledged as such. Those women who did venture outside the home in search of full- or part-time employment did so either out of dire financial need or in an attempt to earn a little "pin money" to subsidize a few household extras. Only in recent years have the everyday tasks of meal-making and home maintenance become less than full-time jobs. When combined with the decrease in family size, large numbers of women became, in the view of many, underemployed and underestimated.

It wasn't until the late 1950s and early 1960s, however, that women once again received "cultural permission" to enter the workforce in search of jobs or careers and a new sense of identity. Contributing to this cultural shift were the feminist movement and its impact on social consciousness, technological advances in the information and communications industries, the conversion from a manufacturing to a service economy, increased access to education, fair employment and affirmative action legislation, and the ever-increasing costs of a higher standard of living. Women now find full-time work outside the home not only possible and desirable, but, in many cases, financially necessary.

At the beginning of the twentieth century, only 5 million of the 28 million working Americans were women. One-quarter of these were teenagers and only a very few were married. As recently as 1947, women accounted for fewer than 17 million of the 59 million employed. Since that time, however, six of every ten additions to the workforce have been women. Between 1969 and 1979 women took on two-thirds of the 20 million newly created jobs;[9] between 1980 and 1992 women accounted for 60 percent of the increase in the American workforce.[10]

In 1984 the Census Bureau reported that for the first time in our history the prototype of American worker—the adult white male—no longer made up the majority of the labor force.[11] Women and minority men now hold approximately 57 percent of all jobs. In 1995, 57.5 million women were in the labor force of 125 million. In 1960, 35.5 percent of all women and 78.8 percent of all men worked full-time; by 1995, those numbers had risen to 55.6 percent of all women and 70.8 percent of all men.[12]

Depending on how you crunch the numbers, women now make up 46 to 49 percent of the entire workforce. Between 1947 and 1995 women's participation in the workforce increased 17 percent. Some demographers predict that women may represent a simple majority of the workforce early in the twenty-first century.[13] The Bureau of Labor Statistics more conservatively estimates that women will maintain but not necessarily exceed their present percentage in the workforce. They project that in 2005 the total labor force will be 150.5 million workers, and that 71.8 million of them will be women.[14]

While single and divorced women have long had relatively high labor force participation rates, fewer than 25 percent of married women were working full-time in 1960. That number today is 33.3 million, or 61 percent of married women. Of these working married women 70.2 percent have children under seventeen years of age.[15] It is estimated that two-thirds of all mothers are now in the labor force. Two-job families now make up 58 percent of married couples with children.[16] One set of statistics indicates that 20 percent of women in double-income families earn more than their husbands.[17] More recent research conducted by the Women's Voice Project, an ongoing study by the Center for Policy Alternatives in Washington, suggests that as many as 55 percent of all married women earn at least half of their family's income.[18]

According to social commentator John W. Wright, an unmistakable sign of the social change going on in the workplace is the significant increase in the number of women who return to work after having a baby. In 1976, about 31 percent of the women who gave birth returned to or entered the labor force, by 1985 it had climbed to 48 percent.[19] In a series of interviews I conducted with human resources specialists, most estimated that at their places of employment 75 percent of new mothers returned to work within twelve weeks of giving birth.

Fueling these rising statistics are the ever-widening professions now open to women. While traditional "women's" jobs such as nurses, teachers, librarians, and clerical workers are still predominantly women, the proportion of female engineers, architects, and public officials—while still small—has more than doubled since 1960.[20] Classes in law and medical schools are now typically composed of 40 to 50 percent women.

According to the Department of Labor special report "Working Women Count," 30 percent of working women are engaged in service and sales jobs, 13.1 percent have factory, craft, construction, or technical jobs or jobs in the transportation industry, 27.6 percent of working women have professional or executive jobs, and 40 percent of all corporate middle-management positions are held by women.[21] In general, although women are grossly overrepresented at the entry and low levels of all kinds of work, it is clear that the historical distinctions between "women's" work and "men's" work have begun to blur.

Obviously, the entrance of women into the labor market has changed the composition of the workforce, the workplace, and the structure of family life. According to "Working Women Count," it is now expected that 99 percent of all American women will work for pay sometime during their lives.[22] The 1950s traditional family—dad at work and mom at home with the kids—is no longer the predominant pattern; nontraditional families are now the majority.[23] Again, depending on whose figures you are willing to accept, it is estimated that fewer than 15 percent of all households fit the traditional family model.[24] As recently as 1960, 43 percent of all families conformed to the single-earner model,[25] but in less than thirty-six years we have become a nation of DINKS (Double-Income-No-Kids) and DISKS (Double-Income-Some-Kids) families. According to sociologist Uma Sekaran, "The number of two-career families, single-parent families, and unmarried working couples living together is steadily increasing. This population constitutes more than 90 percent of today's labor force. Organizations are . . . beginning to feel the impact of this new breed of employee."[26]

In addition, women are now demanding the right to define themselves in the way that men always have —through their jobs. Being a wife, a mother, a homemaker has over the course of the past two or three generations simply changed until it no longer meets the definition of work to which most people now subscribe. It has been suggested that when the first wave of female baby boomers arrived at college in the early 1960s, many expected to marry shortly thereafter and raise children.[27] Not anymore! According to a survey cited by Arlie Russell Hochschild, less than 1 percent of 200,000 female college freshmen wanted to be a "full-time homemaker." In a 1986 survey of female college seniors, 80 percent thought it was "very important" to have a career.[28] Nine years later, 86 percent of recent female college graduates defined themselves as "careerist."[29]

Women now want to be known by their accomplishments and occupations and not merely as "Mrs. John Smith" or "Johnny's mommy." When First Lady Barbara Bush gave the commencement speech at Wellesley College in 1991, many members of the all-female student body protested her appearance because her most significant accomplishment was being somebody's wife.[30] Gloria Emerson has pointed out that every twelve-year-old boy in America knows what must be done to achieve identity and "make it" as a man: Money must be made. Nothing else is as defining or as masculine as this.[31] Women now want to forge their own identity by means of paid employment—the principal definition of work. In the words of demographer Daniel Yankelovich, women now view a paid job as "a badge of membership in the larger society and an almost indispensable symbol of self-worth."[32]

In a very real sense women's desire to define themselves through work was spurred by Betty Friedan, Gloria Steinem, and the feminist movement. The "new breed" of women sought to be autonomous agents, able to guide and direct themselves, determining their purpose and role in life by their own choices and actions. They no longer wanted to be viewed as "second-class citizens," relegated to hearth and home, and totally dependent on men. In addition to the ideological motivations, however, practical reasons played an important role. Many women sought jobs or careers to keep up with the ever-increasing costs of middle-class existence: suburban homes, safe cars, good schools, kids' music lessons, and prestigious colleges.

As recently as 1980, only 19 percent of working women said that their incomes were necessary to support their family, while 43 percent said they worked to bring in extra money.[33] In 1995, however, 44 percent of employed women said that they worked out of necessity, and only 23 percent to earn extra cash. The survey concluded that most married working women now view their incomes as essential to their family's well-being.[34] The new piece of cynical conventional wisdom currently circulating around college campuses today reads something like this: "Guys, look around. Don't just marry the pretty one. Marry the smart one. The one who's got the best chance of landing a good job. Why? Because you're going to need each other to acquire the things and lifestyle that your parents managed to achieve on one salary!" For example, in 1989, 79 percent of homes bought were purchased by two-income households.[35] Some realtors estimate that in the mid-1990s, that number rose to 85 percent.[36]

The bottom line is that women may once have entered the workforce out of desire, but, today, they stay because of need. Not only have they been granted "cultural permission" to seek work, they have now acquired a financial imperative to do so. In the most recent past, most women had three choices about employment: Don't work at all, work part-time, or work full-time. Now, like men, their options have been reduced to one.

As a final note on the many ways in which women's increased presence in the workforce has changed family life, one must mention divorce. Ninety percent of men and women marry, but 50 percent of all first marriages end in divorce, and an alarming 60 percent of second marriages also end in divorce.[37] The traumatic effect of divorce is felt by all members of a family, especially the children. Because of America's rising divorce rates in the last fifty years, 60 percent of all children will live in a single-parent household for a significant period of time before they are eighteen.[38] Although 70 percent of divorced adults will remarry, 25 percent of all children grow up primarily in a one-parent household.[39]

Whatever the causes of a divorce, the practical and financial fallout of the separation is much harder on the woman. According to psychologist Lenore Weitzman, in the first year after divorce women experience a 73 percent loss in their standard of living, whereas men experience a 42 percent gain.[40] Even when divorced fathers dutifully comply with child-support payments and remain emotionally involved with their children, the primary responsibility for children's day-to-day and long-term well-being falls to the mother.

Divorce is now an accepted part of our social tapestry. Another trend gaining acceptance is single motherhood, from unmarried teenage mothers to adult women who choose to have children out of wedlock (à la TV's *Murphy Brown*). One of the major lessons now learned by women and girls alike is self-sufficiency. According to Karen Nussbaum, former head of the U.S. Department of Labor's Women's Bureau, "There should be no girl out there [anymore] who thinks someone else is going to take care of [her]." Life has changed and the expectations of women must also change. For women work is now less of an option and more of a necessity. "If girls [today] aren't working when they get out of high school," Nussbaum has stated, "they will be at some point."[41] While, for many women, work can be a badge of honor and a symbol of self-worth, it has also become a fundamental element of survival.

Justice on the Job

Women are now being recruited more than men for entry positions in various industries. In this way, corporations can claim, at least prima facie, that they are complying with the rules of affirmative action and open employment. The issue for most women is not getting a job, but, what happens to them once they have it. Although not all women encounter prejudicial behavior, too many are forced to endure personal and institutional resistance to their careers and professional advancement.

According to management scholar Judy Rosener, few women encounter a level playing field on the job. Most are forced to cope with a problem she calls "sexual static." Rosener argues that most male managers and workers—especially those over the age of forty—see females in the workplace, first and foremost, as females, not as colleagues. Too many men are unable to see female coworkers outside their traditional sex roles—as mothers, sisters, daughters, and potential mates. Sexual static interferes with communication and hampers normal business conduct between men and women, resulting in mixed signals, misunderstanding, embarrassment, anger, confusion, and fear.[42] Sexual static, suggests business ethicist Patricia Werhane, may make a work environment hostile or just uncomfortable. It may be "sexually charged" or create an atmosphere in which "men and women feel uneasy about their professional interrelationships and how these might be misinterpreted as sexual ones."[43]

Sexual static is not the same thing as sexual harassment. Sexual static is more insidious. Sexual harassment is about inappropriate sexual comments, unwelcome sexual advances, or requests for sexual favors as a condition of an individual's employment, advancement, or success. Sexual static is an attempt to avoid and defuse even the suggestion of sexual harassment. It is the tension that occurs when men and women are not sure how to comport themselves in a business or social environment. The personal sexual insecurity of male managers often leads to dysfunctional corporate decision-making. A senior male attorney at a major firm admitted, "We have a real bright woman who has what it takes to be a partner, but I can't bring myself to vote to promote her because she turns me on, and it gets in my way." Fear of gossip motivates other men. "Every time I promote a woman," reported a fifty-year-old male advertising executive, "I worry about people suspecting I have a romantic interest in her."[44]

Rosener and Werhane agree that although everyone involved loses both personally and professionally in an atmosphere of sexual static, women are the primary victims. Sexual static perpetuates stereotypical female roles, denies women the opportunity to acquire new skills and experiences, too often denies women the support of a senior male mentor who can act as a role model, and, finally, precludes professional objectivity.[45] Professional objectivity maintains that management practices should be unbiased and impersonal. It requires that the most skilled and effective persons be hired and promoted to leadership positions. Unfortunately, concludes Werhane, "we live in a society in which business is conducted in an atmosphere where merit or worthiness is the ideal but not the practice."[46] Not only do we not live in a sex-gender-color-ethnic-age–neutral environment, sexual static reinforces the divisive notion that men and women are two separate and competitive species loosely connected by sex, children, and financial arrangements.

The major organizational problem facing working women is the proverbial glass ceiling—an invisible barrier that keeps women from ascending to the highest levels of management. The glass ceiling does not just apply to elite workers aspiring to corporate management; it also refers to the institutional and personal prejudices that women encounter in every kind of job at every level in the workplace. A majority of American women in the workplace, regardless of race, class, type of job, or job location, feel that the glass ceiling is keeping them in their place. According to the nationally based report "Working Women Count," more than 60 percent of women believe that they have little or no opportunity for advancement.[47]

Even though women now represent 46 to 49 percent of the workforce, more than 97 percent of all senior management is still male. Where women are starting to achieve representation equal with their numbers is in the lower and middle ranks of management. Even those women who manage to pass through this transparent barrier often find themselves in jobs that have a "glass floor," that is, where their every move can be seen and scrutinized, and where their first big mistake has them figuratively crashing down.

Business Week has reported that half the lowest management levels are staffed with female workers and that soon the middle ranks will be, too. Overall, women now occupy an unprecedented 41 to 43 percent of lower- and middle-management positions.[48] However, a report by Catalyst, Inc., released in October 1996 found that only 10 percent of the top jobs at the nation's 500 largest companies are held by women. Alarmingly, 105 of these 500 companies have no female corporate officers at all, and only 2.4 percent of all the women employed in these 500 companies have achieved the rank of chairperson, president, CEO, or executive vice president. Only four of the twenty-four "Best Companies for Women to Work For," featured in a *Business Week* cover story, had women in more than 25 percent of their corporate officer posts in 1996.[49]

In a related report, Catalyst announced that women's representation on boards of directors of Fortune 500 companies had finally exceeded 10 percent. Of the 6,123 Fortune 500 board seats, women now hold 626, or 10.2 percent. Altogether, 83 percent of Fortune 500 companies have at least one woman on their boards. According to Sheila Wellington, president of Catalyst, while these numbers are important, they're "absolutely minuscule. What this shows is that people who say the gains have been made, so let's move on, are dead wrong. It shows that the number of women who have made it to the apex are still so few. . . . Clearly, there's a lot more work to be done."[50]

The absence of women from positions of power in business is also reflected in our political system. In 1995, the seventy-fifth anniversary of women's suffrage in America, The Center for Policy Alternatives reported that across the nation, women represented only 20 percent of state legislators, 25 percent of statewide elective executive officers, 10 percent of U.S. representatives, 8 percent of U.S. senators, and 2 percent of governors.[51] As Katherine Spillar, national coordinator for the Fund for the Feminist Majority, so wryly put it, "At the current rates of increase it will be four hundred and seventy-five years before women reach equality in executive suites."[52]

Some critics suggest that those few women who have broken through the glass ceiling have done so not by embracing feminism but by outperforming men on their own terms. These are classic careerists, who happen to be women. Like any dedicated careerist, they did their jobs, made their numbers, and, when necessary, did battle. In fact, according to Chicago-based consultants Megan Buffington and Jane Neff, some of these successful women are more combative and ruthless than their male counterparts because they feel they have to prove they can be rough, tough, and resilient. Buffington and Neff call this the "only bra in the room syndrome" and cite Chicago's first female mayor, Jane Byrne, as its icon.

By all accounts Byrne may have been "lady" when the situation required but in her heart she was one of the boys. A longtime operative in Richard J. Daley's political machine, Byrne earned her spurs because she did her job, could keep a secret, and over the years built up alliances. After Daley died, she rose to his post. In a tough campaign that "reeked of testosterone," as one pundit put it, she convinced the electorate that she had more of the "right stuff" than her rival. After she was out of office, she said in an interview that she really hated losing the mayor's job because she had worked so hard at it; she had wanted to be an effective mayor, and she feared that people attributed her mistakes not just to miscalculation or shortcomings of character, but to being "just a woman."

According to Buffington and Neff, a characteristic of these types of achievers is their lack of empathy for and support of other working women, especially their subordinates. Having achieved success by playing hardball and working hard, they expect the same from others. Having made it despite being a woman, their focus is on success and not sensitivity. They tend to be intolerant of office schmoozing or signs of friendship in the office, such as birthday celebrations. They leave their private lives at home, and they expect others to do so as well. But, worst of all, out of either a twisted sense of elitism or simple selfishness, too many of these successful women do not reach back to mentor other women. Some of them seem to think "I made it without any help, and if you're any good so will you" or "since I'm already here, there's no more room at the table." Buffington and Neff suggest that consequently, many women do not like to work for female bosses. In a recent Gallop poll conducted in twenty-two countries, women overwhelmingly preferred male to female bosses in all but three countries surveyed (India, where they preferred to work for women, and El Salvador and Honduras, where they were evenly split in their preferences). In the United States 45 percent of men and women surveyed prefer a man as a boss while only 20 percent prefer a woman (the rest did not indicate a preference).[53]

Although the term *glass ceiling* is metaphorical, the effect it describes is very real. Not only does it prohibit some women from advancing to senior corporate management, it also denies women on the shop floor and in the lower offices equal opportunities for training, advancement, and promotion. Worse still, it has a limiting effect on salaries. According to the Department of Labor, the second most common complaint voiced by the 250,000 women surveyed as part of its study "Working Women Count," was "unequal and unfair pay."[54] Even though the Equal Pay Act passed Congress in 1963 and the discrepancy between men's and women's pay has narrowed, the gap remains significant. In 1993 in annual earnings of full-time, full-year workers, women earned 71 cents for every dollar earned by a man in the same job, and in 1996 the International Labor Organization reported that a majority of women in America earn 75 cents for every dollar earned by men doing the same job.[55]

Nationwide it is estimated that, on average, women with college degrees earn slightly more than men with high-school degrees and $10,000 a year less than men with comparable educations. Of the women who took part in the "Working Women Count" survey, 23 percent had part-time jobs (less than 35 hours per week) and 77 percent had full-time jobs (40 hours or more per week). Their income reporting was as follows: 16.3 percent earned less than $10,000 per year; 39 percent earned $10,000 to $25,000; 15.8 percent earned $25,000 to $35,000; 10.4 percent earned 35,000 to $50,000; and 4.8 percent earned $50,000 to

$75,000. It is worth noting that 71.1 percent of these women earned less than $35,000 per year, and 58 percent earned less than $25,000. At the same time, 35 percent of the sample reported being the sole support of themselves and their families.[56] While women may nearly constitute the simple majority of the workforce, it was clear that they are a long way from matching men in pay.

Another factor that impedes women's advancement at work is babies. According to the Women's Bureau of the Department of Labor the greatest concern of working women is finding a way to balance work, family, and child care. Never has the number of women with young children in the workplace been higher. Sixty-seven percent of women with children under eighteen are working or actively seeking employment. This includes 54 percent of mothers with children under three, 58 percent of mothers with children under six, and 75 percent of mothers with school-age children. These mothers report that juggling kids and work results in a constant state of anxiety, fatigue, frustration, and guilt, both on and off the job. As one working woman told me, "I don't even know what I should feel bad about first! The job? Because I always feel I should be working harder? The kids? Because I miss them so much, and I know I'm missing so much. The house? Because it doesn't feel like a home anymore, it's just a place where we live. Or, my husband? Good old—what the hell is his name?!"

In the "Working Women Count" survey, 56 percent of mothers complained about not being able to find adequate, affordable child-care services, 49 percent wanted paid leaves "to care for a newborn and sick relatives," and 35 percent wanted more "flexible working schedules" in an attempt to balance the day-to-day necessities of work and private life.[57] In some sense, these demands and desires reflect a piece of "occupational wisdom" that all working women have been forced to absorb: "You can take time to baby a client, but you can't take time to baby your own baby."[58]

In 1989, in an attempt to address the needs of babies, women, and men, Felice Schwartz published an article in which she proposed that corporations establish two parallel working tracks for female employees: the "career primary" track and the "career and family" track. Those who chose the career primary track would be considered for any and all tasks, and the career and family track women would be given more limited responsibilities than their career primary colleagues. Schwartz also proposed that at different points in a woman's career she could change career tracks. In this way, corporations would be able to retain experienced employees, and women could pursue their careers without being forced to totally abdicate their responsibilities as mothers.[59] Critics immediately attacked Schwartz's ideas and relabeled her categories the "breeders" versus the "achievers." Although Schwartz offered her track system as a means of balancing the needs of women, children, and families, many commentators saw her proposal as a passport to permanent second class status and a one-way ticket to a mediocre career. The "mommy track," as her proposal was commonly called, was seen as singling out women for complete parental responsibility or sacrifice. The mommy track became not a new alternative, but a dead end.

In a 1997 article in *Fortune* magazine Betsy Morris argued that the issues raised by Schwartz—balancing careers, babies, and long-term family responsibilities—have neither been resolved nor gone away. In fact, Morris claims things have gotten much worse. For all their politically correct talk, most companies don't much care about or like kids.

> Today, in the corridors of business as elsewhere, families are getting more lip service than ever. Being on the right side of work and family issues—having the proper programs, letting Mom and Dad slip out to watch a T-ball game—is very PC. But corporate America harbors a dirty secret. People in human resources know it. So do a lot of CEOs, although they don't dare discuss it. Families are no longer a big plus for a corporation; they are a big problem. An albatross. More and more, the business world seems to regard children not as the future generation of workers but as luxuries you're entitled to after you've won your stripes. Its fine to have kid's pictures on your desk—just don't let them cut into your billable hours.[60]

Companies want all their employees to clock as much time as possible. They are interested in results, productivity, and success, not child-care commitments and kindergarten recitals. In the spirit of full disclosure, Morris suggested, all corporate manuals should carry a warning: "Ambitious workers beware. If you want to have children, proceed at your own risk. You must be very talented, or on very solid ground, to overcome the damage a family can do to your career."[61]

Justice at Home

The problems, prejudices, and injustices that women face in the workplace are, unfortunately, mirrored and often intensified on the home front. As Arlie Hochschild put it, "Women can have fame and fortune, office affairs, silicon injections, and dazzling designer clothes. But the one thing they can't have, apparently, is a man who shares the work at home."[62] There is a price to pay for having "made it," and, by all accounts, women are picking up most of the tab. In her important book *The Second Shift*, Hochschild claims that even though women have won certain rights in the workplace, they have not won many rights at home—in fact, many women are losing ground. According to Hochschild, women in dual-income families not only carry the burdens and responsibilities of their profession, but 80 percent of working women also carry the burden of a second job—caring for the home, the kids, and the husband.

On average, Hochschild claims, in the 1960s and 1970s American women worked around the house 15 hours more per week than men did. Over a year, this adds up to women putting in "an extra month of twenty-four-hour days" on household chores. One study showed that "women averaged three hours a day on housework while men averaged 17 minutes; women spent fifty minutes a day of time exclusively with their children; men spent 12 minutes." According to Hochchild's computations, 61 percent of men do little or no housework, 21 percent attempt, on an irregular basis, to do their share of household chores, and only 18 percent of men share housework equally.[63] In effect, the second shift means that women put in a double day: They're on duty at work, they're on duty at home. As one angry woman put it, "I do my half. I do half of his half. And the rest doesn't get done!"[64]

Some of Hochschild's findings are unexpected (for example, working-class husbands did more around the house than ostensibly more liberal, middle-class professional husbands), but the cultural causes of the second shift phenomenon are painfully predictable. Most men feel that their work is more important than their wives' jobs. Although their wives' salaries may be necessary, most men, because they earn more and because they have been traditionally seen as the head of the family, view their work as the primary ingredient defining household status. Although domestic chores may be aesthetically and hygienically necessary, they are neither creative nor important and therefore are not the concern of the progenitor and main provider of the family. Most men believe that women are natural nurturers and are better suited for child care.

Hochschild argues that the sudden surge of women into the workplace has not been accompanied by a new cultural understanding of both marriage and work that would have made this transition smoother. Families have changed, women have changed, work has changed. but most workplaces have remained inflexible in the face of their workers' family demands. At home, most men have yet to fundamentally adapt their lifestyles to accommodate the changes in women's lives. Because of this absence of change, said Hochschild, and because of the burdens of the second shift, the movement of women into the workforce in search of identity, independence, and financial security remains at best a "stalled revolution."[65]

In her most recent book, *The Time Bind*, Hochschild suggests that the revolution not only is still "stalled" but that the burdens and fallout of the second shift have gotten more complex. Even with men actively contributing to child care and household chores, men and women still find themselves desperately trying to juggle their commitments to family and work. The demands of a workaholic corporate system and the needs of families and children have us rushing from one responsibility to another and have us trapped in a "time bind" of guilt. Unfortunately, Hochschild says, "many working families are both prisoners and architects of the time bind in which they find themselves."[66] They want it all: great jobs, great families, and all the goodies that go along with it. But the increased energy and time they pump into work is taken from the home, and their lives become more emotionally stressful. Surprisingly, Hochschild discovered, in her three-year study of a "family friendly" Fortune 500 firm, that for a growing number of two-career couples, when work and family compete, work wins. Many workers choose to escape into work because life at home has become a "frantic exercise in beat-the-clock, while work, by comparison, seems a haven of grown-up sociability, competence and relative freedom."[67]

According to Hochschild, the roles of home and work have begun to reverse. Work has become a form of "home" (a village of associates, peers, coworkers) and home has become "hardwork" (a locus of duty, chores, and demanding personalities). Work is the new "neighborhood," where we spend most of our time, where we talk to friends and develop relationships and expertise. Meanwhile, home is now where we are least secure and most harried. "At home the divorce rate has risen, and the emotional demands have become more baffling and complex. In addition to teething, tantrums and the normal development of growing children, the needs of elderly parents are creating more tasks for the modern family—as are the blending, unblending, reblending of new step parents, step children, exes, and former in-laws."[68] By comparison work is less chaotic, cleaner, more enriching, and much less personal. As one female worker admitted to Hochschild, "I put in for [overtime]. . . . I get home, and the minute I turn the key, my daughter is right there . . . the baby is still up . . . the dishes are still in the sink. . . . My husband is in the other room hollering at my daughter, 'I don't ever get any time to talk to your mother. You're always monopolizing her time!' They all come at me at once."[69]

Is it any wonder that work becomes home and home becomes work? Work is less demanding, a surrogate, a refuge from our troubled private lives. It is also a place where conflicts that originate in the home can be discussed, debated, and subjected to sympathetic scrutiny. In the sanctuary of work, says Hochschild, increasing numbers of women are discovering the "great male secret"—work can be an escape from the pressures of home. In the words of a James Thurber character as he leaves for work after a long weekend of kit and kin, "Ah, thank God it's Monday!" Somewhat reluctantly, Hochschild concludes that for more and more women "the world of 'male' work seems more honorable and valuable than the 'female' world of home and children."[70] The paradoxical result of such a shift, suggests Hochschild, is altogether clear: That for which we work—families—is that which is most hurt by our work!

Hochschild implies that every dual-career family needs a full-time wife. In my review of *The Time Bind* I argued that given Hochschild's findings and insights, perhaps the only way to save the family is to change it.

> In the future, individuals who want to "have it all"—children and a career—without shortchanging one or the other, or both, will be required to enter into a communal marriage involving six precertified adults. Two of them will work full-time in order to support the family; two will be in charge of the house and kids; and two of them will be held in ready reserve, to fill in wherever they are

> needed. Divorce will be forbidden; all property will be owned in joint tenancy; sleeping arrangements are negotiable; and sex will be strictly optional. Hey, why not give it a try? Nothing else seems to be working.[71]

Women have changed. The economy has changed. The workplace has changed. Families have changed. Unfortunately, most men have not changed, either privately or professionally. The rules of work also have not changed sufficiently to accommodate the new reality. Are women in the workplace to stay? Absolutely! Women report that they both need and want to work. Current research also suggests that no matter how taxing and hectic their lives, women who do paid work feel less depressed, have a higher sense of personal worth, and are happier and more satisfied than women who do not have jobs. Do men need women in the workplace? Yes! Demographic trends regarding birthrates, urban population patterns, and college graduation rates necessitate women's active participation in the workplace. Do men want women in the workplace? Yes and no. For a lot of men, women simply represent another group of individuals to compete with for jobs, salaries, promotions; and for some men there yet remains a sense of social awkwardness about women's roles and men's appropriate response.

For too many men, women's commitment to work and their general dependability remains suspect because of "the one immutable, enduring difference between men and women . . . maternity."[72] On the job, families and babies are seen as a vulnerability, an impediment rather than a normal and necessary part of life that should be accommodated. According to Betsy Morris, in an interesting shift in values, the new ultimate male status symbol "is not a fancy car or a fancy second home, or a wife with a fancy career. You've really made it, buddy, if you can afford a wife that doesn't work. She may be a drag on earnings, but she provides a rare modern luxury: peace on the home front."[73]

Finally, will women rise in the ranks and assume power proportional to their numbers in the workplace? I fear not. But the reasons are much more straightforward and much less gender-specific and sexually biased than some social commentators would have us think. To begin with, the rules of work are, by and large, still being written by men, and these rules communicate an indifference to any concerns beyond the job at hand. As both Robert Bly and Gloria Emerson have argued, the primary masculine imperative is to fulfill their role as worker-provider. Consequently, most workplace rules reflect primarily professional, and not personal, issues. Second, although it is true that the predominantly male corporate structure has been unwilling to share the power base, this reluctance is not necessarily misogynistic in its origins. The term *power* comes from the Latin *posse*: to do, to be able, to change, to influence, to affect. Power is about control or the ability to produce intended results. To have power is to possess the capacity to control or direct change. The first maxim of power is self-perpetuation; nobody gladly gives up power. This principle is not testosterone-based or predominantly masculine in its origins. It is purely Machiavellian, that is, those who have power (in this case, men) will give it up only reluctantly. The goal of power, said Machiavelli, is not to allow change, because change always leads to the alienation of power and of the status quo, and an alteration of the status quo is never in the best interest of those who possess power. Although the issue at hand is the power of the "good-old-boy network," we are not talking about a cabal of evil men conspiring to keep women in their place. In effect, the motivating principle involved in this and every power struggle is much more visceral than simple machismo.

Things are not going to radically change anytime soon, but gradual change is occurring. As singer-actress-director Barbra Streisand said upon her 1992 induction into the Women in Film Hall of Fame, "Not so long ago we were referred to as dolls, tomatoes, chicks, babes, broads. We've graduated to being called tough cookies, foxes, bitches and witches. I guess that's progress."[74]

Squeezing Time

No man who is in a hurry is quite civilized.
—Will Durant

AS A SOCIETY WE ARE OBSESSED WITH TIME. IT'S a long-standing part of our national character. Time is money, and we always try to spend it well. We often scoff at the tradition of the siesta in Spain, Italy, and Mexico. We smirk at the French practice of closing down in August and at Sweden's mandated five-week minimum vacation policy. We have never been comfortable with the abstract notion of free time. Unstructured time makes us ill at ease. We see time as our most precious commodity. We try to make the most of our time. We fill time, use time, invest and manage time. We strive to be productive at all times. We live by schedules and lists. We micromanage our work time, much of our play time, and more and more of our family, private time. We have embraced Thomas Edison's admonition that success is 1 percent inspiration and 99 percent perspiration. We believe that successful people always have time to do something more, and unsuccessful people never have enough time to do what must be done. We are in a constant race with and against time.

Historically Americans have viewed the active life as morally superior.[1] The tradition of "busy-ness" is part of our moral fabric. We accord kudos to those individuals who make every moment count, and whose every movement is regulated by the clock. Traditionally, in this society, we measure meaning by productivity. And our obsession with time has always been directly connected to our addiction to work. Labor historian Benjamin Hunnicutt has suggested that, whether by choice or circumstance, we have always lived in "a culture of work."[2] Americans have always been compulsive about what we do and how we do it. How else to explain this nation's accomplishments in such a relatively short period of time? The nineteenth-century union cry for a limited workday was not about our unwillingness to work. It was about our unwillingness to work for bad pay, in horrible conditions, and without the possibility of meaningful advancement. In bad times, we have been forced to work hard simply to endure, but, in good times, we have often chosen to work hard to get further ahead.

In America, being busy or overworked conveys status and self-worth.[3] The busier our schedules, the more important we feel and, often, the more we are able to acquire the possessions that supposedly constitute the good life. As a nation, we learned from the Depression that no matter what abuses can occur, no matter how vulnerable the individual worker can be, no matter what the threats to the human and civil rights of workers, "there is nothing better than work."[4] Having endured no work, all work and any work seemed preferable. We have learned too well that without work, time is unstructured, unproductive, and lacking in both purpose and profit.

In 1946 we came out of the deprivations of the Depression and the lean years of World War II seeking not to escape from or transcend work, but to find transcendence through our work. By the 1950s we seemed to be achieving our goals. We organized our time well, we worked hard, and, thanks to the efforts of our labor, entered the most widely based, longest lasting consumer spending spree in the history of the world. Then the window of unlimited expectations and growth began to close. In the mid-1960s we were once again in a wartime economy. The "Age of Aquarius" precipitated economic and social changes that reverberated throughout the 1970s and 1980s. By the 1990s, less than fifty years and two generations after World War II, the world was a different place and the structure of our lives had once again changed, but not necessarily for the better.

Although we have been a society obsessed with time, we have always felt there was enough time to do what must or should be done. If time was tight it was due to poor organizing, not a real lack of hours. Recently, however, the pace of our lives has changed. In *The Age of Paradox* Charles Handy argues that "time is coming unfixed." Time has changed, as has the way we use time. According to Handy, we are all suffering from a "serious imbalance of time," and this imbalance is affecting the quality of both our work and private lives.[5] Economist and futurist Jeremy Rifkin finds it ironic that in a culture so compulsive about saving time we feel increasingly deprived of the very thing we value the most.[6]

Where we once thought it abundant, we now believe we are suffering from a "poverty of time." We feel there just isn't enough time to fit in all the things that have to be done, and no matter how fast we move, someone or something is bound to get there faster.[7] As a result we have compacted time, accelerated the use of time, and squeezed time in our attempts to compensate for our "poverty of time."[8] Time that once seemed free and elastic has grown tight and elusive.[9]

Our crisis of time, or what has been called "the great American time crunch,"[10] has been fueled by at least four interrelated factors: the new world order, telecommunications technology, the national economy, and the rapid rise of double-income households.

The way we have viewed the world and identified allies and enemies has changed radically in the last ten years. On November 9, 1989, while the world cheered, the wall built by the East Germans to physically divide Berlin, which had come to symbolize the division between democracy and communism, was torn down piece by piece. Political pundits praised the event, as well as the *contemporaneous* breakup of the Soviet Union, as the victory of democracy over communism. I think they were only half right. Communism did fail, but not because people demanded a republican form of government. Instead, it lost to people's desire for a free market system. Capitalism, not democracy, triumphed because communism, as an economic system, had not succeeded. Seventy years of a controlled state economy had failed to produce the lifestyle and benefits people wanted. The Soviet Union was a "land of workers," but the rewards of labor were always limited and meager. In the words of a Communist worker proverb: "We pretend to work, you pretend to pay us, and then we pretend to buy things that are not really there!"

Perestroika, the reform movement initiated by Mikhail Gorbachev, and the independent unionist moment in Poland that preceded it, was a response to an economic system that at the domestic level was unable to raise the living conditions of its citizenry much above the standards of the Third World. In Poland, Lech Walesa demanded rights for the shipyard workers of Gdansk, and by extension all Polish workers. He wanted better working conditions, job security and a seniority system, shorter hours, more vacation days, higher pay and guaranteed overtime, and, last but by no means least, more worker input and participation. Although Walesa sought democracy as a good thing in itself, he also sought democracy as a means to the goods of a free market system. Gorbachev and Walesa, like Henry Ford, understood that the cycles of production and consumption are economically and politically intertwined and interdependent.

The death of communism and the breakup of the Soviet bloc heralded the birth of a new world order, or more precisely, a new world marketplace. As political barriers toppled, former foes were transformed into potential customers and competitors. Even China, which still officially retains its Maoist vision of Marxism-Leninism, began, under the leadership of Deng Xiapong, to embrace a limited market system to meet the needs of China's people and to reap the benefits of the world market.

The new world order is really part of the global marketplace that has been developing since the end of World War II. The economies of the world are now more interconnected and interdependent than ever before. Our old enemies Germany and Japan are our allies and trading partners. Our old European allies have now formed the Common Market and directly compete with us for customers and resources. The Middle East is a political hot spot made up of friends and foes alike. The balancing act between our political best interest and our economic necessity is often difficult to maintain.

The major corporations in the world today are multinational in their outlook, operations, and economic impact. Like super-tankers and cargo ships, although they are officially registered under one flag, they do business worldwide, and their allegiance is often divided or, perhaps more judiciously stated, multibased. Athletic shoes designed in America are engineered in Germany and produced in Taiwan. Japan's largest-selling sedan is produced in Ohio, and the engines for America's most popular domestically manufactured minivans are produced in Mexico by Japanese companies. VCRs and compact disc players sold under different trade names worldwide are produced in Korea by a single manufacturer. French designer dresses are made in Jakarta, ski sweaters in mainland China, and Disney pajamas in Honduras.[11]

At the macro level, the benefits of such a system are obvious and tangible. The global economy offers corporate players more raw materials, resources, market outlets, and potential customers and sales than ever before. The downside is, of course, that along with an increase in customers there is a corresponding increase in potential competitors. In its simplest terms, there are now more companies at the table than ever before competing for the same pool of dollars. At the micro level, expanding markets and sales translate into more jobs and better salaries. But global competition also means that to keep up and stay ahead of the competition individual workers and companies have more to consider, more to compute, and much more to do.

Perhaps the greatest factor in the rise of the global marketplace has been the revolution in telecommunications technology. According to Alvin and Heidi Toffler, authors of the 1970 blockbuster book *Future Shock* and best-selling sequels *The Third Wave* and *Powershift,* we live in a constantly changing society. Change is part of the national evolutionary process of life, but in the twentieth century, the very nature of change has changed. Today what is really changing society is the rapid acceleration of change itself, which is directly caused by our information and telecommunication technologies. The pace of change has increased because of the increased speed of information processing and transmission.

In 1861, when Confederate forces fired on Fort Sumter, Union detachments in the lonely outpost of Los Angeles did not receive news of the momentous event for over six weeks. When square-rigged whaling ships set out from the shores of New England on two- to four-year hunting expeditions, neither the ship owners nor the crew family members had any way to ascertain the crew's whereabouts or well-being during the course of their adventures. In 1927, when Charles Lindbergh completed the first transatlantic flight, he did so without a radio or any direct means of contacting the ground. Being so unconnected now seems almost medieval, but, in fact, all three examples occurred within the last 150 years.

Today we see and know of events, even if they're halfway around the world, as they happen, in real time. Many of us over the age of forty vividly remember the shock of witnessing Jack Ruby killing Lee Harvey Oswald in Dallas on live TV. On July 20, 1969, an estimated 300 million people worldwide watched astronaut Neil Armstrong step from Eagle One onto the surface of the moon and utter the now famous line "That's one small step for man, one giant leap for mankind." On July 17, 1996, when a TWA 747 passenger jet, en route from New York to Paris, exploded and fell out of the sky off Long Island, CNN helicopter cameras arrived in time to capture pictures of the jet fuel burning on the surface of the sea.

We no longer have to wait days or weeks for our news. Today, the world is instantaneously brought to us in words and pictures at a rate that is often faster than our ability to assimilate them.

Futurists and Luddites alike agree that we live in an age of information and that the pace and volume of the information we absorb has changed the structure and meter of our lives. The now almost constant input of radio, television, telephones, faxes, beepers, and computers has altered how we use time and view reality. Social critic Neil Postman believes the surest way to understand a culture is to understand its tools of communication. He posits that the most significant American cultural event of the second half of the twentieth century is our shift from typographic to videographic media, that is, we search for and gather information no longer primarily by means of the printed page, but from the images and sound bites of television and the computer. The printed word and the cathode image are two different media, and they do not communicate information or represent the world in the same way. According to Postman, reading requires time and interpretation, whereas television offers us prefabricated images, and computers present us with bulletlike facts rather than protracted dialogue and debate.[12]

Putting aside Postman's lack of appreciation for the intellectual skills necessary to operate a computer, his main argument remains a cogent one. Ironically, rather than expanding our vision of reality, the telecommunication revolution has telescoped and limited our perspective on the world. Television and computers have made quick-hit information junkies of us all. We have a broader but shallower understanding of the world. The computer has dramatically and irreversibly altered the nature of information, the pace of change, and the importance of time in our lives. Events pass into history instantaneously, the present is in constant change, and the future is happening as we speak. If the "medium is the message" and the medium is the rapid-fire computer, is it any wonder that only immediate and accessible information is relevant to us?

Computers, the engine for the entire telecommunications industry, have reinforced our obsession with efficiency and time. More and more of us are either hard-wired, cellularly connected, or on-line both on the job and at home. The new standard of literacy is computer literacy, and the new "knowledge worker," according to former Secretary of Labor

Robert Reich, is the worker who posseses computer skills, not necessarily someone who is well read. Although it is too sweeping in its scope, it is good to keep in mind the warning of *Time* magazine essayist Lance Morrow regarding dazzling technologies that can induce dullness and even moronism: "Television is a Faustian bargain, and the Internet has the same ominous tendencies."[13]

Like our time, our wallets are being squeezed harder and harder as the American standard of living increases. During the Depression politicians seeking election promised "a chicken in every pot," but after the war they raised the stakes and the tone of their rhetoric considerably. Their new pledge—"a home for every working family"—mirrored the desires of their citizenry, hungry for the amenities of the good life. Owning a home has always been a big part of the American Dream and an index of middle-class existence. It symbolizes community solidarity, commitment to family, and confidence in the future. As one commentator described America's attitude in the 1950s, "Let's make babies and build houses and get down to business."[14] At the time, we had endured much and emerged victorious, and we were in a building mode. Levittowns, tract-home complexes, and starter homes sprang up across the countryside. Suburbia, which as a concept had its origins in colonial time, became an established part of the landscape. And with each new suburban cluster of homes, schools, hospitals, civic buildings, roads, waterworks, and sewage plants also had to be built.[15]

Sociologist Alan Wolfe has pointed out that the "moral life cycle" of most families in postwar America was based on the assumption of a common upward financial and lifestyle trajectory. We wanted and needed to believe that things were good and getting better, and that the future held more of the same. Well into the 1960s people assumed that each generation would live better than the one before, and even if the rich got larger portions, the benefits of economic growth and government policies would eventually trickle down to everybody.[16] Unfortunately, the 1970s and 1980s were only partially able to sustain this cycle.

"The American Dream is very much intact," declares sociologist Paula Rayman. "It's just gotten much more expensive and therefore less attainable."[17] During the last thirty years the costs of all the basic ingredients of middle-class existence—homes, cars, medical coverage, and college tuition—have soared, and they continue to skyrocket. In the 1950s and 1960s it took 15 to 18 percent of the average thirty-year-old man's gross income to pay the principal and interest on a medium-priced home. (The percentage of income does not include local real estate taxes, the cost of utilities, or maintenance and improvement costs.) By 1973, it took 20 percent of his income, and in 1983 it took more than 40 percent.[18] Two independent appraisers and real estate investors estimated that in 1995 it took over 50 percent.[19]

The problem of spiraling costs has also been compounded by inflation, wage stagnation, and the steady erosion of worker buying power. Hourly workers and production and nonsupervisory employees, who make up a majority of U.S. employees, saw their average wage peak in 1973. Since then it has declined substantially, and now, after adjusting for inflation, it stands at its mid-1960s level. According to Juliet Schor's calculations, just to reach their 1973 standard of living, employees must now work 245 more hours, or more than six extra weeks, per year.[20] Before 1973, both blue- and white-collar male workers could expect their wages to double in ten years between ages twenty-five to thirty-five. Men who were twenty-five in 1973, however, saw their earnings grow by only 16 percent in the next ten years, and older men passing from the age of forty to fifty saw their real earnings decline by 14 percent.[21] Many economists believe that the staggering inflation experienced during the Carter Administration (1977–81) leveled or lost many of the gains made by both salaried and hourly workers in the previous twenty-five years. Worse than a decline of spending power and a reduction in pay and benefits, though, is a loss of employment. Since 1987, U.S. companies have eliminated more than 4 million jobs in an attempt to reduce production costs.[22]

Clearly, the "middle-class squeeze" is on, and many of us feel that we fall further behind while trying to get ahead.[23] For many, the American Dream, a system that worked for our parents, is beginning to erode. Many middle-class families today will not be able to do for their children all that their parents did for them. For example, in the 1960s when the baby boomers were getting married and starting families, it has been estimated that 60 percent of them borrowed or received as a gift from their parents the down payment on their first home. Today with the average home costs in metropolitan areas exceeding $160,000, fewer and fewer families are able to carry on this tradition.[24]

At a time when college degrees are essential for good jobs in the global market, college tuition now absorbs 40 percent of a family's income; this figure is up from 29 percent in 1970. Most middle-class families make the necessary sacrifices in order to give their children the passport to a promising career. But even with college there are no guarantees. (Researchers at Dartmouth College and Hofstra University project that only 35 percent of the men between the ages of 25 and 34 in the year 2000 will be able to land a better job than their fathers had.)[25] Consequently, more and more parents are beginning to doubt the American Dream.

All of these factors have led to the unavoidable conclusion that the singular efforts of the traditional male breadwinner are no longer enough. It now takes two paychecks to fund what we imagine as a typical middle-class lifestyle. Single-income families are no longer the norm, and most economic indices of salaries and wages are now based on joint couple or household incomes.

The 1950s are commonly perceived as the "golden age" of the nuclear family, but as Stephanie Coontz has reminded us, *Leave It to Beaver* was a sitcom, not a documentary.[26] The model of dad at work and mom in the kitchen resonated with a deep-seated (and perhaps unexamined paternalistic) bias regarding what we then thought to be natural and proper: Men were providers, women were nurturers.

John Kenneth Galbraith wrote in his 1958 book, *The Affluent Society*, that a "natural division of labor" was the hallmark of successful 1950s, middle-class households. In essence, doing well by providing for your family meant that a man was a success and could afford to have his wife not work outside the home. It was a badge of honor, and people bought into it. A college classmate of mine once told me that one of his biggest priorities in life was finding a job that paid well enough so that his wife would never have to work. His grandmother had worked her entire life, but his mother had not worked since his father returned from the war. His father told him that if his wife had to work, he'd be taking a giant step backward. It would be an admission of personal failure and a dishonor to his family.

Although this model of the modern family was attainable for some middle-class households and although it persists as a nostalgic ideal, Coontz documents that its reality was short-lived.[27] In order to balance the household checkbook, women were often forced to divide their lives between work and family responsibilities. In less than forty years and within one biological generation, the structure of the American family had radically changed.

In contrast to the 1950s and 1960s, when 43 percent of all families (with or without children) made do on a single income, only 14 percent of today's families have just one income earner. So-called traditional families, in which the father is the sole breadwinner and the mother is a full-time homemaker caring for children, are now a small minority of two-parent households with children. As of 1980 this type of family comprised 15 percent of all households, and some experts estimate that that figure is as low as 12 percent.[28] Bradley Googins has put together a handy chart that graphically captures the magnitude of change that the prototypical U.S. family has undergone between 1950 and 1990.[29]

1950	**1990**
Three children	One child
Mother at home	Mother at work
Parents age 22 when first child born	Parents age 35 when first child born
Mother-father married 15 years	Parents divorced/father remarried
Grandmother lives in house	Grandmother in extended-care facility
Family eats out few times per year	Family eats out 3 times per week
Children/mother part of scout troops	Children participate in after-school activities and lessons

According to Googins, it is almost incomprehensible that these radically different families are only a generation apart. Today's families are diverse, defy stereotypes, and operate under a constantly changing series of rules, demands, and expectations. Today's families are more mobile, less stable as units, and much more dependent on institutions, such as day-care centers, schools, restaurants, and elder-service agencies to carry out what were once strictly family functions. No matter how much we romanticize the 1950s model of the traditional family, in reality, it is now nothing more than a statistical anomaly. Today, dad's at work, mom's at work, and we're not always sure who's taking care of the children!

As I have already indicated, the entrance of women into the labor force seeking full-time employment and careers is, perhaps, the single most important demographic trend in the workplace in the second half of the twentieth century. Fueling that trend are the feminist movement, changes in social custom, the evolving needs of business, greater educational achievements, and the need to have an individual identity, and perhaps most immediate, the middle-class financial squeeze.

With women in the workplace, the great American time crunch has become collective, communal, familial. With both mom and dad on the job and working an ever-expanding day, our lives have become hectic attempts to balance work, home, family, and a rapidly diminishing social and leisure calander. Although days are the same length as when wives took care of the home front, there is now twice as much to do and less time to do it.[30] When the hours devoted to home and family responsibilities are added to paid work hours, most working adults today have the responsibility for the equivalent of one and a half to two full-time jobs.[31]

According to Juliet Schor, the 5:00 P.M. dads of the 1950s and 1960s are becoming an endangered species as they transformed into 8:00 or 9:00 P.M. dads. As one hardworking dad put it, "Either I can spend time with my family, or support them—not both. . . . If I don't work the OT my wife would have to work much longer hours to make up the difference."[32] Working women find themselves in the same bind. According to Schor's calculations, the total working time of employed mothers now averages more than sixty-five hours per week, and this figure can jump to seventy or eighty hours depending on marital status, type of job, wage scale, and the number and age of the children.[33]

Perhaps, for the first time in our collective history, the root cause of our obsession with time is less pathological and more practical in its origin. Time has changed. Its pace has quickened. The natural rhythms of human living and human relationships have accelerated. The average double-income household can best be characterized as an experiment in controlled chaos.[34] Our obsession with time has made us addicts of work.

9

Workaholism, Stress, and Fatigue

> Woman to sales clerk: "Do you have any perfume that smells like a desk? My husband is a workaholic."
>
> —Cartoon by Randy Glasbergen

LIKE IT OR NOT, WE ARE "FETTERED TO THE process of work" and captives of our jobs.[1] According to Workaholics Anonymous, given the raw number of hours we put into our jobs, most of us are either active workaholics or potential workaholics. In *The Work Ethic in Industrial America, 1850–1920,* historian Daniel Rodgers argues that we are a nation predisposed to hard work and that the "elevation of work over leisure" is an ethos that has long permeated our lives.[2]

When you add to this inherited infatuation, if not obsession, with work the particular problems of the last third of the twentieth century—the voracious productivity demands of our jobs, the restructuring of corporate work life, stagnant salaries, the ever-increasing cost of living—an argument can be made that we are preordained to be addicted to work. Need, greed, and habit have made us prisoners of a system we helped to design and continue to sustain by our efforts. We have become a nation of workaholics.

John P. Robinson, who heads the Americans' Use of Time project at Penn State, claims that many Americans are addicted to work because they want to be. "Americans now view work as an end in itself—the more of it the better." For some, he believes, it may even have replaced religion.[3] Like religious commitment, work can offer us comfort, guidance, insight, and regulating principles by which to view reality and conduct our lives. While work, like religious commitment, may not be able to offer us ultimate wisdom it can offer us a proactive mechanism by which to handle or at least accept the mysteries and paradoxes of life and living. Working hard may be an addiction, but it's an addiction that produces results. Therefore we value it, granting it the status of a virtue or at least an acceptable vice.

Workaholism is considered a clean addiction, and, not surprisingly, it is prized by businesses and corporations. After all, what company wouldn't rather have a workaholic instead of an alcoholic employee? Workaholics produce worth and achieve success. Workaholism is one of the only addictions that is not merely condoned but actively rewarded. It is socially accepted, even promoted, because it is socially productive. We all know people who brag about working sixty, seventy, or eighty hours per week.[4] Workaholics in effect say, "I know I'm a workaholic, but it's better than a lot of other things I could be! I'm working my rear end off!" They assume, as might their family, friends, and colleagues, that they are being dutiful, industrious, and successful as described by the American Dream.

According to Diane Fassel in her important book *Working Ourselves to Death,* the Protestant work ethic and workaholism are two separate and distinct phenomena. The work ethic is about the role and acceptance of work in our lives. It is about God's calling to work, the dignity and duty of work, the value and purpose of work. It is about personal and communal fulfillment and survival through work. The work ethic is the about life and living. Workaholism, on the other hand, is just the opposite. It is a substitute for life. It is about selfishness, compulsive behavior, and performance fixation. Workaholism is about addiction.

As an addiction, work becomes a narcotic, our coping mechanism for life. Workaholism insulates and isolates us from life. It buffers us from ourselves and others. Workaholism is one way of dealing with reality when other options are unavailable. Work addiction may not be our first or best option, but it is a familiar and well-sanctioned one. "Workaholics," says Fassel, "are no longer 'showing up' for life. They are alienated from their own bodies, from their own feelings, from their creativity, and from family and friends. They have been taken over by the compulsion to work and are slaves to it. They no longer own their lives." Workaholism, she warns, is a progressively fatal disease, which masquerades as a positive trait in the cultural lore of our nation."[5]

In 1964, the World Health Organization (WHO) concluded that

addiction is no longer an exact scientific term because it has been trivialized in popular usage to refer to any kind of personal habitual behavior, such as "TV addiction" and "gambling addiction," that results in either short- or long-term detrimental effects, which are often only cosmetic. In its place, the WHO recommends the term *dependence* or *dependency* because they better emphasize, as a diagnostic criterion, long-term, life-patterning, repetitive behavior that was clearly abusive and maladaptive to an individual.[6] Addiction or dependency involves habitual behavior and fixation. In its strictest sense, behavioral addiction refers to compulsive, repetitive, and oftentimes inappropriate behavior to achieve some external objective or goal or an inner state of personal satisfaction or contentment. True addiction is always dysfunctional because it means depending on something outside of ourselves to feel not necessarily euphoric but good or normal. Ironically, an addict is searching first and foremost for control, seeking the self by surrendering it to the dictates of the addiction.

The most recent edition of *Synopsis of Psychiatry,* the bible of that field, does not list work addiction (or workaholism) as a behavioral disorder. Nor does it recognize it as a medical disease with a specific etiology and remedial protocol. It is instead described as a malaise associated with work. But the growing body of literature in the social sciences argues that workaholism is an addiction and that it in fact fits the standard psychiatric profiles for both dependency disorders and substances abuse.[7] Diane Fassel argues that "workaholics exhibit the same characteristics of addiction that one finds in alcoholics or drug addicts or relationship addicts or compulsive debtors. Whether the addiction is to a substance or a process, the internal design of the disease is the same." Workaholism, she concluded, is an addiction, and our addiction to work is a modern epidemic.[8]

Like the grim lie of the inscription over the entrance to the Nazi concentration camp of Auschwitz—*Arbeit macht frei* (work will set you free)—workaholics' attitude toward work is that it represents freedom, escape, fulfillment. But Auschwitz was the antithesis of freedom. Its purpose was to enslave its detainees and kill the body and spirit of the worker.[9] So too work enslaves: Work does not bring freedom to the workaholics. At best, work for the workaholic produces a false sense of private purposefulness, ersatz personal euphoria, and an anesthetized indifference to the rest of the world. Nevertheless, Fassel says, "for the work addict, the job is like a chocolate factory for an overeater. It is as if an active alcoholic were going to work in a saloon. . . . What is more, you get paid for it." Worse yet, work is god for the compulsive worker, and nothing gets in the way of his religion.[10] Work becomes an end in itself, an escape from family, an inner life, the troubles of the world.

Workaholism is not about working hard or being diligent or being appropriately dedicated to one's work. It is, rather, as Fassel describes, "an entire orientation toward life." It means being obsessed with and preoccupied by work. It is a coping devise, a means of dealing with "life's problems by working harder, always doing more."[11] All life decisions are dictated by the demands of work. Workaholics see work as the means of establishing themselves, outdoing and overcoming any and all obstacles or impediments in their path. Workaholism is a character disorder that goes far beyond time spent on the job; it is about work fixation. According to psychologist Martin Helldorfer, work fixation becomes a work trap, turning every experience—even playing or relaxing—into work. We become work-fixated when all of life becomes something we have to do.

Work fixation is not the same as spending long hours at an office. Nor is it

> necessarily avoided by spending much time pursuing leisure-time activities. Rather, work-fixation has to do with a way of living, of approaching life, and of being present to whatever we are involved in. The person who "works" from morning till night may not be at all trapped in a work-like approach to life, just as the person who has a job for a few hours each day may not necessarily avoid work-fixation. The mark of being fixated is being always and everywhere project-orientated.[12]

By living as if all is work, workaholics believe they can get things done. Workaholics are work addicts, not job addicts, notes Fassel. The addiction does not stop at the front door: It follows the workaholic everywhere. The workaholic lacks boundaries, and uses work to provide everything. Workaholics take work to bed, take it home on weekends, take it on vacation. The workaholic is never without work, because work is the fix. Many children of workaholic parents, reports Fassel, describe vacations as whirlwinds of exhausting activity. Their parents approached vacation the way they did work—full-tilt and nonstop.[13]

In its narrowest sense, Fassel defines as is an addiction to action. The type of action may vary but the process is the same: You leave yourself by losing yourself in your busy-ness. The workaholic cannot say no to work and its demands. As addicts, they are driven by the compulsion to work. Work orients them, affirms them, comforts them, holds out to them the possibility of happiness. Of course, says Fassel, for the addict, work is never done. Thus happiness dangles like the proverbial carrot before the horse, always just the next project away. *Then* they will have succeeded, *then* they will be happy, *then* they will be able to provide for all of their family's wants and needs. Unfortunately, that is the illusion addicts need to believe. In fact, workaholism is a progressively fatal disease. Unchecked, the workaholic's compulsiveness toward work will continue to grow. In the process, workaholics become increasingly unavailable to both themselves and their loved ones. Work addition is never a private disease. Workaholics affect everyone they live with and touch. Families of workaholics are filled with anger and resentment. They feel they are without a spouse or a parent. Ironically, in pursuit of the good life, workaholics lose control of their own lives: "Workaholics have their addictions; they don't have their lives."[14]

According to Fassel, when the workplace rewards workaholism, our very understanding of work is obscured, and the possibility of finding good work or meaningful work is simply not available to us.

> Because work addition keeps us busy, we stay estranged from our essential selves. An aspect of that estrangement is that we cease asking ourselves if we are doing our right work. Are we actually performing the task or pursuing the vocation we need to be doing? Is it good for us, for our families, and the universe? I believe the social implication of workaholism is that we don't ask the questions for two reasons: 1) We aren't doing our true work, and 2) in our society, few people have access to their right work.[15]

Of course, compounding the problem for the workaholic is a social and business structure that actively rewards work addiction. We are a nation of addicted workers primarily because we are a nation of addictive work organizations. In an addictive society, workaholism does not shock us. There is no dissonance in this disease; it feels normal because it is the norm. Workaholism is the status quo. We have created a series of positive myths about workaholism: No one ever died of hard work; workaholism is always profitable for individuals and corporations; workaholics always get ahead; hard work keeps you out of trouble; no effort goes unrewarded; success comes to those who work for it; work proves worth; fitness addicts have better bodies, but workaholics make more money; having it all is not an illusion. Homilies such as these hide the truth. We have adapted to workaholism, says Fassel, in much the same way a frog can adapt to a pot of boiling water. If you suddenly drop a frog into boiling water it will leap out immediately, but if you put a frog in a pot of cool water and gradually heat the water to the boiling point, it will remain in the pot until it dies. Fassel contends that this is the perfect metaphor for the state of workaholism in our society today.[16]

At its core, workaholism is about attitude: Work is the key; work is the answer; work is the way. Although all workaholics are committed to a belief in the efficiency and necessity of work, not all workaholics are alike, and not all workaholics are motivated by the same issues. The spectrum of workaholic types ranges from the absorbed, focused, and relatively benign to the obsessive, frenetic, and destructive. For some, workaholism is a manageable habit, and for others it is an all-consuming addiction that can never be satisfied. Where one winds up on this spectrum of addiction is dependent on a number of variables. Some people choose to be "hooked on work," or are culturally and ideologically seduced into addiction, some embrace it in the pursuit of philosophical and psychological tranquility and insight, and others degenerate into workaholism out of financial necessity.

There are at least ten different types of work addiction. Each type refers to a specific series of circumstances, symptoms, or causes. Each type can, in itself, cause and sustain workaholism, but it has been my experience that most addicts are affected by multiple causes simultaneously. The ten types and their origins are as follows.

1. The Protestant Work Ethic—Like mathematics, this ethic may not lead you to passion but, it is a powerful and long-established cultural imperative. "Work is good" has been drummed into our heads with the same frequency and intensity as has "Cleanliness is next to godliness." We have been told again and again—work is part of humankind's punishment, destiny, mandate and blessing. Hard work, successful work is part of Christian theology and proof of our private and collective redemption.

2. Role Models—Robert Bly has argued that both boys and girls learn their place and purpose in a community through the example and witness of others.[17] Gender roles and cultural standards and patterns are not innate or intuitive but learned and reinforced. As products of culture, they change with the times. For example, in today's world both boys and girls want to grow up to be firefighters, police officers, teachers, and ministers. Work addiction is a generational disease. Families that are always doing things produce children who primarily value what they do.

3. Your Job Is Your Perk—Economic necessity is perhaps the most obvious catalyst for work addiction. Diane Fassel calls those individuals who are economically forced or frightened into long hours or multiple jobs "reluctant workaholics."[18] Economic hard times and fear of them have made many of us insecure. We are afraid of losing our jobs, our stability, and our lifestyles. At least in part, this fear comes out of the legacy of the Reagan era—downsizing.

Downsizing is the defining reality of the workplace today. Corporations driven by the need to reduce costs, increase their competitive advantage, and expand profit margins decided that the easiest and fastest way to cut costs was to "gut itself of excess workers."[19] As I have already indicated, since 1987 U.S. companies have eliminated 4 million jobs, and in 1995 alone more than 375,000 workers lost their jobs to workforce reductions.[20] This single-minded and rampant strategy of severing salaries as the best means of saving the company money has led many workers to feel endangered.

Social critic Ralph Nader has found that American workers are genuinely frightened about losing their jobs and their lifestyles. Although stock market prices and corporate profit gains are at their highest level in two decades, workers have neither shared in these financial dividends nor gained greater job security because of them. Today's workers have resurrected a Depression-era mentality about their jobs: Stay busy, don't make waves, and be thankful when you don't find a pink slip in your pay envelopes. Today's work ethic is maintained by fear of reprisals and lack of realistic options rather than loyalty or even basic gratitude.[21]

Kafkaesque cartoonist Scott Adams of *Dilbert* fame claims that losing a job to downsizing is the final insult and degradation. As Adams sees it, the employer is saying to the employee, "We've squeezed your benefits. We've taken all your power and soul. We've taken the best years of your life. We made you sit in a cardboard box. We drove you crazy. And now you can't stay!"[22] Downsizing, suggests Adams, views workers as necessary but, taken individually, as expendable and transitory. Products and profit are the only perennial truths of business. And, as is his habit, Adams encapsulated the issue in a three-frame cartoon: 1) The boss talking to a group of employees admits that he was mistaken when he previously claimed that "employees are our most valuable asset." 2) "Actually," he explains, "they're ninth." 3) "Eighth place?" asks an employee. "Carbon paper!" says the boss.[23]

Workers' fears and frustrations are not abstract. They are directly connected to the size of their paychecks and the volatile nature of both the marketplace and job security. In losing a job workers lose much more than a paycheck. Without work we are bereft of identity as well as finances. And so, to borrow another image from *Dilbert,* being a corporate cubicle dweller, working in an air-conditioned sweatshop sixty hours a week for bad pay is better than not working at all.

4. Fast-Track Careerists—Summarizing the cultural acceptance of workaholism, Arlie Hochschild has written, "In America, we don't have family coats of arms anymore, but we have the company logo."[24] Making it on the job. Being successful. Carving out a career. These are the lessons, values, and the vision of middle-class America. Successful careers require ambition, commitment, and the willingness to outwork, outpractice, outperform both the competition and your coworkers. Time spent on the job and terrifying work habits are viewed as indications of dedication. A lot of people who don't make it to the top work long hours, but all the people who do make it put in the time.[25] As one interviewer informed a job candidate: "We feel that anybody serious has got to be willing to work at least sixty hours a week. If you're not, we know we can get someone who will."[26]

5. Job Requirements—Personal temperament and ambition aside, some people, such as surgeons, CEOs, and politicians, simply have jobs that require inordinate amounts of time, energy, and commitment. These jobs both attract work addicts and produce addiction. These are jobs that people want to do and need to be done, but they prohibit moderation. They produce "bionic grinds" rather than balanced personality types.[27] As one management type put it, "It's going to be a long time before somebody becomes the CEO of a company saying, 'I'm going to be a wonderfully balanced person'—because there are just too many others who aren't. The environment [at this level] is very competitive."[28]

6. Work as Fun—There are those lucky few who find their work so engaging, so creative, so fulfilling that they love their work, live their work, thrive on their work, and seek it out in ever-increasing measure. For them the line between work and play has been dissolved. They feel work is fun and, if need be, would do it for free.

7. Low Self-Esteem—According to Diane Fassel, work addicts either have an inflated or depleted perception of themselves. Those with low self-esteem have a hard time evaluating themselves honestly and accepting themselves for who they are. They fear that they have little or no ability and are not worthy of the love or regard of others. Consequently, says Fassel, in order to feel good and convince others to love them, they must accomplish something. Accomplishments are the workaholic's primary means of establishing who they are. In working hard, in staying busy, in demonstrating competence and proficiency, addicts justify their existence both to themselves and others.[29] Ironically, the self-centeredness of many workaholics is a compensating mechanism for a lack of appropriate self-esteem.

8. Sanative Device—Sanative means the power to heal, to cure, to restore. Work for many addicts is a means to overcome the emptiness or unhappiness in other parts of their lives. In being busy they keep others and themselves at bay. In being competent, in being successful, addicts create an image of themselves as healthy or normal. As a sanative device, work is narcotic escapism. Work keeps a workaholic sane!

9. Command and Control or The God Thing—Being obsessive, being a perfectionist, being a control freak does not explain life, but at least it reassures the organizer that "everything is in place and there is a place for everything." Compulsive behavior is time-consuming, energy-consuming and, if done well, an almost foolproof diversionary tactic and strategy for getting through life.

10. Metaphysical Angst—Hannah Arendt has said that "work [can] bestow a measure of permanence and durability upon the futility of mortal life and the fleeting character of human time."[30] This is the philosophical darkside of work addiction. Work will not set you free, will not offer comfort, insight, control, or happiness, but it can preoccupy our lives, and our efforts can, if not make a difference, at least make a mark so that we will not be entirely forgotten. An even darker philosophical interpretation of work can be found in Ernest Becker's *The Denial of Death,* in which he posits that work is a way for us to temporally transcend death. To work is to live without thoughts of dying. To work is to be creative, and in our creativity we block out other issues in our life that we are unable or unwilling to handle directly. Work can be a response to the chaos and seeming nihilism of life. Work is a defense against metaphysical anxiety and our despair over the thoughts of death and finitude.[31]

Whatever the particular reason for work addiction, the results are always the same: frenzy, fatigue, burnout, breakdown. Life is a stress test, and the longer you're in the game the greater your chances of getting hurt.

According to the "Mitchum Report on Stress in the 1990s," 74 percent of the American public admit to living with a notable amount of stress in their lives, and 26 percent say they have "a lot" of stress in their lives. Fifty percent say that their lives are more stressful than five years ago, and one in three Americans cites work as the single most common source of stress.[32] In another, more recent *Wall Street Journal* and NBC poll, 40 percent of the population surveyed would choose more time over more money, 59 percent described their lives as too busy and too stressful, and 19 percent reported that their lack of time resulted in serious personal stress.[33]

According to Dr. Paul J. Rosch, president of the American Institute of Stress, more than 66 percent of all visits to primary-care physicians are for stress-related complaints, as are more than half of the 550 million workdays lost to absenteeism at an estimated cost of more than $200 billion annually.[34] The last ten years of medical research has been able to identify some of the more serious consequences of high and increasing stress levels. One of every five healthy people respond to stress in a manner destructive to their cardiovascular system (it's one of two for anyone with high blood pressure). Stress causes cholesterol levels to increase as much as, and sometimes more than, dietary habits do. Depression is now more closely linked to stress than to genetics, and depression is up threefold among young people since World War II, even when allowing for the population boom.[35]

In a 1995 cover story, *Newsweek* reported that 25 percent of us say we're fried by our work, frazzled by the lack of time, and just plain exhausted.[36] Our lives are fuller and busier but not better. Arlie Russell Hochschild suggests that our lives and schedules are so exhausting that we talk about sleep in the same longing way that hungry people talk about food.[37] Symptoms of exhaustion and fatigue are now among the top five reasons people consult with their doctors. Although physicians are quick to point out that exhaustion is an umbrella term and not a medical term or a diagnosis, fatigue symptoms can herald any number of serious illnesses. (However, chronic fatigue syndrome, also called Epstein-Barr and Yuppie's Disease, is very rare, affecting only 5 percent of those who suffer long-term fatigue.) According to Dr. Sheldon Miller, chair of psychology at Northwestern University, exhaustion is the body crying out "I've had it." Most commonly, exhaustion is a sign of depression, and more than half of the burnout cases that make it into a doctor's office are depressed patients.[38]

Psychologist Charles R. Figley defines burnout as a state of physical, emotional, and mental exhaustion caused by long-term involvement in emotionally demanding situations. The most widely used measurement of burnout is the Maslach Burnout Inventory. It measures three areas: emotional exhaustion ("I feel emotionally drained by my work."), depersonalization ("I worry that this job is hardening me emotionally"), and reduced personal accomplishment ("I don't feel I'm positively influencing other peoples' lives through my work"). Burnout, says Figley, is a process rather than a fixed or sudden condition that begins gradually and becomes progressively worse. Burnout, he reports, has five identifiable categories of symptoms.

1. Physical symptoms (fatigue and physical depletion/exhaustion, sleep difficulties, loss of libido, specific somatic problems such as headaches, gastrointestinal disturbances, colds and flu).
2. Emotional symptoms (e.g., irritability, anxiety, depression, guilt, sense of helplessness).
3. Behavioral symptoms (e.g., aggression, callousness, pessimism, defensiveness, cynicism, substance abuse).

4. Work-related symptoms (e.g., quitting the job, poor work performance, absenteeism, tardiness, misuse of work breaks, thefts).
5. Interpersonal symptoms (e.g., perfunctory communication with inability to concentrate or focus, withdrawal from clients or coworkers, and then dehumanizing, intellectualizing clients).[39]

Clearly the most exotic example of fatigue disease is the Japanese variant *karoshi,* or sudden death from overwork. This disease, which is linked to too much work and not enough play, typically affects blue- and white-collar men who put in 12- to 16-hour days over many years. The 30,000 victims a year are usually between the ages of forty and fifty and have no previous health problems. They apparently just work themselves to death. Two-thirds of the deaths are from brain hemorrhages, and one-third from myocardial infarction. According to Japan's Ministry of Health and Welfare, *karoshi* is the second-leading cause of death, after cancer, among Japanese workers.[40]

Neuropsychologist Walter Tubbs believes that *karoshi* is primarily caused by the stress of prolonged overwork, but that it is also the body's reaction to a whole array of physical and psychosociological stress factors. The *karoshi* victim, says Tubbs, succumbs to the cumulative stress we are forced to endure and absorb. He argues that *karoshi* is caused by feelings of depression and helplessness combined with overwork. "Helplessness," says Tubbs, is not merely a vague, emotional term. It is a technical term for the psychological state that frequently results when events are uncontrollable—when there is nothing we can do about the situation we are in and when nothing we do matters. *Karoshi,* says Tubbs, results from the despair of being trapped in a vicious cycle over which we have no control, and from which there is no chance of change or escape. It is due to the stress of helplessness.[41]

Tubbs warns *karoshi* will flourish as a social phenomenon unless we learn how to protect ourselves from or actively prevent stress. The first step in that process is to analyze our stress absorption and decide how we will manage the unavoidable and remove the unnecessary stress factors in our lives. He offers as an assessment tool the Holmes-Rahe List of Stress-Rated Life Issues and Events, a reliable instrument to predict health breakdown as a consequence of stress overload.

The Social Readjustment Rating Scale

(Gunderson and Rahe, 1979, and Albrecht, 1979)

Check off each of the life events that has happened to you during the previous year

		Life Change Unit Values
Family:	Death of spouse	100
	Divorce	73
	Marital separation	63
	Death of close family member	63
	Marriagc	50
	Major reconciliation	45
	Major change in health of family	44
	Pregnancy	40
	Addition of new family member	39
	Major change in arguments with spouse	35
	Son or daughter leaves home	29
	In-law troubles	29
	Spouse starting or ending work	26
	Major change in family get-togethers	15
Personal:	Detention in jail	63
	Major personal injury or illness	53
	Sexual difficulties	39
	Death of a close friend	37
	Outstanding personal achievement	28
	Start or end of formal schooling	26
	Major change in living conditions	25
	Major revision of personal habits	24
	Changing to a new school	20
	Changing residence	20
	Major change in recreation	19
	Major change in church activities	19
	Major change in social activities	18
	Major change in sleeping habits	16
	Major change in eating habits	15
	Vacation	13
	Christmas	12
	Minor violations of the law	11

Work:	Being fired from work	47
	Retirement from work	45
	Major business adjustment	39
	Changing to different line of work	36
	Major change in work responsibilities	29
	Trouble with boss	23
	Major change in working conditions	20
Financial:	Major change in financial state	38
	Mortgage or loan over $10,000	31
	Mortgage foreclosure	30
	Mortgage or loan less than $10,000	17

A person who scores below 150 points on this inventory has a chance of a serious health problem in the next two years of less than one in three. A score between 150 and 300 gives a likelihood of about 50 percent. A score of over 300 indicates a risk of over 80 percent of a major health breakdown. Note that the risk period is two years, and the causal factors in stress death lie not in the previous day's work or in the previous week's work, but in the total context of the previous one year.[42]

Tubbs suggests we emulate the teachings of the Japanese sage Sontoku, who believed that the place of work can or should be the place in which salvation and enlightenment can be found. But far from being the place where self-actualization and fulfillment is found, work for many people is the place that robs their life of meaning and, in extreme cases, even kills them. When this amount of overwork is demanded or allowed by companies, it is not only poor business practice, but damnable business ethics.[43]

Barbara Ehrenreich has observed that "busyness has become an important insignia of upper-middle-class status. Eating is giving way to 'grazing'—the unconscious ingestion of unidentified foods while drafting a legal brief." Leisure, recreation, and unstructured time are given over to either chores or a semicomatose state caused by utter exhaustion.[44] The central problem of our work lives is not so much the work as the overwork. Even good work when done too much is dispiriting and enervating. In doing too much, we lose perspective, purpose, and the pleasure involved in the doing. Vince Lombardi, NFL coach and football legend, is reported to have said that "fatigue makes cowards and fools of us all and more often than not results in mediocrity." Working longer and harder does not mean we are working smarter or better. Working too long and too hard may not necessarily result in *karoshi,* but it will produce a persuasive form of fatigue that can erode morale and morals.

In a 1997 study entitled *Time for Life: The Surprising Ways Americans Use Their Time,* time-use experts John Robinson and Geoffry Godbey of Penn State University argued that despite all the intrusions and demands of work upon people's lives these days, Americans in the 1990s have more leisure than ever before. Not everyone, of course. A working single mother of two children doesn't have as much time as a sixty-five-year-old empty nester. In general, though, the authors found that Americans are working less than they did thirty years ago—about fifty hours per week, including paid work time, household chores, and commuting—and now enjoy close to forty hours of leisure per week, five more hours than we had in 1965. "People think they are working longer hours," says Godbey, " but in reality, they mistake the pace of work for length of time spent working. On average, the number of hours people spend working has diminished."[45]

Needless to say, this is a controversial thesis, and it has received a lot of criticism because it refutes the pace and feel of our lives. The authors aren't entirely surprised by this reaction. They claim that "being busy has become a status symbol." We brag about being busy because being busy means we're important. Hence, claim the authors, when people are asked how many hours they work, commute, tend to children, do chores, and so on, they exaggerate. Instead of just asking them, then, Robinson and Godbey required the 10,000 survey participants to keep a minute-by-minute, twenty-four-hour diary of how they spent their days. Their results were surprising. When asked, women claimed that they put in 40.4 hours week on the job, and men claimed 46.2 hours. When calculated from diary entries, however, women actually put in 32 hours per week and men worked 40.4 hours per week.[46]

Even though Robinson and Godbey's research may cause a reevaluation of our time management, it doesn't change how this society sees itself and deals with the issues of work, time, and addiction. Although people may mistake working faster and being more rushed with working longer, Robinson and Godbey's data also reinforce the premise that rushing and stress are huge problems in our society. No matter what the numbers, work addiction is primarily about attitude, compulsion, focus, fixation, and orientation. Work addiction seems to be our inescapable legacy, and our current response to it seems steadfastly schizophrenic. In this society, we praise people who seek balance in their lives, but we only reward those who diligently work themselves to death!

So, are you a workaholic or do you just really love your job? Answer the following questions with a simple yes or no (rationales, justifications, excuses do not count).

1. Do you get more excited about your work than about family or anything else?
2. Are there times when you can charge through your work and other times when you can't get anything done?
3. Do you take work with you to bed? On weekends? On vacation?
4. Is work the activity you like to do best and talk about most?
5. Do you work more than forty hours per week?
6. Do you turn your hobbies into money-making ventures?
7. Do you take complete responsibility for the outcome of your work efforts?
8. Have your family or friends stopped expecting you on time?
9. Do you take on extra work because you are concerned that it won't otherwise get done?
10. Do you underestimate how long a project will take and then rush to complete it?
11. Do you believe that it is O.K. to work long hours if you love what you are doing?
12. Do you get impatient with people who have priorities beside work?
13. Are you afraid that if you don't work hard you will lose your job or be a failure?
14. Is the future a constant worry for you even when things are going very well?
15. Do you do things energetically and competitively, including play?
16. Do you get irritated when people ask you to stop working so you can do something else?

17. Have your long hours hurt your family or other relationships?
18. Do you think about your work while driving, falling asleep, or when others are talking?
19. Do you work or read during meals?
20. Do you believe that more money will solve the other problems in your life?

According to Workaholics Anonymous, anyone who agrees with at least *three* of the above questions is either a workaholic or a potential workaholic.[47] Scary, huh!?

10

The Work, Spend, and Debt Syndrome

> The source of status is no longer the ability to make things but simply the ability to purchase them.
>
> —Harry Braverman

IT ISN'T ONLY WORK THAT LABELS AND IDENTIFIES us. *Tu sei quello che fai* (You are what you do). We are also known, identified, and labeled by what we consume, purchase or buy. *L'uomo e' quello che compra* (Every man is what he buys, or You are what you buy). In an advertisement-intense, capitalistic economy people are known by *where* they shop, *how* they shop and *what* they buy and own. More than a century ago Henry David Thoreau observed that "Americans know more about how to make a living than how to live." By and large, his critique remains true today. We organize our lives around our economic institutions and measure our value and worth by our success on the job and our choices as consumers. As another American scholar, Van Wyck Brooks, has put it:

> The typical American has not been taught that life is a legitimate progress toward spiritual or intellectual ends. . . . He has had it embedded in his mind that the getting of a living is not a necessity incidental to some higher and more disinterested end, but that it is the prime and central end.[1]

In her most recent book, *The Overspent American*, Juliet Schor argues that we are both children and captives of a culture of consumerism. For far too many of us, "shopping till we drop" is not just a satirical cliché, but rather an honorific—a lifestyle to be wished for and sought after. To put the point in a mix of Italian and Latin idioms—it isn't only *Laboro, ergo sum* (I work, therefore I am), it's also *Emo, ergo sum* (I shop, therefore I am).

In 1959 distinguished historian Arthur Schlesinger, Jr., in the pages of the *Saturday Evening Post,* cast a worried eye to the future. He warned us about the impending abyss of free time and the dangers of "the onrush of a new age of leisure." In the same year, the scholarly *Harvard Business Review* also warned of the "crises of leisure" and "the intellectual and emotional stultification" brought on by excessive amounts of unstructured time. The *Review* warned that "boredom, which used to bother only aristocrats," had become "a common curse." Experts proclaimed that the four-day workweek was at hand and that by the turn of the century employees would work either a twenty-hour week or a six-month year, and that the new standard retirement age would be thirty-eight.[2] High school teachers of Home Economics quizzed their students about how they would deal with all that extra free time. How would housewives cope with their husbands' being around for four-day weekends? What would men do to keep busy or at least stay out of the way? For many, the impending onslaught of free time seemed more like a burden than an opportunity.[3]

In his fascinating book *The Day before Yesterday,* journalist Michael Elliot said that the "leisure scare" was, in part, precipitated by the somewhat unexpected economic boom that occurred after World War II. In 1945, based on the "twin rocks of its economic and military might" America "bestrode the . . . world like a colossus" wrote Elliot.[4] Not only had we defeated the Axis powers in the field, but we had also produced the military hardware needed by ourselves and our Allies to do so. After the war the challenge became how to reconvert to a peacetime economy. Could we beat and bend our bullets back into plowshares? By 1946, the United States accounted for more than 40 percent of the world's total economic output, higher than any nation before. Cars were once again rolling off the assembly lines that had been producing tanks, household goods were back on the shelves at Sears and Roebuck and Montgomery Ward stores, rationing was over, and universities were jammed with former GIs eager to better themselves. The general economy was in high gear. We embraced these "golden years" as the fruition of the American Dream. We had survived the Depression, won the war, and had officially become a "people of plenty." The postwar boom economy was a benchmark to maintain, expand, and pass on to future generations.[5]

Based on Juliet Schor's calculations, since 1948, the level of production in America has more than doubled. In other words, we can now produce enough goods and services to live at our 1948 standard of living (measured in market-available services and goods) in less than half the time it took in 1948. If we chose to, we could work four-hour days, six months per year, or every worker in America could take every other year off with pay. So why, given our poverty of time and the burdens of work, haven't we traded our prosperity for leisure?[6] As Daniel Bell put it, what keeps the worker, "like the mythical figure of Ixion," chained seemingly forever to the endless revolving wheel of work?[7]

Bell contends that we are no longer motivated to work by a sense of duty, necessity, or utilitarian pleasure. The Protestant work ethic no longer commands or motivates us to labor long and hard. Due to an elaborate web of social checks and balances, physical hunger is no longer the driving force that necessitates our labor and effort. Nor, suggests Bell, do the "satisfactions of craftsmanship" or the pleasures of a "job well done" motivate and guide our work efforts. Bell proposes that what drives us is a "new hunger." We now want "immediate gratification." The desire for goods and services, aided and abetted by advertisement and the installment plan, is the "new candied carrot," to use Bell's phrase, that keeps us at our jobs and motivates our work efforts. The new American worker has been formed not by discipline, ideology, or need, but by boredom, want, and desire. He submits himself to work because he is primarily interested in money and all of the things it can buy. Bell writes that capitalism breeds a "culture of consumers" and consumerism breeds a "culture of hedonism." The modern worker in modern industry labors for the sake of pleasure of consumption and not for the sake of the work itself.[7]

The dangers of consumerism are, of course, not only a phenomenon of the post–World War II experience in America. Historically, a tension has always existed between the philosophical-spiritual appeals of austerity and the celebration of material abundance and comfort. Legend tells us that Socrates set a tone of asceticism by never shaving, wearing the same toga every day, and donning sandals only on occasion. He believed things distract our attention from the life of the mind and the reality of pure ideas. During the fourth century, St. Augustine found himself attracted to the Persian sect called Manichaeanism, which posited that the world was divided between good and evil, light and darkness, and the spiritual and the material. Manichaeanism held that these polarities were in constant conflict for supremacy and the control of the human soul. In the Middle Ages, Francis of Assisi lamented that no matter how strong the calling of his spiritual nature, the needs of his body had to be accommodated. Oliver Cromwell of England and Jonathan Edwards of New England preached and practiced a code of simplicity and the eschewing or purification of worldly symbols, standards, and status.

Simultaneous feelings of desire for and disgust with material comfort have always been a part of our emotional and intellectual history. In truth, though, it wasn't until the industrial revolution created an "economy of scale" that consumer products and material goods become plentiful enough to threaten public, not just individual, morals.

In 1835 in *Democracy in America* Alexis de Tocqueville argued that the establishment of a mass-production and a mass-consumption society is both a triumph and a necessary condition for democratic rule. Citizens with a modicum of wealth and goods find it in their best interest to try to perpetuate economic prosperity and maintain political stability. On the other hand, Tocqueville argued that excessive materialism and self-indulgence are "dangerous diseases of the human mind." He warned that the American "love of well being" and lack of "self restraint" would cause citizens to "lose sight of the connection that exists between the private fortune of each and the prosperity of all."[9]

Despite Tocqueville's warnings, clearly, indulgence rather than prudence became the order of the day. Consumption has become one of the pillars of prosperity. We believe it creates rather than destroys value. With each thing that we consume, replace, discard, or wear out we are creating the need for more production and consumption. Wanting more is neither excessive nor a vice in a consumer society. Consumerism assumes that having more is being more and, if some is good, more must be better! It identifies well-being with accumulating and displaying consumer goods and services. Consumerism is perceived as an acquired right and national characteristic. Though we poke fun at our materialistic obsessiveness—"I shop, therefore I am!"; "He who has the most toys wins!"; "Nothing succeeds like excess!"; "So many malls, and so little trunk space!"—we do not renounce it.[10] Instead of disparaging the tendency to want more than we need, we have elevated it to the status of a private duty and a public virtue. We are, seemingly, in complete accord with Adam Smith's dictum "Consumption is the sole end and purpose of all production."[11] Simply put, we have become addicted to the fruits of our production. We have traded our time and remain "chained to our jobs" in order to obtain consumer products and services. We have deconstructed Aristotle's adage—"the purpose of work is the attainment of leisure," to the far baser notion—"I work, in order to consume and possess." We have become a society of conspicuous consumers for whom want equals need and needs clamor for instant fulfillment and gratification. The equation reads as follows: I want. If I want something, I must need it. If I need it; I have a right to it. If I have a right to it; then someone should provide it or produce it so that I can consume it!

Over a century ago Karl Marx used the term *commodity fetishism* to express the idea that because in capitalism labor exists to serve the process of production, workers, in turn, attempt to restore their humanity by comforting themselves through the accumulation of commodities and services. Commodity fetishism, or product idolatry, as it's also known, is an attitude that evaluates the quality of human life in terms of commodity acquisition, private material comfort, and satisfaction with one's general standard of living.[12] Marx argues that in lieu of finding meaning in our work, we seek satisfaction, meaning, purpose, and fulfillment in the things we own. In effect, Marx believes, we substitute *having much* for *being much.*

According to Erich Fromm, *having* and *being* are two fundamentally different modes of existence. The central difference between being and having is that one connotes a society centered on persons and the other, one centered on things.[13] The having orientation is a fundamental characteristic of Western industrial society, in which the desire for money, fame, and power has become the dominant theme of life.[14] The great promise of American capitalism, said Fromm, was the that of unlimited progress, the domination of nature, material abundance, and unimpeded personal freedom. These are the promises that have sustained Americans since the dawn of the industrial age. In modern society *citizen* and *consumer* are synonymous terms, and most consumers believe "I am what I have and what I consume."[15] Consumption, Fromm suggests, produces pleasure and comfort, relieves anxiety, and allows us to assert our place in the social pecking order. But, consumption produces only a transitory effect on the consumer. Consumption, as Tibor Scitovsky has pointed out in *The Joyless Economy,* quickly loses its power to satisfy. Purchases cannot long sustain our enjoyment level, so we must consume regularly and in ever larger measures to meet a basic threshold of pleasure.[16] Like a drug addict whose tolerance keeps rising, we consume and consume to maintain the same feeling of normalcy and balance.

In his now classic antiestablishment text *One-Dimensional Man,* Herbert Marcuse first described this phenomenon as a tautology: The goods of life are equal to the good life. Marcuse contends that as a society we are infatuated with the benefits of science, technology, and industrialism. In the words of Roger Bacon, they have become "the idols of the mob" because they have produced a lifestyle to which we have become both accustomed and addicted. Modern-day capitalism, suggests Marcuse, has, for the majority of Americans, fulfilled an age-old dream of humankind—freedom from want. No matter what the political limits and drawbacks, the system has proven its capacity to produce a seemingly unlimited variety of products and services. People find comfort and recognize themselves in their commodities. They find their soul in their car, and their status and identity in their stereo, their home, their wardrobe.[17]

Of course, warns Marcuse, this prosperity comes at a price—the loss of freedom, or what he calls "unfreedom" or "one-dimensional thinking—the unquestioning acceptance of the real or actual as the rational or good."[18] Material affluence and liberty (the right to buy and consume) overrides our individual and collective search for real opposition and the critical questioning of the system. Gripes and grievances are allowed, but revolution or even real change is forbidden. Instead, citizen-consumers work to perpetuate and expand the system, not change it.[19] The political needs of society, said Marcuse, became individual needs and aspirations, and the whole appears to be the very embodiment of reason.[20] After all, a job, a home, television, regular time off, and an annual vacation are a lot more than our Depression-era grandparents had.

The goal of capitalism, Marcuse argued, is to produce a "happy consciousness"—a contented citizen-worker-consumer. Perhaps the ultimate citizen that Marcuse had in mind is best captured in W. H. Auden's poem, "The Unknown Citizen."

> He was found by the Bureau of Statistics to be
> One against whom there was no official complaint,
> And all the reports on his conduct agree
> That, in the modern sense of an old-fashioned word,
>   he was a saint,

For in everything he did he served the Greater Community.
Except for the War till the day he retired
He worked in a factory and never got fired,
But satisfied his employers, Fudge Motors Inc.
Yet he wasn't a scab or odd in his views,
For his Union reports that he paid his dues,
(Our report on his Union shows it was sound)
And our Social Psychology workers found
That he was popular with his mates and liked a drink.
The Press are convinced that he bought a paper every day
And that his reactions to advetisements were normal in every way.
Policies taken out in his name proved that he was fully insured,
And his Health-card shows he was once in hospital but left it cured.
Both Producers Research and High-Grade Living declare
He wasn't fully sensible to the advantages of the Installment Plan
And had everything necessary to the Modern Man,
A phonograph, a radio, a car and a frigidaire.
Our researchers into Public Opinion are content
That he held the proper opinions for the time of year;
When there was peace, he was for peace; when there was war,
he went.
He was married and added five children to the population,
Which our Eugenist says was the right number for a parent of
his generation.
And our teachers report that he never interfered with their
education.
Was he free? Was he happy? The question is absurd:
Had anything been wrong, we should certainly have heard.[21]

Martin Heidegger, in *Being and Time,* suggested that in lieu of being able to address the serious questions and issues of life, we busy ourselves with cocktail party conversations or escapist behavior. To shop, for example, is not merely to pass time or simply to acquire goods and services that we want and need. To shop is to be.

Juliet Schor contends that we live in the most consumer-oriented society in history. The average American is consuming more than twice as much as he or she did forty years ago. This holds true not only for the jet set, but all the way down the income scale. Every stratum of worker has participated in the postwar consumption boom. Today, on average, Americans spend three to four times as many hours per year shopping as do their counterparts in western European countries. Shopping has become a leisure activity in it own right. Going to the mall is a common evening's entertainment not only for teenagers, who seem to live and breed there, but for adults as well. Shopping is also the most popular family weekday-evening out-of-home entertainment.

The simple fact, says Schor, is that outside of watching television, shopping is the chief cultural activity in the United States. Americans used to travel to see the sights and meet people. Regretably, that is no longer the case. *Born to Shop* guide books are rapidly outselling Fodor and Baedeker. Once a purely utilitarian chore, shopping in America has been elevated to the status of an obsession.[22] As one women put it, "[I realized] I was a compulsive shopper when it dawned on me that I knew all of the UPS drivers in my neighborhood. They all waved and said hello by my first name!"[23]

Malls are now everywhere and growing by the moment. Over 1 billion square feet of our total land area has been converted into shopping centers. That's about sixteen square feet of mall-space for every man, woman, and child in America.[24] The Mall of America, Bloomington, Minnesota, is the largest enclosed shopping and entertainment complex in the United States. It has more than four hundred stores, a theme park, two food courts, a 1.2-million-gallon aquarium, arcades, minigolf couses, and a fourteen-screen movie theater. A mall brochure claims it's big enough to hold a total of thirty-two 747 airplanes or seven Yankee Stadiums. The mall also claims to attract more visitors annually than do the Grand Canyon and Disney World combined.[25]

There can be little doubt that the malling of America has been an extraordinary financial success for everyone involved: investors, builders, retailers, and local communities. The larger suburban malls have contributed to a retailing revolution by creatively blending specialized boutique shops with larger, old-fashioned department stores under one roof. The smaller urban six-store pocket malls, typically anchored by an all-night minimarket, have created new commerce, added to neighborhood stability, and helped to create a new generation of small-business owners.

For all of the benefits malls produce, there are, of course some dramatic drawbacks. To begin with, malls, big and small, have nearly decimated large urban downtown areas as well as the main streets of small-town America. Central downtown and neighborhood shopping areas are generally losing the battle with the satellite suburban malls, and prosperous Main Streets now exist almost exclusively in the stories of Sherwood Anderson and Garrison Keillor.

Second, at the aesthetic level, the malling of America is homogenizing America. Although some developers design mall exteriors to fit the materials and general architectural style of the local areas, the internal organization has become increasingly standardized. Retailers have studied malls to determine which locations within a mall are best and why, and with this information in hand, they negotiate with mall developers to have their stores placed in the same location in every mall. In addition, malls feel strikingly similar because they contain the same kinds of stores, the same types of products, and often the same national chains. What results is a boring conformity. Most of us shop the same stores, buy the same kinds of products, and wind up at least looking and sometimes behaving much too much alike. Sloan Wilson's man in the gray flannel suit is back, and his children are wearing jeans from The Gap, shirts from Banana Republic, hats from Eddie Bauer, and shoes from Foot Locker.

Finally, and perhaps most important for our purposes, malls and mall-shopping strongly reinforce the equation of shopping + consumption = pleasure. But malls are by no means the only purveyors of consumption. You don't even have to leave your home to shop any longer. Phone lines, mailboxes, and the Internet are direct conduits to thousands of potential products. Most homes, Schor finds, are now virtual retail outlets, with cable shopping channels, mail-order catalogues, toll-free numbers, and computer hookups. Fifty-three percent of all Americans bought something by phone or mail in 1996, and, although Internet transactions remain comparatively minuscule, experts agree the potential audience for on-line commerce is unlimited.[26]

Marx once suggested that religion is the opiate of the people. Matthew Fox now suggests that shopping maybe the new opiate of the people or maybe even the new religion of the people.

> We have lost a sense of Sabbath [religious celebration] in our lives—a sense of joy and delight, a sense of what we do when we come face-to-face with the mystery of existence itself. . . . The Sabbath serves, in our secularized society, as one more shopping

> day—perhaps *the* shopping day of the week, and thereby religion not so subtly legitimates the idolatry of work and spend that a consumer economy demands of us. We think that what we buy makes up for all we suffer.[27]

We love to shop, we want to shop, and, at a very basic level, we need to shop and consume. The desire to consume is not wrong. Critics of the consumer economy are not simply attacking every pleasure that can be associated with the products or services that we need. The issue is not consumerism itself, but consumption as an addiction, an obsession, or a metaphysical orientation toward life.

The nationally syndicated comic strip *Cathy* by Cathy Guisewite specializes in satirizing "Yuppie" and middle-class lifestyles and consumer patterns. In the late 1980s Guisewite did a Sunday story line that perfectly captures the spirit of "commodity fetishism" or "product idolatry." In each frame of the carton are a man and a woman surrounded by a sea of high-end consumer goods. He says, displaying and describing each item in turn: "An anodized aluminum multi-lens three-beam mini excavation spotlight that will live its life in the junk drawer with dead batteries. A professional designer's magnifying draft lamp that will never be in a room with an idea." She says, holding up her goodies for all to see: "An industrial stainless steel pasta vat that will never see a noodle or a group." He says: "Architectural magazines we don't read. . . . " She says: A 10-function answering machine with anti-tap device for a telephone that never rings. . . . " He says: "A deep sea dive watch that will never get damp." She says: "Keys to a four-wheel drive vehicle that will never experience a hill. . . . " And in the final frame, he announces: "Abstract materialism has arrived." "Yes," she sadly concurs, "we've moved past things that we want and need and are buying those things that have nothing to do with our lives!"

Work, according to historian Theodore Roszak, is a necessary ingredient of human personality; limitless consumption is not.[28] Karl Marx, Christopher Lasch, and Erich Fromm all agree: Excessive consumerism is the dark side of meaningless work and the degradation of our labor.[29] According to Peter Drucker, the only meaning left in the job is the paycheck, not in anything connected with the work we do or the products we make.[30] When money becomes the "report card," human identity is no longer defined by what one does, but by what one owns.[31]

"Money is the mirror of our self-image," says psychologist Kathleen Gurney. "Each of us spends money for different reasons—be it love, security, power. People who use money to make themselves feel good often have a hole in their self-esteem that they are trying to fill."[32] Whether we hate our jobs, are bored by them, or simply put too much time into them, buying stuff is an immediate response. In lieu of other forms of meaningful activity, shopping can be seen as a creative outlet, a playful event, or at the very least a temporary escape. "After all," as one citizen-consumer said to me, "what's the sense of working if I can't buy stuff?"

Ironically, the more we shop to compensate for or temporarily escape from work, the more we owe and the more we must work to compensate for our shopping. Just paying off a standard mortgage, a modest car loan, and an average credit card balance can make long hours necessary. Add to that the seductive qualities of the market's latest fad and the psychological comforts associated with compulsive shopping, and it is all too easy to become prisoners on the "treadmill of consumerism." The "squirrel cage" of "work-and-spend" has resulted in what Juliet Schor refers to as the "debt and dependency syndrome." According to Schor, consumerism traps us. Work-and-spend have become two sides of the same coin—a seamless, sticky web that we somehow keep choosing, perhaps without even meaning to.[33] The more we spend, the more we go into debt and the more we are captives of the system and dependent on work to pay our bills. Or, in the succinct phraseology of a popular bumper sticker, "I owe, I owe—so off to work I go!"

Former Czechoslovakian president and playwright Vaclav Havel warns us of the spiritual and moral disease engendered by a consumer culture. Consumerism, he says, is a "desperate substitute for living." When life "becomes reduced to a hunt for consumer goods," freedom becomes trivialized to mean "a chance to freely choose which washing machine or refrigerator we want to buy." Consumer bliss, Havel points out, diverts people's attention from the community to the self. A consumer culture makes it easy to accept the slow erosion of social, political, and moral standards because their passing is hardly noticed—we're all too busy shopping. Havel suggests that a lifestyle is not the same thing as a life.[34]

In 1917 America and the world experienced a severe influenza epidemic that killed an estimated 20 million victims. Today, we are all suffering from a pandemic of *affluenza,* the disease of consumerism. At the moment there is no known cure or immunization for this malady, and all of us are at some risk of "shopping ourselves to death." Or, as Chicago playwright Belinda Brenner puts it, "shopping ourselves into anesthetized transcendance":

> And on Sunday, the end of the endless work week, we worship at the shrine of the holy half-price. We rejoice and are exceedingly glad in the bargain and the deal and the promise of a perfect life if we just buy this one more _______________ (fill in the blank!). We have traded scapulars and tallithes for new badges of faith—designer logos and labels. No longer afraid to utter the name of the Almighty, we wear it writ large on every item. We purge our pain when we splurge our gain. Ritual cleansing shopping! Shop therapy! Baptism by fire sale! Next year in the Mall of America—we long to go on a pilgrimage of purchase. We make the stations and try on the mysteries. All the while believing that if we but search hard enough—the peace that passeth all understanding can be found at 40 to 70 percent off![35]

11

Moral Leadership and Business Ethics

> Those who really deserve praise are the people who, while human enough to enjoy power, nevertheless pay more attention to justice than they are compelled to do by their situation.
>
> —Thucydides

A BIG PART OF THE REASON MANY OF US DON'T like our jobs is the people we work for—our bosses or leaders—and the values of the workplace itself. In more than a thousand daily newspapers across the land, in best-selling books, in calenders, and even on coffee mugs, Scott Adams and his alter-ego comic strip character Dilbert have made a career out of critiquing and satirizing the frustrations, failures, and foibles of the workplace. The main target of Adams's rapier wit and cutting invective is the stupidity of business management and leadership. In Adams's world, *all* bosses are incompetent, unethical, uncaring, or a combination of all three. He believes that the main problems facing the average worker on a day-to-day basis are boredom, emptiness, lack of purpose, and petty bureaucratic politics, and that the cause of all of these—and many more problems—are the mistakes, myopia, and mismanagement of those in charge. Furthermore, Adams' maintains that his thesis is beyond debate, part of the "natural order of the universe," and can be validated by anyone who has spent as little as one day on the job.[1]

Adams gets two hundred e-mail messages a day complaining about "bad bosses." Both his own experiences in the workforce—seventeen years in cubicle 4S700R at Pacific Bell—and his fan mail led him to the belief that only "idiots get promoted to management." In the old days, says Adams, we used to explain away inept leadership in terms of the Peter Principle, which states that capable employees are promoted until they reach their level of incompetence. We didn't always appreciate it then, but the Peter Principle provided us with bosses who fundamentally understood what they were doing for a living. They may have made lots of bad decisions—after all, they had no management skills—but at least the decisions were the informed choices of seasoned veterans who had spent time in the trenches. Their mistakes lacked mental malfeasance, maliciousness, or demonic intent. Now, though, the Peter Principle has given way to the Dilbert Principle—incompetent workers are promoted directly to management without ever passing through a competency stage, thereby allowing them to do the greatest amount of damage.

Adams's comic critique of bosses centers on the ineptitude of middle managers, but it is easy to recognize that his commentary also applies to the executive boardroom and, in fact, to the entire class of people we call "leaders" in business and elsewhere.[2] Scott Adams's satirical musings may not be totally accurate, but they do resonate with a growing body of literature on the state of business leadership today. This literature focuses less on technical ability and mental competence than on the philosophical dimensions of management, specifically, business ethics and leadership.

When workers are asked what they dislike most about their jobs, the list always includes other people: customers, colleagues, and, especially, bosses. Management philosopher Charles Handy is convinced that workers want more than just trading time for money. They want to be valued, respected, and to feel like a vital part of the enterprise. They want to be regarded by management as assets rather than as adversaries. They want to be seen as contributors, not just another capital cost. In the traditional top-down management style, however, rank and file are two separate categories that rarely meet on common ground for debate or discussion.[3] Psychotherapist and worklife consultant William Lundin insists that the management of most companies is "more concerned with what Wall Street is doing than what Main Street thinks."[4]

A 1997 survey of 1,324 emplooyees found that 51 percent complained of "poor leadership." The overwhelming majority of the respondents want management to take on issues of both morals and morale in the workplace. Fifty-seven percent want people in management to address the "continuously mounting pressure" to perform and be productive; 48 percent want them to reduce the pressure to "cut corners" and even engage in "unethical and illegal activity" in the pursuit of the bottom line; 73 percent want a commitment to "better communications and open dialogue; 51 percent want management to address the related issues of work hours and work load; and 52 percent want to see the problem of balancing work and family life addressed. Finally, 71 percent agreed that the best solution to both economic and ethical problems of the workplace would be better standards of business ethics and moral leadership.[5]

The terms *business ethics* and *moral leadership* are commonly cited as oxymorons, in part because we have so few models of businesses and leaders operating on ethical principles. At best, these terms remain as utopian ideals. Nevertheless, I am convinced that without better standards of business ethics and better examples of moral leadership we will improve neither the lot of the worker nor the future viability of the workplace.

A *New York Times*/CBS News Poll conducted in 1985 revealed that 55 percent of the American public believe that the vast majority of corporate executives are dishonest, and 59 percent think that executive white-collar crime occurs on a regular basis. A 1987 *Wall Street Journal* article noted that one-fourth of the 671 executives surveyed by a leading research firm believed that ethics can impede a successful career and that over half of all the executives they knew bent the rules to get ahead.[6]

A 1990 national survey published by Prentice Hall concluded that in the area of ethical standards of practice and moral leadership, business leaders merit, at best, a C-average. Sixty-eight percent of those surveyed believed that the unethical behavior of executives is the number-one cause of declining business standards, productivity, and success. The survey further suggested that because of the perceived low ethical standards of the executive class, workers feel justified in adhering to similar standares, responding with absenteeism, petty theft, indifference, and a generally poor performance on the job. Many workers openly admitted that they spend more than 20 percent of their time at work (or eight hours a week) goofing off. Almost half of those surveyed admitted to chronic malingering and calling in sick on a regular basis when they were not sick. One in six of the workers surveyed said that they drank or used drugs while on the job. Three out of four workers reported that their primary reason for working was "to keep the wolf from the door"; only one in four claimed that they gave their jobs their "best effort."

The survey concluded that the equation for assessing ethics in the

American workplace is a simple one: Workers are as ethical or dutiful in doing their jobs as they percieve their bosses and companies to be ethical or dutiful in leading them. Sadly, ample evidence suggests that this cynical cycle often starts long before one enters the workplace.[7] Recently in the Chicago public high school system, one of the teacher-coaches in the citywide Academic Decathlon Contest not only encouraged his students to cheat, he fed them the answers. According to the eighteen-year-old student captain of the team, "The coach gave us the answer key. . . . He told us everybody cheats, that's the way the world works and we were fools to just play by the rules."[8] Unfortunately, these students followed the guidance of their teacher just as workers often mirror the standards set by their bosses.

The ethics of leadership affects the ethos of the workplace and thereby helps to form the ethical choices and decisions of the workers in the workplace. Leaders help to set the tone, develop the vision, and shape the behavior of all those involved in organizational life. The behavior and attitude established by leaders set the patterns for individual and collective worker behavior. Although business ethics and moral leadership are abstractly distinguishable, in practice, they are inseparable components in the life of every organization.

The fundamental principle that underlies my thesis regarding leadership and ethical conduct is age-old. In his *Nichomachean Ethics*, Aristotle suggested that morality cannot be learned simply by reading a treatise on virtue. The spirit of morality is awakened in the individual only through witnessing the conduct of a moral person. We now refer to this as "patterning," "role modeling," or "mentoring," and it is predicated on a four-step process: 1) As communal creatures, the actions of significant others is one of the primary means by which we learn to conduct ourselves; 2) When the behavior of others is repeated often enough and proves to be peer-group positive, we emulate these actions; 3) If and when our actions are in turn reinforced by others, they become acquired characteristics or behavioral habits; 4) The final step in the process must include reflection, evaluation, choice, and conscious intent on the part of the actor, because ethics is always "an inside-out proposition" involving free will.[9]

According to behavior psychologist B. F. Skinner the first three steps complete the process. In affecting the actions of individuals through modeling and reinforcement, the mentor in question (in Skinner's terms, "the controller of the environmental stimuli") has succeeded in producing the type of behavior sought or desired. Skinner's experiments showed that the primary goal of the process did not need to take into consideration either the value (or worth) of the action or the interests (or intent) of the reinforced or operatively conditioned actor. The bottom line for the psychologist is simply the response evoked.[10] From a philosophical perspective, however, the completion of the fourth step is key. Even role modeling that produces a positive or beneficial action does not fulfill the basic requirements of the ethical enterprise at either the descriptive or normative level. Modeling, emulation, habit, results—whether positive or negative—are neither the sufficient nor the final goal.

John Dewey argued that at the precritical, prerational, preautonomous level, morality starts as a set of culturally defined goals and rules that are external to the individual and are imposed or inculcated as habits. Real ethical thinking, though, begins at the evaluative period of our lives, when as independent agents we freely decide to accept, embrace, modify, or deny these rules. Dewey maintained that every serious ethical system rejects the notion that one's standard of conduct should be a simple and uncritical acceptance of the rules of the culture we happen to live in. Even if it is the case that custom, habit, convention, public opinion, or law are correct in their mandates, to embrace them without critical reflection does not constitute a complete and formal ethical act and might be better labeled "ethical happenstance" or "ethics by virtue of circumstantial accident." For Dewey, ethics is essentially "reflective conduct," and the distinction between custom and reflective morality is clear. The former bases the standard of conduct solely on habit; the latter appeals to reason and choice. The distinction is as important as it is definite, for it shifts the center of gravity in morality. Ethics, according to Dewey, is a two-part process—reasoned choice and action. It is never enough to simply do the right thing.[11]

In claiming that workers derive their models for ethical conduct from leaders, I am in no way denying that workers share responsibility for the overall conduct and culture of an organization. I do not exonerate the culpability of workers, but try to explain the process involved: The witness of leaders both communicates the ethics of our institutions and establishes the desired standards leaders want and often demand from their fellow workers and subordinates. Although it would be naive to assert that employees blindly absorb the manners and mores of the workplace, it would be equally naive to suggest that they are unaffected by the standards of their respective places of employment. Work is how we spend our lives, and the lessons we learn there play a part in the development of our moral perspective and how we formulate ethical choices. Most business ethicists believe that without active, effective moral leadership, the lower ranks are doomed to forever wage a rear-guard action. Observers of organizational development are never really surprised when poorly managed businesses wind up doing unethical things.

Jean-Paul Sartre argued that we are by definition moral creatures because we are "condemned" by the fact of our collective existence to continuously make choices about what we "ought" to do in regard to others.[12] Ethics is primarily a communal, collective enterprise, not a solitary one. When Robinson Crusoe found himself marooned, all things were possible, but when Man Friday came along Crusoe was then involved in the universe of others, an ethical universe. Ethics is the attempt to work out the rights and obligations we have and share with others.

According to Harvard philosopher John Rawls, ethics is elementally the pursuit of justice, fair play, and equity. It has to do with developing standards for judging the conduct of one party whose behavior affects another. At minimum, good behavior intends no harm and respects the rights of all affected, and bad behavior willfully or negligently tramples on the rights and interests of others.[13] Ethics, then, tries to protect one person's individual rights and needs against and alongside the rights and needs of others. Of course, the paradox and central tension of ethics lies in the fact that while we are by nature communal and in need of others, at the same time we are by disposition more or less egocentric and self-serving.[14]

Most ethicists argue that business has a moral obligation to make a profit. But business is also about people—the people who work above, alongside, and below you. Business is an interdependent, intertwined, symbiotic relationship. Moreover, life, labor, and business are all of a piece. They should not be separate "games" played by different "rules." Therefore, like other areas, business is required to ask the question "What ought to be done in regard to others?"

While most people understand the role of ethics in our private lives, they apply a different standard to business; many people believe that "business is business" and that the stakes and standards involved in business are simply different from the principles of ethics.

As Matthew Fox has pointed out, we often lead schizophrenic lives because we either choose or are forced to abandon our personal beliefs at the door when we enter the workplace. This "destructive dualism" of the workplace separates our lives from our livelihood, our personal values from our work values, our personal needs from the needs of the community. Money becomes the sole reason for work, and success becomes our excuse to justify the immoral consequences of our behavior.[15] This dualism produces and perpetuates the kind of occupational schizophrenia recently articulated by nationally known jurist Alan Dershowitz: "I would never do many of the things in my personal life that I have to do as a lawyer."[16]

According to ethicist Norman Bowie the disconnection of business and ethics and the dualism of the workplace stem from the competing ways that economists and ethicists view human nature. Economics is the study of the betterment of self, and most economists have an egoistic theory of human nature. Their analyses focus on how an individual rationally pursues desires. Within the economic model individuals behave rationally when they seek to maximize their own perceived best interests. They need only take the interests of others into account when and if such considerations work to their advantage. Economics is singular and radically subjective in its orientation. It does not judge whether the individual's preferences are good or bad.

Ethics, on the other hand, is plural in nature. Its paradigm of evaluation is always self in relation to others. The ethical point of view requires that an individual take into account the impact of her action on others. Economists ask, "What can I do to advance my best interests?" Ethicists ask, "In pursuing my best interests what should I do in regard to others?" Where economics breeds competition, ethics encourages cooperation.[17]

For R. Edward Freeman of the Darden School of Business, these competing paradigms are firmly entrenched in our collective psyches and give rise to what he calls the "problem of the two realms." One is the realm of business: the realm of hard, measurable facts, such as market studies, focus groups, longitudinal studies, production costs, managed inventory, stock value, research and development, profit and loss statements, quantitative analysis. The other realm is that of ethics. This is the soft realm of myth, meaning, metaphor, purpose, quality, significance, rights, values. While the realm of business can be easily dissected and judged, the realm of philosophy is not open to precise interpretation. Freeman asserts that in our society these two realms are accorded unequal status. Only in moments of desperation does the realm of business solicit the insights of ethics. Otherwise, the realm of business operates under the dictum of moral legalism: Everything is allowed which is not strictly forbidden.

In Freeman's view, the assertion that "business is business" and ethics is private simply does not hold up to close scrutiny. Business is a human institution, a basic part of our collective experience, arising out of the human need for order, security, and fulfillment. The goal of all business should be to make life more secure, more stable, more equitable. Business should exist to serve more than just itself. No business can view itself as isolated, unaffected by the demands of individuals and society. For Freeman, business ethics, rather than being an oxymoron, is really a redundancy in terms.[18] As Henry Ford, Sr., once said, "For a long time people believed that the only purpose of industry is to make a profit. They are wrong. Its purpose is to serve the general welfare."[19]

What business ethics advocates is that people apply in the workplace those rules and standards learned at home, from the lectern, and from the pulpit. The moral issues facing a person are essentially the same issues facing a business, but perhaps writ large.[20] According to Freeman, ethics is "how we treat each other, every day, person to person. If you want to know about a company's ethics, look at how it treats people—customers, suppliers and employees. Business is about people. And business ethics is about how customers and employees are treated."[21]

The ethical standards being asked of the business community are neither extraordinary nor excessive: a decent product at a fair price; honesty in advertisements; fair treatment of employees, customers, suppliers, and competitors; a strong sense of responsibility to the communities it inhabits and serves; and a reasonable profit for the financial risk-taking of its stockholders and owners. In the words of General Robert Wood Johnson, founder of Johnson & Johnson:

> The day has passed when business was a private matter—if it ever really was. In a business society, every act of business has social consequences and may arouse public interest. Every time business

> hires, builds, sells or buys, it is acting for the . . . people as well as for itself, and it must be prepared to accept full responsibility.[22]

Philosopher George Enderle has argued that business leadership would be relatively simple if corporations had only to produce a product or service, without being concerned about employees; if management had only to deal with concepts, structures, and strategies, without worrying about human relations; if businesses had only to resolve their own problems, without being obligated to consider the interests of individuals or society.[23] But such is not the case.

Leadership is always about self and others. Like ethics, labor, and business, leadership is a symbiotic, communal relationship between leaders, followers, and all stakeholders involved. And, like ethics, labor, and business, leadership seems to be an intrinsic part of the human experience. Charles de Gaulle once stated, "Men fundamentally can no more get along without direction than they can without eating, drinking or sleeping." Leadership is a necessary requirement of communal existence. It tries to offer guidance and a plan by which to handle the seemingly random and arbitrary events of life. Depending on the type of leadership, this can be achieved by consensus, fiat, or cooperative orchestration. Whatever techniques are employed, leadership is always, at bottom, about stewardship. To paraphrase St. Augustine, no matter what the outcome, the first and final job of leaders is serving the needs and the well-being of the people they lead.

What is leadership? While the terms *leadership* and *leader* are not strictly synonymous, the reality of leadership cannot be separated from the individual leader. Given this caveat, and leaning heavily on the research and insights of leadership scholar Joseph C. Rost,[24] leadership can be defined in the following manner: "Leadership is a power- and value-laden relationship between leaders and followers/constituents who intend real changes that reflect their mutual purposes and goals." For our purposes, the critical elements of this definition that need to be examined are, in order of importance, followership, values, and mutual purposes and goals

Followership—Perhaps the single most important thesis developed in leadership studies in the last twenty years has been the evolution and now almost universal consensus regarding the role of followers in the leadership equation. Pulitzer Prize–winning historian Garry Wills argues that we have long had a list of the leader's traits—determination, focus, a clear goal, a sense of priorities, and so on—but until recently we overlooked or forgot the first and all encompassing need: "The leader most needs followers. When those are lacking, the best ideas, the strongest will, the most wonderful smile have no effect."[25] Followers set the terms of acceptance for leadership. Leadership is a "mutually determinative" activity on the part of the leader and the followers. Sometimes it's cooperative, sometimes it's a struggle, and often it's a feud, but it is never one-sided. Although "the leader is one who mobilizes others toward a goal shared by leaders and followers," according to Wills, leaders are powerless to act without followers. In effect, then, successful leaders need to understand their followers far more than followers need to understand leaders.[26] Scott Adams claims that this rarely happens in Dilbert's cubicle world, or in the workplaces of most real-life worker-followers.

Leadership, like ethics, is always plural; it always occurs in the context of others. Although the leader is the central and often the most vital part of the leadership phenomenon, followers are important and necessary factors in the equation.[27] All leadership is interactive, and all leadership should be collaborative. Perhaps *collaborator* is a more precise term than either *follower* or *constituent* to explain the other side of the leadership process.[28] Whichever term is used, as political theorist James MacGregor Burns wrote, one thing is clear: "Leaders and followers are engaged in a common enterprise; they are dependent on each other, their fortunes rise and fall together."[29]

From an ethical perspective, leadership is dependent on the recognition of the roles and rights of followers. The principle of followership denies the Machiavellian assertions that "politics and ethics don't mix" and that the sole aim of any leader is the acquisition of personal power. Followership requires that leaders recognize their true role within the commonwealth. Like the Guardians of Socrates' *Republic,* leaders must see their office as a social responsibility, a trust, and not as a symbol of their personal identity and prestige.[30] In more contemporary terms, social commentators James O'Toole and Lynn Sharp-Paine have separately argued that the central ethical issue in business is the rights of stakeholders and the obligation of business leaders to manage with due consideration for the rights of all stakeholders involved.[31]

Management guru Peter Senge has stated, in *The Fifth Discipline,* that of all the jobs of leadership, being a steward is the most basic. Being a steward means that leaders recognize that the ultimate purpose of their work is others and not self, that "they do what they do" for something larger than themselves. That their "life's work" may be the "ability to lead," but that the final goal of this talent or craft is "other directed."[32] If the real business of business is not just to produce a product or service and a profit but to help "produce" people, then the same demand can be made of leadership. Given the reality of the presence of others, leadership, like ethics, must confront the question "What ought to be done with regard to others?" Unfortunately, in most workplaces, this question is rarely addressed because employees are seen neither as assets to be protected nor as individuals whose rights and personal integrity must be guaranteed.

Values—Ethics is about the assessment of values, because all of life is value-laden. As the writer Samuel Blumenfeld emphatically pointed out "You have to be dead to be value-neutral."[33] Values are the beliefs that influence and direct our choices. Values—even bad values—guide how we make decisions and the kinds of decisions we make.

I believe that Tom Peters and Bob Waterman were correct when they stated, "The real role of leadership is to manage the values of an organization."[34] All leadership is value-laden. All leadership is ideologically driven or motivated by a certain philosophical perspective, which upon analysis may prove to be morally acceptable. All leaders have an agenda, a series of beliefs, proposals, values, ideas and issues that they wish to at least "put on the table." In fact, as James Burns has suggested, leadership asserts itself and followers only become evident only when there is something at stake—ideas to be clarified, issues to be determined, values to be adjudicated.[35] In the words of Franklin D. Roosevelt:

> The presidency is . . . preeminently a place of moral leadership. All our great presidents were leaders of thought at times when certain historic ideas in the life of the nation had to be clarified.[36]

Although we regularly hold up for praise the moral leadership of Lincoln, Churchill, Gandhi, and Mother Teresa, we must also evaluate within a moral context Hitler, Stalin, Saddam Hussein, and David Koresh.

All ethical judgments are in some sense a "values-versus-values" or "rights-versus-rights" confrontation. Unfortunately, the question of "what we ought to do" in relation to the values and rights of others cannot often be reduced to a simple litmus-paper test. In fact, I believe that all of ethics is based on what William James called the "will to believe," that is, we choose to believe, despite arguments to the contrary, that individuals possess certain basic rights that cannot be willfully disregarded by others. In "choosing to believe," James stated, we establish this belief as the baseline of our thought process for all considerations in regard to others. Without this "reasoned choice," James concluded, the ethical enterprise loses it "vitality" in human interactions.[37]

If ethical behavior respects the rights of all affected and unethical behavior willfully or negligently tramples on the rights of others, then ethical leaders cannot deny or disregard the rights of others. Leaders should not see followers as potential adversaries to be bested or as servants with no needs of their own, but rather as fellow travelers with similar aspirations and rights. One commentator encapsulated this goal when he said, "Ethics should be an automatic norm of the leadership process."

How do we judge the ethics of a leader? Clearly, no leader can be expected to be perfect in every decision and action made, just as no follower can. As business analyst John Gardner has pointed out, particular consequences are never a reliable assessment of leadership.[38] The quality of leadership can be measured only by what a leader intends, values, or stands for—in other words, by character. In *Character: America's Search for Leadership*, Gail Sheehy argued, as did Aristotle before her, that character is the most crucial and most elusive element of leadership. The root of the word *character* comes from the Greek word for engraving. As applied to human beings, it refers to the enduring marks in our personality, which include our innate talents as well as our traits learned through life and experience. These engravings define us, set us apart from others, and motivate behavior.

For leadership, Sheehy argued, character is fundamental and prophetic. The "issues [of leadership] are today and will change in time. Character is what was yesterday and will be tomorrow."[39] She believes character establishes both our day-to- day demeanor and our destiny. Therefore, it is not only useful but essential to examine the character of those who desire to lead us. As a journalist and longtime observer of the political scene, Sheehy contends that the Watergate affair of the early 1970s serves as a perfect example of the links between character and leadership. As Richard Nixon demonstrated so well, said Sheehy, "The presidency is not the place to work out one's personal pathology."[40] Leaders rule us, run things, wield power, so we must be careful in choosing them. Who we choose is what we shall be. If, as Heraclitus wrote, "character is fate," the fate of our leaders will also be our own.

Watergate has come to symbolize the failings of people in high places. It now serves as a turning point in our nation's concern for integrity, honesty, and fair play from all kinds of leaders. It is not mere coincidence that the birth of business ethics as an independent, academic discipline dates from the Watergate affair and the trials that came out of it. No matter what our failings as individuals, Watergate sensitized us to the importance of ethical conduct from those who direct our political and public lives. Society now demands and business ethics now advocates that our business leaders and public servants should be held to an even higher standard of behavior than we might demand and expect of private citizens. Sadly, suggests Sheehy, for far too many people in public life, the bar is set too high.

Mutual Purposes and Goals—The character of a leader, or any individual, is not developed in a vacuum. Leadership, even in the hands of a strong, confident, charismatic leader, remains relational. Leaders, good or bad, great or small, arise out of the needs and opportunities of a specific time and place. They require causes and, of course, a constituency. Leaders may devise plans, establish an agenda, bring new ideas to the table, but these actions are a response to the environment and membership of which they are a part. If leadership is an active and ongoing relationship between leaders and followers, then a central requirement of leaders is to elicit consensus in their constituencies. At the same time, followers must inform and influence their leaders. This is done in at least two ways—through the use of power and education.

Power is the capacity to control or direct change. All forms of leadership must make use of power. The central issue in leadership is not "Will power be used?" but, rather, "Will it be used wisely and well?" According to James MacGregor Burns, leadership is not just about directed results; it is also about offering followers a choice among real alternatives. Hence, leadership assumes competition, conflict, and debate whereas brute power denies it.[41] "Leadership mobilizes," said Burns, "naked power coerces."[42] Power need not be dictatorial or punitive to be effective. It can also be used in a noncoercive manner to orchestrate, direct, and guide members of an organization in the pursuit of a goal. Leaders must engage followers, not merely direct them. Leaders must serve as models and mentors, not martinets. "Power without morality," wrote novelist James Baldwin, "is no longer power."

Peter Senge believes teaching is one of the primary jobs of leadership.[43] The "task of leader as teacher" is to provide people with information, insights, new knowledge, and alternative perspectives on reality. The "leader as teacher," said Senge, not just teaches people how "to achieve their vision" but, rather, fosters learning, offers choices, and builds consensus.[44] Effective leadership recognizes that in order to build and achieve community, followers must become equally accountable in the pursuit of a common enterprise. Through their conduct and teaching, leaders must try to make their constituents aware that they are all stakeholders in a joint activity that cannot succeed without their involvement and commitment. Successful leadership believes in and communicates some version of the now famous Hewlett Packard motto, "The achievements of an organization are the results of the combined efforts of each individual."

In the end, says Harvard's Abraham Zaleznick, "leadership is based on a compact that binds those who lead with those who follow into the same moral, intellectual and emotional commitment."[45] However, the nature of this compact is inherently unequal because the influence held by leaders and by followers is not equal. Responsive and responsible leadership requires, as a minimum, that democratic mechanisms be put in place that recognize the right of followers to have adequate knowledge of goals, programs, and alternative options, as well as the capacity to choose between them. "In leadership writ large," states Joseph C. Rost, "mutually agreed upon purposes help people achieve consensus, assume responsibility, work for the common good and build community."[46]

There is, unfortunately, a dark side to the theory of the "witness of others." Howard S. Schwartz, in his radical but underappreciated managerial text *Narcissistic Process and Corporate Decay,* argued that corporations are not bastions of benign, community-oriented ethical reasoning, nor can they, because of the demands and requirements of business, be models of moral behavior.[47] The rule of business, said Schwartz, remains the survival of the fittest, and the goal of survival engenders a combative "us against them mentality," which condones getting ahead by any means necessary. Schwartz calls this phenomenon "organizational totalitarianism": Organizations and the people who manage them create for themselves a self-contained, self-serving worldview, which rationalizes anything done on their behalf and which does not require justification on any grounds outside of themselves.[48]

This narcissistic perspective, Schwartz suggests, imposes Draconian requirements on all participants in organizational life: Do your work; achieve organizational goals; obey and exhibit loyalty to your superiors; disregard personal values and beliefs; obey the law when necessary, obfuscate it when possible; and deny internal or external information at odds with the stated organizational worldview. Within such a "totalitarian" logic, neither leaders nor followers operate as independent agents. To maintain their place, or to get ahead, all must conform. The agenda of "organizational totalitarianism," according to Schwartz, is always the preservation of the status quo. Within such a logic, change is rarely possible. Except for extreme situations in which "systemic ineffectiveness" begins to breed "organization decay," transformation is never an option.

In *Moral Mazes* Robert Jackall parallels, from a sociological rather than a psychological perspective, much of Schwartz's analysis of organizational behavior. According to critic and commentator Thomas W. Norton, both Jackall and Schwartz seek to understand why and how organizational ethics and behavior are so often reduced to either loyalty or the simple adulation and mimicry of one's superiors. While Schwartz argued that individuals are captives of the impersonal structural logic of organizational totalitarianism, Jackall contends that "organizational actors become personally loyal to their superiors, always seeking their approval and are committed to them as persons rather than as representatives of the abstractions of organizational authority."[49] In Scott Adams's terms, employees are forced to "suck up" to their bosses. All three authors agree that workers are prisoners of the systems they serve.

According to Jackall, who studied American businesses, all organizations are examples of "patrimonial bureaucracies" wherein "fealty relations of personal loyalty" are the rule of organizational life. Jackall argued that all corporations are like fiefdoms of the middle ages, wherein the lord of the manor (CEO or president) offers protection, prestige, and status to his vassals (managers) and serfs (workers) in return for homage (commitment) and service (work). In such a system, says Jackall, advancement and promotion are predicated on loyalty, trust, politics, and personality at least as much as on experience, education, ability, and accomplishments. The central concern of the worker-minion is to be known as a "can-do guy," a "team player," being at the right place at the right time and "master of all the social rules." That's why in the corporate world, says Jackall, a thousand "atta-boys" are wiped away with one "oh, shit!"

As in a feudal system, employees of a corporation are expected, Jackall maintains, to become supporters of the status quo. Their loyalty is to the powers that be, their duty is to perpetuate performance and profit, and their values can be none other than those sanctioned by the organization. Jackall contends that the logic of every organization and the collective personality of the workplace conspire to override the desires and aspirations of the individual worker. No matter what a person believes off the job, on the job all of us are required to some extent to suspend, bracket, or only selectively manifest our personal convictions. He wrote:

> What is right in the corporation is not what is right in a man's home or his church. What is right in the corporation is what the guy above you wants from you.[50]

In Jackall's analysis, the primary imperative of every organization is to succeed. This goal of performance, which he refers to as "institutional logic," leads to the creation of a private moral universe that, by definition, is self-sustained, self-defined, and self-centered. Within such an environment truth is socially defined and moral behavior is determined solely by organizational needs. The key virtues, for all, become the virtues of the organization: goal-preoccupation, problem-solving, survival or success, and, most important, playing by the "house rules." In time, says Jackall, those initiated and invested in the system come to believe that they live in a self-contained world that is above outside critique and evaluation.

For both Schwartz and Jackall, the logic of organizational life is rigid and unchanging. Corporations perpetuate themselves, both in their strengths and weaknesses, because corporate cultures clone their own. Given the scenario of even a benign organizational structure that produces positive behavior and results, the etiology of the problem and the opportunity for abuse that it offers represent the inherent dangers of applying the "witness of others" to leadership theory. Within the scope of Schwartz's and Jackall's allied analyses, normative moral leadership may not be possible. The model they offer is both absolute and inflexible, and only "regular company guys" make it to the top. Mavericks, radicals, and reformers are not long tolerated. The "institutional logic" of the system does not permit disruption or deviance.

The reason, says Scott Adams, that all leaders think alike, act alike, and in his cartoons even look alike is that they are alike—otherwise they never would have been put in charge. Adams implies that "business ethics" and "moral leadership" are not just oxymorons but perfect examples of what the existentialists meant by "absurdity" and "nothingness."[51] Business and bosses, Adams contends, are only about seeming to be ethical. Their only imperatives of bosses are to manage for profit and ensure their own success and sinecure. They will do this by any means possible, even if they occasionally must resort to telling the truth or intentionally doing the right thing for the right reason. In lieu of the reasoned moral approach, says Adams, bosses prefer demagoguery, denial, deviant behavior, and duplicitous double-speak to get their way. As a service to workers everywhere, Adams compiled a numbered list of the most popular management lies of all time.[52] Now when you're telling a story about the idiocy or treachery of your boss, you can simply refer to each lie by its number—"She told me number six, again!"—and save a lot of time and energy that can be better channeled into whining about other problems in our lives.

Great Lies of Management

THE LIE	THE TRANSLATION
1. "Employees are our most valuable asset."	"No they're not, they're ninth!"
2. "I have an open-door policy."	"Just don't ever bother to come in!"
3. "You could earn more money under the new plan."	"Emphasis on the term 'could'!"
4. "We are reorganizing to better serve our customers."	"Profits are down! Quick, do something—or else!"
5. "The future is bright."	"The way things are going, things have got to get better and soon!"
6. "We reward risk-takers."	"But only if they succeed—failures are fired!"

7. "Performance will be rewarded."	"If not in this lifetime, certainly in the next!"
8. "We don't shoot the messenger."	"Who said!?"
9. "Training is a high priority."	"But, not here! So just do it—and, it better be right!"
10. "I haven't heard any rumors."	"Believe me, I've heard everything! So, watch it!"
11. "We'll review your performance in six months."	"Your chances of getting a raise are deader than a fishstick at a cat festival."
12. "Our people are the best."	"Bullshit!"
13. "Your input is important to us."	"But your output is the only thing that counts."

Scott Adams is convinced that the workplace doesn't contain more absurdity than everyday life, but the absurdity is more noticeable there. Adams is convinced that bad bosses make work degrading and humiliating. Although satirical, Adams's insights are in accord with the scholarship of Jackall and Schwartz and their portrait of the dark side of the "witness of others." Bosses are seen as adversaries, others, and obstacles to be overcome. Sooner or later bad leadership erodes "internal and even external standards of morality."[53]

Sociologist Kathleen McCourt has stated that it is difficult to be a good person in a society that is itself not good. People, after all, live and learn through the institutions of society—family, school, church, community, and the workplace—and these institutions must support the positive development of individuals if society is to produce succeeding generations of positive individuals.[54] In *Business as a Calling,* theologian of capitalism Michael Novak argues that the real social purpose of work comes out of a complicated nexus of human aspirations and needs that are much larger than just the simple desire for money. The aim of business, Novak says, is not simply acquisition or increase but rather the optimization of the human social condition.

Essentially, Novak argues that there ought to be more to business than the maximization of profits because there is more to life than merely having. We are not intended solely for ourselves, writes Novak. Work is not a private enterprise. It is a social one. In work we labor with and for others. If "our work is us," then, Novak suggests, business is, or ought to be, a morally serious enterprise. Therefore, a career in business is not only a morally serious vocation but a morally noble one. "Moral conduct is in the long run," Novak writes, "more in keeping with the probabilities of [social] success than is immoral behavior." Because the institution of business (work) is so important, so vast, so time-consuming in our lives, the lessons and values we learn there tend to determine our nonwork behavior as well. Unfortunately, observation shows that many business executives are blind to the social destructiveness of some of their behavior. Executives who cut corners or vacillate morally shame their profession. Executives such as these see their jobs solely in terms of personal success. Within such a moral milieu, Novak suggests, work for bosses and employees alike can not be a "calling" but only an enervating burden, and neither our workaday lives nor our private lives will be made better.[55]

Leadership is hard to define, and moral leadership is even harder. Nevertheless, I am convinced that without the "witness" of moral leadership, standards of ethics in business and organizational life will not occur or be sustained. Leadership, even when defined as a collaborative experience, is still about the influence of individual character and the impact of personal mentoring. Good behavior does not always beget good behavior, but it does establish tone and offer options. Although it is mandatory that an organization as a whole make a commitment to ethical behavior to actually achieve it, the model for that commitment has to originate at the top.[56]

Or, am I wrong? Is it always about the money?

The End of Work: Is Rifkin Right?

> The factory of the future will be staffed by only two living things, a man and a dog. The man's job will be to feed the dog. The dog's job will be to keep the man from touching any of the computer driven machines!
>
> —Carlos M. Früm

MY LIFE HAS ENCOMPASSED THE ENTIRE SECOND half of the twentieth century. I have witnessed and experienced many changes and events, some of them insignificant and a few that were actually momentous. Two of my most vivid childhood memories deal with events most of us now take to be utterly commonplace. In 1949 my family purchased the Three-Way Admiral Home Entertainment Unit, which consisted of a twelve-inch television, an AM radio, and a phonograph, and in 1950 my father bought his first postwar new car. It was a dark green Ford coupe, with a V-8 engine, stick shift, and huge whitewall tires, and it cost an astonishing $1,000. At the time, these two purchases changed how we spent our evenings, where we shopped, how we got around, and where we went on vacation—if we went on vacation. Then there was, in no particular order of importance: commercial jet airlines, central air-conditioning, 45-r.p.m. vinyl records, Sputnik, the Pill, the civil rights movement, TV dinners, expressways, nuclear energy, the electric guitar, the Vietnam War, Sony Walkmans, microwave ovens, AIDS, and the cloning of Dolly the sheep. All of these have somehow affected the general quality of our existence. After each of them, life was never the same.

Of all the changes, events, and inventions of the latter half of the twentieth century, the two that I believe will have the most profound and long-lasting effects are the entrenchment and ideological victory of capitalism or market economics over its chief rival, communism, and the development of computer technology and its penetration into every aspect of our educational, business, and industrial life.

William Greider says, in *One World Ready or Not,* that, like it or not, free-market capitalism is the secular religion of our time. Its creed is triumphant, and its practice the talisman for personal success.[1] Capitalism won the Cold War, and then the political battle in Washington, says Greider, turning liberal Democrats into "Eisenhower Republicans" and ordinary Republicans into small-government zealots. The philosophies of Reaganism rules the day: market decisions over government decisions; greed is good; me first. Political designations no longer matter. Whether one belongs to the Democratic or the Republican Party, everyone is now a fiscal "centrist." Even if, argues Greider, such an atmosphere contains the seeds of its own destruction, for now "global capitalism" and its promise of continuous progress reign as if "to the manor born."[2]

According to Jeremy Rifkin, in his bleak and blistering critique of conventional economic theory and industrial practices, *The End of Work,* life and work as we know it are being altered in fundamental ways by the computer.[3] The impact of computers has been so vast, so sweeping, it seems mythical. Edward Fredkin, a prominent computer scientist, goes so far as to claim that the new technology represents the third greatest event in the whole of cosmic history: "Event one is the creation of the universe. . . . Event two is the appearance of life. . . . And third, there's the appearance of artificial intelligence."[4]

Although Fredkin is perhaps overstating the case, Rifkin believes that computers can and will alter the direction of human history. Computers are not just our latest tool or gadget, nor are they simply the most advanced machines devised to date. Computers, suggests Rifkin, represent a quantum leap in intellectual capacity and decision-making ability. They represent a monumental difference in kind and not merely degree. They are "intelligent engines of productivity," "machines that perform functions that require intelligence," and they can compute faster and more accurately than Descartes, Pascal, Newton, or Einstein could on their own. Rifkin admits that although "scientists, philosophers and social critics often disagree as to what constitutes 'genuine' intelligence as opposed to rote computation, there is no doubt that computers are taking on tasks of increasing complexity and, in the process, changing our concepts of self and society in fundamental ways."[5]

In 1943 Tom Watson of IBM said, "I think there is a world market for about five computers." As recently as 1977, Ken Olson, former CEO of Digital Equipment, stated, "There is no reason anyone would want a computer in their home." Currently there are more than 100 million computers in the world, and it is estimated that every white-collar worker in America has access to over $810,000 in information-processing hardware. The major computer companies predict that more than 1 billion computers will be in use by the turn of the century.[6]

Perhaps computer technology's starkest feature is its inexorability. Today, the power of a personal computer microchip doubles every eighteen months.[7] Rifkin argues that it is the ability to be elegantly dumb and redundant as well as intricately complex that makes the computer the most adaptable, far-reaching, and potentially dangerous tool or machine ever created by humankind.

Even though, as of this writing, we are in the midst of a booming economy with national unemployment hovering at 4 percent, Rifkin argues that computers have changed the geography of the world and the workplace and that these changes have only just begun. In the future, computer technology will determine how work, where we work, what we do at work, and, most fundamentally, how many of us will be actually working. What Rifkin fears is that better technology means better processes and fewer and fewer workers.[8] He wants to avoid the chilling prophecy of French philosopher, politician, and computer consultant Jacques Attali, "Machines are the new proletariat. The working class is being given its walking papers."[9] For Rifkin the real question of the near future is not whether you are a white- or blue-collar worker, but whether you have a job at all. Redefining the role of the individual in a society without mass, formal work is, said Rifkin, the seminal issue of the coming age.[10]

Rifkin contends that we are in the first fifty years of the last phase of the industrial revolution, or what he calls the "third industrial revolution." According to Rifkin, the third industrial revolution is not just the mechanistic culmination of the first and second phases, but it is, in and of itself, the beginning of a new era and a new formulation of how we define economic well-being, work, and our theories regarding social justice and stability.

E. F. Schumacher has argued that most of human history has been entirely dependent on a six-inch crust of topsoil, atmospheric conditions, and solar energy.[11] Humankind's literal survival, success, and progress were directly tied to growing conditions, a modicum of human ingenuity, luck, and the annual size of the harvest. Social anthropologist Lewis Mumford contends that human progress from dependency to domination over nature began long before James Watt and the application of his revolutionary steam engine to industrial machinery of all kinds. In his opinion, the real beginnings of the industrial revolution were the introduction of hand tools, the domestication of animals, and the use of water and wood for energy. Tools, like machines, give the user more control, power, energy, accuracy, and reliability. At bottom, Mumford suggests, this "prerevolution" was all part of the long mechanical march from simple hand tools to complex computerized machines.[12]

The popular demarcation of the first industrial revolution is, as I suggested, associated with the Scottish engineer and inventor James Watt and an Englishman named Thomas Savory who designed a steam-driven pump to flush out excess water from underground coal mines. This union of coal, machines, and steam marked, according to Rifkin, the modern beginning of the first leg in the long journey to replace human labor with mechanical power. In the first industrial revolution, steam was used to mine its own source of power—coal, produce textiles, and manufacture consumer products on an economic scale far surpassing that of hand-crafted goods. Coal and steam powered the engine that drove the machines that produced more products and power that exceeded the power of animals and human beings combined.[13]

Oil, electricity, and the development of the "modern" mechanized assembly line were the hallmarks of the second industrial revolution, in Rifkin's view. Between 1860 and World War I, petroleum oil began to compete with coal, and electricity was harnessed to run our engines, propel our machines, and light our streets. As with the impact of steam, oil and electricity continued to shift the burden of physical toil and economic activity from people to machines. In every segment of industry and agriculture, inanimate sources of power combined with the increasing horsepower of machines to amplify and replace more and more human and animal tasks in the industrial-economic process.[14]

The third industrial revolution, as defined by Rifkin, assumes energy, electricity, and increasingly complicated machinery. It emerged immediately after World War II and is still proceeding at full speed. The third revolution is primarily the information age: concerned with facts, figures, analysis, digital decision-making, sophisticated software, and complicated hardware. The information age has evolved into one of artificial intelligence, thinking machines, silicon-based computers that can process information and perform tasks more efficiently and exactly than is humanly possible. It is the age of computers, which are increasingly capable of performing manual, conceptual, managerial, and administrative functions. It could be the "age of computopia," when mere mortal thinkers of flesh and blood are freed of most of the grueling and demanding tasks and repetitive toils of the workplace. It is an "age" whose motto unabashedly reads: "Better technology, better processes, and fewer, better workers." In it, Rifkin warns, the computer helps us, does for us, and possibly replaces us.[15]

At the outset of the industrial age, Lewis Mumford wrote, the machine was looked at as the new Messiah. Machines held out the promise of continuous materialistic progress, since they were capable not only of making more of the same, but also of producing new and better products while at the same time improving the working conditions of the worker.[16] There is, of course, a price to pay for progress: when machines move in, workers move out—sometimes lots of workers. According to Robert Heilbroner, economists have long granted the argument that new machinery may displace a few workers here and there, but they contend that in the end productivity will be vastly augmented, as will the GNP and general social well-being. The history of man and machine in the industrial age, said Heilbroner, is one of a great migration of workers leaving lesser jobs that technology has displaced, looking for better jobs it has newly created.[17] Conventional economic wisdom holds that new technologies boost productivity, lower the costs of production, and increase the supply of cheap goods, which in turn stimulates purchasing power, expands markets, and in the long run generates more jobs.[18]

The belief that the dramatic effects produced by advances in technology eventually filter down to the mass of workers in the form of cheaper goods, greater purchasing power, and more jobs has been traditionally known as "trickle-down economics." The trickle-down theory dates back to the writings of the early-nineteenth-century French economist Jean

Baptiste Say who argued that supply creates its own demand. He wrote, "A product is no sooner created than it, from that instant, affords a market for other products to the full extent of its own value. . . . The creation of one product immediately opens a vent for other products." According to Rifkin:

> Say's ideas on markets . . . were taken up by neoclassical economists who argued that new labor saving technologies increase productivity, allowing suppliers to produce more goods at a cheaper cost per unit. The increased supply of cheaper goods, according to the neoclassical argument, creates its own demand. In other words, falling prices resulting from productivity advances stimulate consumer demand for the goods being produced. Greater demand in turn stimulates additional production, fueling demand again, in a never-ending cycle of expanding production and consumption. The increased volume of goods being sold will assure that any initial loss of employment brought about by technological improvements will quickly be compensated by additional hiring to meet the expanded production levels. In addition, lower prices resulting from technological innovation and rising productivity will mean consumers have extra money left over to buy other products, further stimulating productivity and increased employment in other parts of the economy.
>
> A corollary to the trickle-down argument states that even if workers are displaced by new technologies, the problem of unemployment will eventually resolve itself. The growing number of unemployed will eventually bid down wages. Cheaper wages will entice employers to hire additional workers rather than purchase more expensive capital equipment, thereby moderating the impact of technology on employment.[19]

Over the years, the idea that technological innovation stimulates perpetual growth and employment has met with serious opposition from a number of different quarters. As early as 1867 Karl Marx argued that producers continually attempt to reduce labor costs and gain greater control over the means of production by substituting capital equipment for workers wherever and whenever possible. Marx foresaw a steady progression of increasingly sophisticated machines substituting for human labor. He predicted that the increasing automation of production would eventually eliminate the worker altogether, and, as Rifkin states, Marx believed that:

> the ongoing effort by producers to continue to replace human labor with machines would prove self-defeating in the end. By directly eliminating human labor from the production process and by creating a reserve army of unemployed workers whose wages could be bid down lower and lower, the capitalists were inadvertently digging their own grave, as there would be fewer and fewer consumers with sufficient purchasing power to buy their products.[20]

John Maynard Keynes, in his groundbreaking publication *The General Theory of Employment, Interest and Money*, warned of a new and dangerous phenomenon whose impact was likely to be profound:

> We are being afflicted by a new disease of which some readers may not yet have heard the name, but of which they will hear a great deal in the years to come—namely "technological unemployment." This means unemployment due to our discovery of means of economizing the use of labor out running the pace at which we can find new uses for labor.[21]

In 1937 President Franklin D. Roosevelt reiterated Keynes's and Marx's warnings in an address to a special session of Congress that had been convened to deal with worsening unemployment that year:

> What does the country ultimately gain if we encourage businessmen to enlarge the capacity of American industry to produce unless we see that the income of our working population actually expands to create markets to absorb that increased production.[22]

The question, said Rifkin, is as timely and significant today as it was when Roosevelt asked it more than sixty years ago.

Rifkin suggests that although Say's Law remains extraordinarily influential and the backbone of neoclassical economic theory, it is, at best, a very tightly argued and logically sophisticated tautology or, perhaps, nothing more than a long-standing, self-fulfilling prophesy, that is that a system works if and only if everything in the system keeps working. However, the system is no longer working. Moreover, suggests Rifkin, even if Say's Law once had partial validity in regard to early stages of technology, it is no longer defensible in the face of the kinds of sweeping changes being brought on by the information age. Although once the operating rationale for the economic policy of every industrialized nation in the world, Say's Law is now leading to "unprecedented levels of technological unemployment, a precipitous decline in consumer purchasing power, and the specter of a worldwide depression of incalculable magnitude and duration."[23] Our continued commitment to Say's Law, says Rifkin, will result in the loss of work, the loss of workers, and the loss of economic, social, and political well-being.

The landscape of the workplace, in regard to the type of work available and the kinds of skills necessary to work, has been radically altered since the founding of the United States more than 225 years ago. In the late eighteenth century, 97 percent of the workforce was directly engaged in farming. In 1850, 60 percent was employed in agriculture. By 1900 only 33 percent was involved in farming, and in 1940 the number had dropped to 20 percent. Today, less than 2.7 percent of the workforce is engaged in agriculture. Since World War II, more than 15 million men and women have left farming in the United States.[24] According to Robert L. Heilbroner, in 1810 a mere 75,000 persons worked in America's infant industrial system. Fifty years later 1.5 million worked in the factories; by 1910 over 8 million; and by 1960 over 16 million.[25] In the 1950s, 33 percent of all U.S. workers were employed in manufacturing. By the 1960s, it had dropped to 30 percent, and to 20 percent in the 1980s. Today, says Rifkin, less than 17 percent of the workforce is engaged in blue-collar industrial work, and some estimates predict that employment in manufacturing will continue dropping to less than 12 percent of the entire workforce in the next decade.

Although the number of industrial workers continues to decline, says Rifkin, manufacturing productivity is soaring. From 1979 to 1992, productivity in the industrial-manufacturing center increased by 35 percent while the workforce shrank by 15 percent. According to William Winpisinger, former president of the International Association of Machinists, studies conducted by the International Metalworkers Federation predict that within thirty years, as little as 2 percent of the world's current labor force "will be needed to produce all the goods necessary for total [global] demand."[26] Rifkin has made a even more dire predictions since his book's publication. He said that it is possible that by 2020 there will be no industrial, blue-collar, assembly-line workers whatsoever.[27]

As labor left the farms and moved out of the factory it entered into the twentieth century's only growing segment of employment: the service sector. Service employment offers a wide range of jobs—doctors and lawyers, teachers and social workers, nannies and maids, government bureaucrats and traffic cops, janitors and window-washers, sales representatives, file clerks, typists, and secretaries. Heilbroner estimates that by 1870 there were perhaps 3 million in the diverse branches of the service sector and by the 1990s nearly 90 million. For thirty years, service employment, said Heilbroner, saved every modern national economy from devastating unemployment, and then the "knowledge sector" developed, propelled by the photocopier, the fax, and the computer.[28]

Quietly and without a great deal of fanfare the birth of the information age and knowledge sector of the economy arrived in 1944 when scientists from Harvard and MIT invented America's first programmable computer, the Mark I:

> The machine was more than fifty feet in length and eight feet high and was nicknamed "the monster" by its inventors. Just two years later, scientists at the University of Pennsylvania's Moore School of Engineering unveiled an even more advanced computing machine. The Electronic Numerical Integrator and Computer, or ENIAC, was made up of 18,000 radio tubes, 70,000 resistors, 10,000 capacitors, 6,000 switches, was forty feet long and over twenty feet high, and weighed more than thirty tons. Though complex and gangly, the machine was a marvel of modern technology. ENIAC was the first fully electronic general-purpose [programmable] digital computer. It was said that the giant thinking machine was so powerful that the lights of Philadelphia dimmed when its creators first switched it on. Yoneji Masuda, the Japanese computer savant, summed up the historical importance of the new invention, observing that "for the first time a machine was made to create and supply information.[29]

The knowledge sector is staffed with many of the same workers who labored in the service sector, but its core is a new cosmopolitan elite of "symbolic analysts" who control the technologies and the forces of production. These new knowledge workers come from the fields of science, engineering, management, mathematics, consulting, teaching, marketing, media, and entertainment. While this core continues to grow, they will remain a relatively small percentage of the workforce in comparison to the number of workers displaced by each succeeding generation of "thinking machines."[30] Both Rifkin and former Secretary of Labor Robert Reich believe that we are developing a "boutique labor sector" of knowledge workers who represent just 20 percent of the workforce. Although knowledge workers have become the most important group in the economic equation and constitute the "new aristocracy" in the global economy, their sinecure is not absolute. With progress, even this sector is doomed to downsizing. Nevertheless, those who remain will be in charge of the direction, pace, and quality of our collective economic life.[31]

With each new development of the computer, more and more can be automated and less and less need be done manually. In a very short time, predicts Rifkin, knowledge workers will end mass wage labor just as the industrial revolution ended the economic rationale for slavery.[32] The information age, depending on how it is handled, has the potential, says Rifkin, to either liberate or totally destabilize civilization in the coming century.

To begin with, more than 75 percent of the labor force in most industrial nations engages in work that is little more than simple, repetitive tasks. In the United States alone, that means that more than 96 million jobs in a labor force of 129 million are potentially vulnerable to replacement by machines.[33] An equally frightening set of statistics has been generated by authors Edward Gordon, Ronald Morgan, and Judith Ponticell. They claim that 84 million Americans—from managers to production workers—are currently undereducated and incapable of handling almost any job in a high-tech twenty-first-century workplace. As a result, most Americans are destined to become the "new peasants of the information age," and most will not be able to find any work, anywhere, at any time in the future."[34] Rifkin reluctantly agrees:

> The few good jobs that are becoming available in the new high-tech global economy are in the knowledge sector. It is naive to believe that large numbers of unskilled and skilled blue and white collar workers will be retained to be physicists, computer scientists, high-level technicians, molecular biologists, business consultants, lawyers, accountants, and the like.[35]

Presently, in the United States alone, corporations are eliminating in excess of 2 million jobs a year. The *Wall Street Journal* reports: "Most of the cuts are facilitated, one way or another, by new software programs, better computer networks and more powerful hardware." All this gadgetry allows companies to do more work with fewer workers.[36]

In October 1929, fewer than 1 million Americans were out of work, but in December 1931, more than 10 million people were unemployed. At the height of the Depression, March 1933, more than 15 million people were out of work.[37] In 1993, nearly 16 million American workers, or 13 percent of the labor force, were either totally unemployed (8.7 million) or underemployed (7.3 million), that is, they were either working part-time or so discouraged that they stopped looking for work altogether. [38] Moreover, according to the Department of Labor, in 1996 only 70 percent of those people who had jobs had full-time conventional jobs with conventional hours and standard pay and benefits packages. Thirty percent of the workforce held temporary jobs or worked part-time at one or more jobs, at substandard pay and without benefits.[39] In the European Common Market countries, official unemployment is approaching 13 percent. According to Matthew Fox, in so-called Third World countries, as well as in Ireland, on Indian reservations, and in pockets of American inner cities, unemployment ranges from 40 to 60 percent.[40] Global unemployment, reports Rifkin, has now reached its highest level since the 1930s: A staggering 800 million people are unemployed or underemployed in the world today.[41]

At the same time, all around the world, 40 million people enter the job market every year, looking for work. To put all these people to work, within the next thirty years, the world must come up with 1.3 billion new jobs—which is equal to half of the jobs that now exist on the planet. This is more jobs than have been created since World War II, the greatest period of sustained prosperity in world history.[42] "The problem is simple," Richard J. Barnet and John Cavanagh wrote in their book *Global Dreams.* "An astonishingly large and increasing number of human being are not needed or wanted to make the goods or to provide the services that the paying customers of the world can afford."[43]

Rifkin contends that computer-driven machines are quickly replacing human labor and promise an economy of near automated production by the middle of the twenty-first century. He writes, "Workers with years of education, skills, and experience face the very real prospect of being made redundant by the new forces of automation and information."[44] The American underclass, which has traditionally been made up of African Americans and other urban minorities, will become increasingly white and suburban as the new "thinking machines" relentlessly make their way up the economic ladder, absorbing more and more skilled jobs along the way. Perhaps less than 20 percent of the entire national and global workforce will be necessary to produce all the goods and services necessary, 80 of those still employed will be "knowledge workers"; and the other 20 percent will consist of "common laborers" who will toil at handyman chores or be ingloriously relegated to the task of being nothing more than "machine minders."[45]

When Ned Ludd, an eighteenth-century English working man, and his fellow workers smashed the new machines in their Leicestershire mill, they did so because they feared the machines would take away many of their jobs. Subsequent followers of Mr. Ludd—called Luddites—have not always been so violent, but have always been very vocal in their denunciation of technological change. They have, in turn, decried the loom, electric motors, and the automobile. Each time, they have been overly pessimistic. Technology has created millions more jobs than it destroyed. This time, however, says Rifkin, there is some reason to believe the modern-day Luddites are right.

In July 1997 President Bill Clinton accepted an invitation to speak at the national conference of the AFL-CIO in Pittsburgh. Former Democratic presidents who attended AFL-CIO conventions could expect to receive a standing ovation and a great deal of support, but not this time—and perhaps never again, whether the president is Democrat or Republican. Clinton was greeted by a round of boos and received only polite applause when he finished. The rank and file of the AFL-CIO felt betrayed by a man they had endorsed for reelection in 1996, but who had, nevertheless, signed the North American Free Trade Agreement with Mexico (which labor feared would mean a great loss of American jobs), and was actively pushing for "fast track" authority to negotiate trade agreements with other Latin American countries. (Clinton was unable to muster sufficient support for this legislation and withdrew it from congressional consideration in November of 1997.) The union membership felt abandoned. Their own president was giving away their jobs. As one disgruntled member put it, "We liked him. We voted for him. But he's got to make more low-skilled, low-tech jobs available to us, and not just give them away to NAFTA."[46]

According to Rifkin, unions are fighting a rear-guard action with no real chance for success. Low-skilled, low-tech jobs are an endangered species and doomed to early extinction no matter on which side of the border they are presently found. Moreover, the rest of the American workforce is becoming increasingly aware that they too are at some risk of following the "trail of the dinosaurs" in the not too distant future.

In a four-year survey of worker attitudes and opinions conducted by International Survey Research Corporation and published in 1996, CEO John R. Stanek reports that although workers are becoming more and more satisfied with their pay and their general working conditions, they are becoming more fretful about suddenedly being pink-slipped out of a job. According to Stanek, these fears of losing their place are not simply the results of the current downsizing trend or undue concern about company shutdowns and failures. Increasingly, workers fear being displaced from the economy by cybernation. "Anyone who thinks he's got a job for life has been in a lead mine for the past 10 years or [is] a Supreme Court justice," says Stanek. "People are living their lives in chapters now"—that is, day to day and job to job.[47]

Industrial and intellectual workers of all kinds and all skill levels are caught in the middle of what experts are calling the battle of "shifting paradigms" regarding the definition and longevity of labor. As technology continues to advance, "small is beautiful" has become the mantra of business life. "Sophisticated computers, telecommunications, and robots," says Rifkin, "are fast replacing entire job categories."[48] What is happening in factories and offices across America and around the world is less about *downsizing* workers than *eradicating* them. We are, in effect, creating not only "virtual corporations" but a "virtual workforce" as well. Our "intelligent engines of productivity" are also proving to be engines of human displacement. As one technology advocate gleefully proclaimed, "The new generation of computer-driven numerical control tools marks our 'emancipation from human workers!'"[52] As the father of cybernetics, Norbert Weiner, lamented, "The cybernetic revolution will undoubtedly lead to the factory without employees."[50]

Workers are being seen as contingent and, more often than not, redundant and unnecessary in regard to the long-term needs of a business. Employers increasingly want a "just-in-time" workforce, or what Charles Handy calls "portfolio workers," "career gypsies," "project workers," "temps," "task-consultants" who come in to do the work of a specific but transitional job.[51] According to William Bridges, in his ironically titled book *Job Shift: How to Prosper in a Workplace without Jobs,* "the conditions that created jobs 200 years ago—mass production and the large corporation—are disappearing. In place of jobs, there are part-time and temporary work situations. . . . Today's organizations are rapidly being transformed from a structure built out of jobs into a field of work needing to be done." In effect, says Bridges, we've entered the era of "dejobbing" and the "post-job corporation."[52] In many parts of the world, reports a 1994 United Nations Human Development Study, we are beginning to witness a very new and disturbing phenomenon—"jobless growth."[53] No category of worker seems to be immune. The technology of the information age is rapidly eliminating huge segments of the traditional workforce. For example, in 1980 United States Steel, the largest steel company in the country, employed approximately 120,000 workers. By 1990, due to increased automation, it was producing roughly the same output using only 20,000 workers. In a fourteen-year period the entire American steel industry eliminated more than 220,000 jobs, or half of its routine workforce.[54] In the summer of 1996, Navistar International Corporation announced its intention to lay off 3,000 assembly-line workers. The announcement was succinct and to the point: "As truck assembly is made more efficient through computers and programming we need fewer and fewer people on the production lines."[55]

According to Rifkin, the automobile and its related industrial enterprises is responsible for generating one out of every twelve manufacturing jobs in the United States. In 1993, John F. Smith, Jr., then president of General Motors, announced that much-needed upgrades in automation techniques would allow GM plants to eliminate as many as 90,000 auto jobs, or one-third of its workforce, by the turn of the century. These new cuts would come on top of the 250,000 jobs GM had already eliminated since 1978.[56]

White-collar service work and the retail industry have also been affected by the computer revolution. Secretaries were among the first casualties of the new electronic office space. Between 1983 and 1993, the country's secretarial pool shrank 8 percent, to about 3.6 million workers.[57] In a 1996 survey conducted by the Olsten Corporation, a staffing-services firm, 42 percent of more than 400 corporations surveyed reported that they have radically trimmed their secretarial and administrative staffs over the past five years, citing cost-cutting (78 percent) and increased automation (74 percent) as the big reasons. The automation involved includes e-mail, voice mail, and the rise of computer literacy among managers.[58] Andersen Consulting Company estimates that in just one service industry, commercial banking and thrift institutions, technological changes will eliminate 30 to 40 percent, or 700,000 jobs, in seven years.[59] Thanks in part to automated warehouses, pricing bar codes, and electronic scanning equipment that allows up-to-the-minute inventory control, 400,000 jobs, which includes cashiers, bookkeepers, sales, and stock persons, have been lost in retail employment since 1990. The retail giant Sears alone eliminated a staggering 50,000 jobs from its merchandising division in 1993, reducing employment by 14 percent. These same cutbacks occurred in a year when Sears's sales revenue rose by more than 10 percent.[60]

Similarly, knowledge workers and middle management are not immune from the fatal effects of the silicon chopping-block. Michael Hammer, who wrote *Re-engineering the Corporation,* estimated that up to 80 percent of those engaged in middle-management tasks are susceptible to elimination. Traditionally, argues Rifkin, middle managers have been responsible for coordinating the work flow up and down the organizational ladder. Today, a growing number of companies are deconstructing their organizational hierarchies and eliminating more and more middle management jobs by compressing several jobs into a single process. With the introduction of increasingly sophisticated computer technologies, many middle management jobs have become both costly and unnecessary. Between 1986 and 1994, even IBM cut 171,000 jobs. The reality, as Michael Hammer so aptly put it, is, "We are in the midst of a major polarization of work. Organizations need fewer and fewer of better and better people. The [only] jobs organizations are going to have are going to be better jobs."[61]

Nobel Laureate economist Wassail Leontief has warned that with the introduction of increasingly sophisticated computers "the role of humans as the most important factor of production is bound to diminish in the same way that the role of horses in agricultural production was diminished and then eliminated by the introduction of tractors."[62] Rifkin argues that the loss of jobs and the subsequent loss of purchasing power will prove to be the Achilles heel of the information age. As it becomes more efficient to replace mass labor with computer technologies and an elite high-tech workforce, there will not be enough people left with rising incomes to absorb the increased production.[63] Management patriarch Peter Drucker states quite bluntly, "the disappearance of labor as a key factor of production" is going to emerge as the critical "unfinished business of capitalistic society." The economic question is simple and direct: If workers no longer produce, how will they be able to consume?[64]

In the most elemental terms, says Rifkin, after centuries of defining human worth in terms of productivity, the wholesale replacement of human labor with machine labor leaves the workforce without self-definition, an economic base, or a societal function.[65] "The idea of a society," Rifkin asserts, "not based on work is so utterly alien to any notion we have about how to organize large numbers of people into a social whole, that we are faced with the prospect of having to rethink the very basis of the social contract."[66] In other words, in a world fast phasing out mass employment, how do we find alternative ways for individuals to earn a living, find meaningful and creative outlets for expression, and establish their own sense of self-worth and identity? How will we define ourselves? How will we stay sane? If we cannot address these issues, warns Rifkin, we are in danger of creating a broad and permanently based technological and economic "underclass," and in so doing destroying the traditional means by which people have viewed themselves and the world. Sadly, many believe that this process has already begun.

In 1996 longtime University of Chicago sociologist William Julius Wilson, now of Harvard University, published his eagerly awaited study on inner-city life, *When Work Disappears: The World of the New Urban Poor.* As a scholar, Wilson has been researching and gathering statistics on the African-American ghetto experience for decades. *When Work Disappears* is the third in a series of books on the growing black underclass, after *The Declining Significance of Race,* and *The Truly Disadvantaged,* and is primarily based on three in-depth surveys he and his colleagues conducted between 1987 and 1993, primarily in Chicago. While perceived by others as both an academic and political liberal, Wilson tries to eschew the ideological labels of both the right and the left. He prefers to cite hard research, statistics, and surveys that point to measurable structural explanations behind social problems, and consequently Wilson is often alternately praised and damned by both sides involved in the political debate.

Like Rifkin, Wilson believes that the overall structure of the workplace and the composition of the workforce has been radically affected by our ever evolving "means of production." Specifically, as a student of the African-American experience, Wilson is convinced that "technological unemployment" has fundamentally altered the sociology, value structure, and work ethic of the black community.

The mass exodus of blacks from the rural South in pursuit of "low-tech" jobs in northern industrial cities began after World War I and peaked between 1940 and 1970 when more than 5 million black men, women, and children migrated north in search of work. Although race and class helped to fuel this migration, the main motivation for most individuals was economic. Northern industries spurred on by a war economy and then a postwar consumer boom were in desperate need of labor, and simultaneously the introduction of the mechanical cotton picker, which could do the work of fifty people a day, had killed the southern sharecropper system. For most southern rural blacks, the choices seemed obvious.[67]

Although many African-American laborers found work as skilled tradesmen and as clerical workers in the industries and corporations of Detroit, Cleveland, and Chicago, and thus began the long climb to economic and social middle-class status, the vast majority of black workers could find employment only in semiskilled and unskilled jobs. As the boom ended and automation began to affect even the most skilled job categories, those at the lowest end of the totem pole, primarily but not exclusively African-Americans, began to be systematically eliminated from the workplace and relegated to a permanent underclass. Social scientists define the underclass as a permanently unemployed or badly underemployed part of the population whose unskilled labor is no longer required or marketable and who live hand-to-mouth, generation-to-generation, on part-time jobs or as wards of the state. Of the 8.5 million people considered to be in the nation's underclass (or to use a less loaded term, the jobless poor) about 50 percent are African-Americans.[68]

Wilson argues that it is not the "culture of race" or ethnicity that created an underclass, but the "culture of poverty" and the conditions that arise out of permanent unemployment. For Wilson such social ills as the breakdown of families, out-of-wedlock births, assaults, robberies, street gangs, random violence, and drugs are the results of grinding poverty and the powerful, complex role of the social and economic environment in shaping and structuring the life experiences, attitudes, and options of inner-city residents. It is an environment, Wilson insists, that people are caught in, but over which they have little or no control. For Wilson, this does not justify certain behavior, but it does help to explain its structural etiology. The root of the problem is not the moral fabric of individuals, but the social and economic structure of society.[69]

For the first time in the twentieth century, says Wilson, most adults in many inner-city neighborhoods are not working in a typical week. In some of the ten wards that make up the historical core of Chicago's "black belt," as it's locally known, the jobless rate is in excess of 45 percent, which does not take into account the "invisible unemployed"—those who gave up looking for work long ago, and part-time workers who want full-time jobs but can't find them—who do not show up in government reports.[70] Wilson also claims that in the poorest areas of the nations hundred largest cities, there are ten adults without a job for every six who have one.[71] Wilson has found that "the consequences of high neighborhood joblessness are more devastating than those of high neighborhood poverty. A neighborhood in which people are poor but employed is different from a neighborhood in which people are poor and jobless." Work is all-important, says Wilson. "Regular employment provides the anchor for the special and temporal aspects of daily life," he writes. "It determines where you are going to be and when you are going to be there. In the absence of regular employment, life, including family life, becomes less coherent."[72] Work is not just a means to making a living; it also imposes discipline. When people are working, their lives are organized. People who work on a regular basis develop predictable habits. They eat at the same time. They organize their recreational life around work. Kids growing up in that environment automatically develop the same kinds of patterns.[73]

Without work, says Wilson, both individuals and communities can die psychologically and physically. Without jobs people lose hope, standards and expectations are diminished, and there is a general breakdown in civility, cooperation, and the rudiments of "social networking" and "social organization."[74] Community networking and organizing is called "social capital" by Robert D. Putnam, who touted its importance in his now-famous article "Bowling Alone." Social capital is the energy, commitment, and intelligence that overlapping community structures and organizations bring to group life. Social capital, or civic engagement, produces social norms and expectations, breeds trust, coordination, and cooperation, and engenders a sense of connectedness, solidarity, and reciprocity. Putnam maintains that social capital is a precondition for economic vitality and success because it leads to dialogue, conviviality, a wider sense of self, a diverse sense of group, and the concept of commonwealth. Putnam argues that the quality of both our private and public lives is radically influenced by the quality and quantity of our civic participation and our commitment to the principle that communal well-being is a precondition for private well-being.[75] Wilson agrees. Racially and economically segregated neighborhoods, he argues, are less conducive to employment and employment preparation, in large part, because of the lack of appropriate social models, social action, and social reinforcement:

> Neighborhoods that offer few legitimate employment opportunities, inadequate job information networks, and poor schools lead to the disappearance of work. That is, where jobs are scarce, where people rarely, if ever, have the opportunity to help their friends and neighbors find jobs, and where there is a disruptive or degraded school life purporting to prepare youngsters for eventual preparation in the workforce, many people eventually lose their feelings of connectedness to work in the formal economy; they no longer expect work to be a regular, and regulating, force in their lives. In the case of young people, they may grow up in an environment that lacks the idea of work as a central experience of adult life—they have little or no labor-force attachment. These circumstances also increase the likelihood that the residents will rely on illegitimate

sources of income, thereby further weakening their attachment to the legitimate labor market.[76]

For Wilson the most destructive and long-lasting effects of joblessness are the loss of a sense of self-efficacy and a balanced sense of identity. Self-efficacy refers to the belief in one's own ability to take the steps necessary to achieve the goals required in a particular situation. It is built on self-confidence and self-discovery. In social cognitive terms, work requires organization, focus, and regularity. In work we are challenged, we acquire skills, accomplish tasks, influence events, achieve objectives, recognize our abilities as well as our limits, and, if we are lucky, receive reinforcement from others. The inability to influence events, to take on a challenge, even if we fail, or at the very least to organize one's behavior in a regulated and orderly way leads to feelings of futility, despondency, and lack of worth. Wilson hypothesizes that lacking the framework of a regular job and trapped in a neighborhood plagued by low employment will lead to the loss of self-efficacy, as well as the fundamental psychological prerequisites necessary to establish and sustain a viable "work ethic." The social arithmetic involved, suggests Wilson, is easy to compute. Those who do not live in a culture of work are unable to define themselves by what they do, and as a result they drift deeper into despair and desperation.[77]

William Julius Wilson is quick to point out that his thesis regarding the culture of poverty and what has happened to the African-American underclass can happen to any and every worker regardless of race or ethnicity. The chilling sociological and economic effects of "structural-technological unemployment" have simply happened to the black community first. For Wilson, the marginalization of the black underclass and the chronic social pathologies that grow out of segregated existence is the harbinger of the future for all of us—if and when work disappears.

Sadly, Jeremy Rifkin agrees the underclass has become expendable, invisible, and economically unnecessary, and their fate seems permanently cast. Their experience, he warns, should serve as an eye-opener. It portends what may be lurking on the horizon for all workers in every job category. Work should and can offer us identity, integrity, and purpose, but "without work," as Albert Camus reminds us, "all life goes rotten." Nearly fifty years ago, at the dawn of the computer revolution, Herbert

Marcuse, in his troubling book *Eros and Civilization*, made a prophetic observation—one that Rifkin believes has come to haunt our society as we ponder the transition into the information age:

> Automation threatens to render possible the reversal of the relation between free time and working time: the possibility of work time becoming marginal and free time becoming full time. The result would be a radical transvaluation of values, and a mode of existence incompatible with traditional culture.[78]

Rifkin is no Luddite. His thesis is not a purely personal agenda, but, rather, an interpretation of the facts as he understands them. Writing as an economist and a social historian he sees the information age as a triumph of human ingenuity as well as the possible epiphany of a long-term tragedy. I think his gloomy prognostications correct. Of course, only time will tell, but even if he is only partially right, the possible negative impact on the global economy and the psychological well-being of individual workers is staggering. Rifkin has said that he wrote *The End of Work* not as a "doomsday chronicle," but as a warning, albeit apocalyptic, of what could and would happen if we let economic-technological progress proceed unabated. He wrote the book to begin a debate on the options we face in the future—a debate, he says, we have yet to seriously address.[79]

Having said that Rifkin is no follower of Ned Ludd, let me conclude with a richly ironic tidbit. Rifkin has written more than a dozen books, hundred of articles, and innumerable of speeches in his career. In an interview in the comfortable study of Rifkin's home A. J. Vogel made a startling discovery: Jeremy Rifkin belongs to an almost extinct tribe—he does all of his writing by hand![80]

13

The Failure of Work

> The significant problems we face cannot be solved at the same level of thinking we were at when we created them.
>
> —Albert Einstein

DESPITE JEREMY RIFKIN'S DIRE WARNINGS OF NO work in the future, a recent survey by the *Los Angeles Times* found that just 22 percent of workers were putting in fewer than forty hours per week, 50 percent worked more than forty hours, and close to 30 percent logged more than fifty hours per week.[1] Although the twenty-first century may prove to be the age of joblessness, the twentieth century has made work a fetish. Benjamin K. Hunnicutt, a professor of work and leisure studies at the University of Iowa, asks, "Has any previous age been so obsessed with [work], so troubled by it, or tried so desperately to find enough of it to go around? Have humans ever before struggled so hard to have more rather than less work to do?" Work, says Hunnicutt, sits squarely in the center of twentieth-century life, and some have even argued that work has emerged as a modern religion. In other words, the more secular we become, the more we expect our jobs to answer the ultimate questions of meaning and purpose in our lives.[2]

Even as we are entering into the new millennium, we continue to proselytize the age-old virtues and values of the work ethic. Jesse Jackson continually preaches from the pulpit and the political rostrum, "Get a job, work hard—*be somebody!*" Richard Todd, contributing editor of *Worth* magazine, points out that when Cal Ripkin, Jr., completed 2,131 consecutive professional baseball games, the stadium went wild. The president of the United States, who was in attendance, praised Ripkin's "discipline, determination, and consistency," and ABC correspondent Chris Wallace referred to him as "a paragon of the work ethic." Newt Gingrich, in his book *To Renew America,* laments "pauperism as a condition of passive dependency in which the 'work ethic' has been completely lost." And Pete DuPont has written in the *National Review*, "The work ethic is at the core of a healthy society, and the individual responsibility of doing a job, earning a living, and striving for improvement is crucial to restoring opportunity and self-respect to underclass Americans."[3]

Organized labor trumpets the benefits of the work ethic to its membership by regularly extolling the vision of one of its founding fathers, Samuel Gompers, president of the AFL from 1886 to 1925:

> What does labor want? It wants the earth and the fullness thereof. There is nothing too precious; there is nothing to beautiful, too lofty, too ennobling, unless it is within the scope and comprehension of labor's aspirations and wants. We want more school houses and less jails; more books and less arsenals; more learning and less vice; more constant work and less greed; more justice and less revenge. In fact, more of the opportunities to cultivate our better nature, to make manhood more noble, womanhood more beautiful, and childhood more happy and bright.[4]

Although somewhat adversarial in tone, Gromper's overall message is both pro-worker and pro-work. Gompers believed that workers want to work and that their commitment to a work ethic should be justly rewarded by a fair share of the benefits and results of their efforts. John Sweeney, the new president of the AFL-CIO, has recently called for a genuine partnership between business and labor. "American labor no longer takes the position that quality, productivity and profits are not our business," Sweeney recently told a group of corporate executives. "We want to help American business compete in the world and create new wealth for your shareholders and your employees. . . . It's time for business and labor to see each other as natural allies, not natural enemies." Both business and labor, suggests Sweeney, should be in pursuit of the common good for all, and the primary means to that end is a solid work ethic.[5]

There is, of course, much more to life than just work. To thrive and achieve balance, the human condition requires both work and leisure, but in the twentieth century we have fostered a culture in which neither pursuit exists in proper balance in our day-to-day lives. J. Dwayne Roush, a successful automotive engineering executive, nicely captured our national fascination and fixation with work when, in an interview, he explained why he had recently turned down a lucrative early retirement package, "With or without the package, I've got enough money now to retire. So either way I can retire, but I'm not about to. Work keeps me going. It's the only thing I really like or know. How many times a week can I go golfing? How many vacations a year can I take? What am I supposed to do with myself? Forget it! I'm staying on the job. I don't want to get old and die too soon."

As much as many of us would wish otherwise, work remains the center of our lives. Unfortunately, most employees feel that they are trapped in a cycle of "work without end." Work rules, runs, and often ruins our lives, and yet, as in the psychological phenomenon known as the "Stockholm effect," in work we often become eager and willing prisoners of that which we may have originally rejected or rebeled against. Many of us come to love or at least need that which holds us captive. To tweak the classic Cartesian formula one more time, maybe in the most elemental sense it isn't the descriptive *Laboro, ergo sum* (I work, therefore I am) but, rather the imperative *Sum, Ergo laboro* (I am, therefore I [must] work).

For most of us the impetus to work is necessity and fear rather than desire or fulfillment. Most of us must work! And for most, work provides a major component of self-definition. In a series of surveys reported in *Poor Richard's Principle,* sociologist Robert Wuthnow reinforces the idea that "We find meaning and are defined by our work." Relying on two hundred in-depth interviews with working people and a general survey of two thousand other working Americans, Wuthnow asked people if they find meaning in their jobs. The short answer is that they do. Wuthnow argues that people not only work to make money, but also "to give a legitimate account of themselves" to themselves and others. For better or for worse, suggests Wuthnow, work is one of the places in which people learn, not only about the job, but also the wider world outside of themselves.[6]

By our work we acquire knowledge, meaning, relationships, and a general philosophy or attitude toward life. Any job, every job gives us these "skills," and no matter how high or low the task, for some workers, genuine satisfaction can be found. As "Lovin' Al," a parking attendant, told Studs Terkel:

> When people ask what I do, I tell 'em I park cars. Only thing you got is a white-collar, that's okay with me. Working behind a typewriter, that's fine. You're a doctor, that's cool. Everybody got a job to do. My friends never feel superior to me. . . . After thirty years I can drive a car like a baby, like a woman changes her baby's diaper. I can handle that car with one hand. I had a lot of customers would say, "How you do this? The way you goes around this way?" I'd say, "Just the way you bake a cake, miss, I can handle this car." A lotta ladies and gentlemen come to you, say, "'Wow! You can drive!" I say, "Thank you, ma'am." They say, "How long you been doin' it?" I say, "Thirty years, I started when I'm sixteen and I'm still doin' it."[7]

At the very least, work is a "structuring activity," a process whereby we impose order and meaning on the raw data of life and the activity of others. We see the world through the lens of our labor, and we understand and evaluate life by the metaphors, models, and lessons we have learned on the job.

It is an interesting aside to briefly consider the fact that work not only consumes our days, but also pervades our pastimes. According to media critic Neil Postman, the most commonly shared cultural experience in America is watching television. Household televisions are turned on, even if not closely watched, an average of 6.8 hours per day. Educators lament that school-age children often watch in excess of four hours of television per day. Postman suggests that most adults huddle around the television set for at least a couple of hours each night. Television may be the primary medium by which most of us gain information and relax.[8]

Although cable and satellite dishes have changed our watching patterns, the backbone of commercial broadcasting remains weeknight prime time programming, from 8 to 11 P.M. Dedicated to sitcoms, serial dramas, and magazine news shows, many of the fictional programs are about friends, neighbors, schoolmates, roommates, husbands and wives, and families. Recently there have been more and more sitcoms based on the problems, idiosyncracies, and personalities that people encounter at work. In the fall of 1997, ABC, CBS, and NBC aired at least eleven successful shows that were work-based in their theme: *Suddenly Susan* (magazine publication), *Fired-Up* (PR firm), *Caroline in the City* (cartoonist), *Naked Truth* (magazine publication), *Murphy Brown* (TV news), *News*

Radio (radio news), *Just Shoot Me* (magazine publication), *Spin City* (city government), *Drew Carey* (retail sales), *Veronica's Closet* (lingerie designing/marketing), and finally and appropriately enough *Working* (life in the corporate cubicle).

And then there are the serials. These action-packed dramas depict cops, lawyers, and doctors dealing with the compelling tragedies and misfortunes of others. The main characters are usually dedicated professionals who alternately love and loathe their work, but always do it with a passion for the betterment of others. Some of these shows include *NYPD Blue* (police), *ER* (doctors and nurses), *Law and Order* (lawyers and police), *Chicago Hope* (doctors and nurses), and *The Practice* (lawyers).

Certainly part of the appeal of these shows is that they are clever, well written and well acted. These shows also appeal to us because, at least ostensibly, they are about something that we intimately know—work. We see in them people like us, trying to do the right thing, trying to get by, trying to do a job. Even though these shows may not be realistic, we see in them little moments of ourselves, maybe not as we really are on the job, but as we would wish to be. Perhaps they simply offer us a new perspective on what we do and why we do it, or perhaps they offer us new models to follow. Whatever the reason we like them, millions of us watch these mythic playlets faithfully each week. Ironically, even at home when we're relaxing, we can't get away from work.

If it can be argued that people have an economic and psychological need to work, that work is a necessary condition for human existence, then it can also be argued that people have a "right to work." In *Centesimus Annus,* Pope John Paul II clearly stated, "The obligation to earn one's bread by the sweat of one's brow also presumes the right to do so. A society in which this right is systematically denied, in which economic policies do not allow workers to reach satisfactory levels of employment, cannot be justified from an ethical point of view, nor can the society attain social peace."[9]

For Pope John Paul II, "protecting the rights and dignity of those who work" is part of his belief system, and a sacred trust of his ministry, but he also suggests that the "right to work" has political and economic dimensions. The right to work is based on philosophical and ethical propositions about how we define human nature and individual rights.

It is a fundamental human right, because it is a necessary condition for personhood at the most primary physical, moral, and psychological levels and, as such, "applies to all human beings simply by virtue of their being human." It is based not only on the accumulated teachings of the Catholic Church but also on a tenet of the Enlightenment: that no person is expendable. Recognition of this fact is required for individuals to have rights that must be respected by others. Since work is the way we establish and maintain ourselves, assert and come to know ourselves, work is one of the most fundamental of human rights.[10]

Alan Gerwirth, one of the leading ethicist of the day, has argued that the right to work is essential for individual survival, self-respect, and self-esteem. Therefore, he maintains that "all prospective purposive agents have a right to employment, a right to be effectively able to earn their livelihoods through their own productive work." As with all rights, says Gerwirth, the right to work is correlated with a "duty or responsibility to work." The duty to work suggests that no one has the right to be an intentional burden on others; moreover, individual workers cannot and should not, by their actions, impede or interfere with the rights of others to work. According to Gerwirth, both individuals and the state have a duty to refrain from interfering with a person's gaining productive employment. Such interference occurs when employment is denied due to a person's race, creed, ethnic status, sex, or sexual orientation, or any other criteria irrelevant to the performance of the job. Furthermore, Gerwirth argues that the state, as representative of the community of human rights, must, when necessary, correct market deficiencies to ensure that everyone who can work and is willing to work has a job. Gerwirth argues, echoing Franklin D. Roosevelt's New Deal and the United Nations' Universal Declaration of Human Rights, "Everyone has the right to work . . . and to protection against unemployment." Governments must play a major role in protecting the rights of individual workers because of their unique position to offset market inequities.[11]

For Gerwirth, Pope John Paul II, and many others who have written on the topic, the right to work does not mean a perfect job, a great salary, and a middle-class lifestyle. These are privileges, not rights; and within the present socioeconomic system they must be earned. The right to work is not about economic prosperity as measured by the sum total of goods and wealth that an individual possesses; it's about an "existence worthy of human dignity," "useful employment, just wages and decent work conditions," and a "fair share of earthly goods, sufficient for oneself and one's family." It's about individual rights and collective responsibilities. It's about establishing a just and secure threshold of opportunity.[12]

John Paul II was surely on to something when he observed that it is always men and women who are the purpose of work, not the other way around.[13] Few would disagree. And yet, while this statement may be true, for most of us the world of work remains an enduring mystery and paradox. Work, says social historian Theodore Roszak, can be a chance to innovate, fraternize, and serve. It can be an opportunity to learn and grow. It can be a fulfilling expression of the person, but it only rarely is. For most people, he says, work is a bore and a burden. It is something done for other people's profit, rarely for love.[14] In the words of one working mother, "The only reason I'm working is that every time I go to the grocery store the bill is twenty dollars more. I'm not working to develop myself. I'm not working to discover my identity. No way!"[15]

We have made work simultaneously compulsory and unsatisfactory. Work isn't about what we want to do, but what others tell us to do. Generations of Americans have viewed work as a place to make a living, but the living itself takes place only after hours—if at all. We accept that boring work is part of the human condition and hope that "living for the weekend" will at least be palliative if not curative.[16] We want work to offer us recognition and appreciation, the opportunity to be effective and to make a difference, the chance to really belong, but only rarely does any of this occur. "Do what you love, and the money will follow" is scoffed at as a pathetic example of management mottos. In work, says Matthew Fox, we are filled as well as emptied and rendered tasters of ecstasy as well as nothingness. And our work can bring out the divine or the demonic in us. "Was it not workers," asks Fox, "who built the ovens in the concentration camps and worker-politicians who conceived of the evil final solution in the first place?"[17]

In *The End of Ideology,* Daniel Bell wrote that work has "always stood at the center of moral consciousness" in Western culture—as a need, a duty, a corrective to idleness and as a necessary condition for the attainment of personal identity and the potential realization of our collective humanity.[18] It is this last component, "our collective humanity," or the concept of community, that Robert Bellah argues is conspicuously missing from our places of employment. Work, suggests Bellah, may be a right, a necessity, and our most common experience, but it is not a connecting link or a community-building experience.

Freedom is perhaps the most resonant, deeply held American value. The language of freedom—radical individualism—denigrates dependency and advocates self-reliance. It leads us to define and measure ourselves against others, not alongside them. It suggests that we find ourselves independently of other people and institutions, not through them.[19] The myth of rugged individualism suggests that we are self-created and self-sustaining, that we are competitive rather than cooperative by nature. It holds self-interest as a virtue, not a vice. Sadly, says Bellah, this emphasis on individual freedom, self-reliance, and hard work goes hand and hand with an isolating preoccupation with self. "The problem is not so much the presence or absence of a work ethic as the meaning of work and the ways it links, or fails to link, individuals to one another."[20]

Bellah believes we do not experience work as "a moral relationship between people."[21] Work is not "a way of cooperating" or a means of "dwelling together meaningfully and well."[22] Work is seen as the means by which we create our own history. The workplace is first and foremost where we compete to establish ourselves and only secondarily, when tied directly to a job description or the requirements of a specific task, to cooperate. It means that while we may be on a work team, we are not truly *members* of the team. The team is only a vehicle for the achievement of individual well-being. Our membership and cooperation is based on necessity and need, not genuine camaraderie. Like many professional athletes in the age of free agency, we are all playing for ourselves.

The problem, according to Bellah, is that the way work is organized and rewarded in America today exacerbates rather than eliminates workers' feelings of isolation and dissatisfaction. And just how is modern work organized and rewarded? According to Robert Kanigel, there is only one possible answer—Taylorism, named after efficiency expert Frederick Winslow Taylor, which states "The application of scientific methods to the problem of obtaining maximum efficiency in industrial work or the like." Taylor, champion of Scientific Management, is long dead, but his legacy—or enduring curse—lives on says Benjamin Hunnicutt: Study, measure, and regiment every aspect of work life in order to guarantee the most efficient outcome and profit.[23]

Kanigel, author of the Taylor biography *The One Best Way,* believes that Taylor must be credited with modern business life's "fierce" and "unholy concern" with efficiency. Taylorism, says Kanigel, has forever changed the tempo and production levels of our working lives. Although the particular calculations of Taylor's original time-motion studies are no longer discussed and *The Principles of Scientific Management,* is no longer read, Taylor's credo of rational efficiency has burned itself into the modern mind.[24] Taylor's vision of man and machine working by a "system" has been applied, as an approach and a general way of looking at the world, to every aspect of work and life.

Jeremy Rifkin has written that Taylor "made efficiency the *modus operandi* of American industry and the cardinal virtue of American culture. His work principles have been transported to every sector of the globe and have been responsible for converting much of the world's population to the modern time frame."[25] "Organized, planned, scheduled to the hilt?" asks Kanigel. "No time to stop and smell the roses? Taylor deserves a dollop of the blame."[26] Taylorism, writes Neil Postman, constitutes "the scaffolding of present-day American Technolopy . . . the idea that society is best served when human beings are placed at the disposal of their techniques and technology."[27]

Henry Ford and Frederick Winslow Taylor are recognized as the twin icons of the modern industrial state, but, Kanigel suggests that Taylor has had the more profound, long-lasting, and wide-ranging impact. Ford may have created and perfected the first major assembly-line system, but it was built on the foundations of Taylor's theories.

Part and parcel of Taylor's theories of how "best to work," says Benjamin Hunnicutt, were his assumptions about the nature of work and why workers bother to work. According to Hunnicutt, for Taylor "work exists to make products and services people need, not to act as some sort of eleemosynary academy for the improvement of workers' personalities and souls."[28] Work is about making something, earning a living; it is not supposed to be fun. People work for money, so that they can have a life off the job, not on it. Pay people more, said Taylor, for doing more, working faster and more efficiently, and everybody comes out ahead. Then as now, suggests Hunnicutt, "decision making by costs goes to the very heart of a market economy."[29] No matter what bromides we use, capitalism and, by extension, the security of its workers are dependent on achieving output and profits and doing so in the most efficient man-

> ner possible. For Taylor, romantic notions about work being creative, providing some sort of community of brothers, and so on, are pipe dreams—products of the overheated imaginations of people who have little contact with real work and real workers.[30]

In a setting where individual workers must constantly compete with the system, themselves and fellow workers, a genuine sense of community cannot and will not occur. This competition of each against the other may be a partial explanation for the growing phenomenon of individuals and families moving to small towns across America.

In 1997 *Time* magazine reported that a new kind of "white flight" is happening in America today. Unlike the middle-class exodus from large multiethnic cities of a generation ago, the new migration is from suburbia to small towns and rural counties. In the 1980s rural areas suffered a net loss of 1.4 million people, but in the 1990s it has enjoyed a net inflow of 2 million people. In other words, 2 million more people have moved from metropolitan centers to rural areas than have gone the opposite direction. Most of these emigres from urban life are able to move, of course, because of the powerful technological forces that are decentralizing the American economy. The Internet and the overnight-shipping industry are enabling industries once tied to urban centers to settle in the countryside, thereby creating jobs for skilled workers literally anywhere. As Jeremy Rifkin has pointed out, the information age has made work more portable and less dependent on the concentration of large factories and heavy machinery. With computers, information workers are at work anyplace they can plug into an outlet, boot up, and get on-line. But beyond the fact that many cutting-edge firms are relocating to small towns, workers are not just following them for the jobs. Besides wanting to escape from the noise, congestion, and high costs of urban existence, they want to improve their "quality of life."

Time suggests that these new migrants are acting out a fantasy shared by tens of millions of Americans. They want the chance to reinvent their lives in places that seem purer, safer, more secure, and more close-knit. They believe that in rural America they won't get lost. They'll become a part of a community where people actually know their neighbors and maybe even make a difference and leave a mark.[31]

In *City Life,* architect and social commentator Witold Rybczynski reflects on why people live in cities and what we want out of them.

Although, says Rybczynski, we did not begin as a nation of urban dwellers, we are one now.[32] At the time of the Revolutionary War only 3 percent lived in urban settings; the rest lived in rural-agricultural areas. By 1993, this ratio was more than reversed with 98 percent of us living in urban enclaves and only 2 percent living in the rural areas. To be exact, most of us don't live in *cities,* but in metropolitan areas—central cities and their adjacent residential and commercial suburbs. To qualify for the designation, a metro area must contain fifty thousand people. Currently there are more than three hundred metro areas in the United States and twenty-five in Canada.[33]

Even though the vast majority of Americans will forever remain urban dwellers, both out of choice and necessity, many of us are not entirely happy with our living arrangements. According to Rybczynski, when Americans were asked "Where would you choose to live if you could live anywhere: in a city, suburb, small town, in the country?" well over one-third said they would prefer a small town. Even more striking, says Rybczynski, is when those surveyed are asked to mentally sketch out their picture of a small town, the images they came up with were all very familiar and very much the same: A population of not more than 10,000, to allow for more effective self-government, a main street lined with stores and offices, well lighted, and with broad sidewalks, a town hall in the center of downtown and surrounded by a public park, churches at the ends of Main Street that serve as pillars of the town, private homes well spaced, with broad lawns and front porches facing the street, and, finally, an abundance of large-canopy trees.[34]

Part of the reason so many of us prefer Main Street to Wall Street is, of course, romanticism. Think of some of our most cherished plays, films, TV and radio shows: Thorton Wilder's *Our Town*, Frank Capra's *It's a Wonderful Life, The Andy Griffith Show,* Garrison Keillor's *A Prairie Home Companion.* All of these evoke images of secure, pedestrian-based, well-manicured small towns that are insulated from the fast-paced urban world.

Rybczynski suggests that it is not just the physical attributes of a small town that attract us. The longing for community, stability, and a sense of permanence play a large role. It may well be that the best and worst part of living in a small town is the same thing—everybody knows everybody. The appeal of a small town speaks to one of the central paradoxes of the human condition: We are by nature at one and the same time egocentric and self-centered and in need of others and desirous of community. If we cannot find it in our work, we will search for it where we may.

Charles Handy perhaps said it best:

> We are not meant to stand alone. We need to belong—to something or someone. Only where there is mutual commitment will you find people prepared to deny themselves for the good of others. . . . Loneliness may be the real disease of the next century, as we live alone, work alone, and play alone, insulated by our modem, our Walkman, or our television. . . . It is no longer clear where we connect or to where we belong. If, however, we belong to nothing, the point of striving is hard to see.[35]

No matter what our individual jobs and circumstances, too many of us feel that our lives as workers have been a failure because work has failed to give us what we need. The failure of work manifests itself in many ways: diminished self-esteem, toil without dignity, long hours on the job, poor pay, and the growing financial disparity between rank and file (the typical CEO in the 1990s made 150 times the average worker's pay),[36] petty bureaucratic politics, the purposelessness of many of our tasks, the gnawing lack of creativity, fulfillment, and genuine sense of involvement on the job, the absence of autonomy, the increasing sense of isolation, excessive competitiveness, ineffective and inept leadership, physical and psychological enervation, feeling trapped in a system that primarily promotes products and profits over people, and the absence of the simple expectation of reward and recognition for a job well done. Unless these and other failures are addressed, work will remain for most of us a "disutility"—something that people do as a means to put bread on the table, not as an end—and the term *meaningful work* will forever remain an oxymoron.

And now to add to our collective woes are the warnings of the possibility of no work and the specter of permanent joblessness for the vast majority of the global workforce. Jeremy Rifkin's worst-case scenario is a formula for despair and disaster. No society can long sustain itself when most people do not work and are maintained by the efforts and taxes of an elite working minority. What is more likely to ensue is a model much like the one William Julius Wilson offers us in regard to the African-

American experience: a disenfranchized, unemployable underclass caught in a "culture of worklessness" and sequestered in urban pockets where the only options are welfare or crime.

There are, of course, some commentators who look on Rifkin's predictions of a workerless world as the fulfillment of the utopian dreams of the working class—plenty, or at least sufficiency, without struggle or strife and the unlimited leisure to enjoy it. The machine in the service of humankind can mean freedom, redemption, and relief from the burdens of labor. It can mean that every man and woman will no longer have to spend their lives grubbing for a living but rather can give themselves over to creative thinking, to art, to science, or to play. But, says science fiction writer Frederick Pohl, be very careful what you wish for, because sometimes the excesses of wealth can be as destructive to the human spirit as the burdens of poverty.

In his novel *Midas World,* Pohl creates a futuristic scenario wherein technology is king. Cold fusion has been achieved. Power became plentiful and cheap. It was used to rebuild cities and restore the ecology. Deserts were made to bloom. Crops multiplied. Automatic machines became smart machines, human-sized robots, and androids. These robots became the workforce, the servants and slaves. They did everything for society, or almost. They made gadgets and hardware, built the homes, maintained the cities, cooked the meals, and so on. The only thing that robots couldn't do was to solve the fundamental conundrum of a capitalist economy: Production requires consumption. Robots can build cars, but robots cannot buy them. This task was left to their masters. In Pohl's fictional world, plentitude had to be consumed for plenty to be maintained. The human nonworkers of this plentiful world had but one task—to continuously consume. Everyone was required to have "too much of everything" in order to keep the system going. Plenty became a duty, and consuming became a constant chore. But there were also rewards built into the system. If, over time, one proved to be a model citizen, he or she was granted the "ultimate prize"—a job, real work, something to do besides consuming.

In Pohl's vision of technological utopia, the truly rich consume less, have less, and, most important, have a job. The poor, on the other hand, were condemned to live in houses designed for their comfort and entertainment. Their grinding poverty further condemned them to never being hungry and never lacking for anything—except for the "greatest luxury in the world, work!"[37]

Although it is true that the information age will make us less dependent on human capital or human labor to do some of the jobs that must be done, work and the need of workers to work will never entirely go away. It is not in our nature to be idle. Tasks that machines cannot handle will still need to be done. Toil and tinkering are still basic requirements of the human condition. As a society we cannot choose to disregard the human need for work in order to better satisfy the utilitarian needs of production.

In a bizarre but believable mystery entitled *The Ax,* Donald F. Westlake paints a dark tale of Burke Devore, a quiet, ordinary, middle-aged victim of technological downsizing who, in the pursuit of the last possible job available for a man of his age and qualifications, goes about it in a most extraordinary way: He systematically murders all of the other potential candidates. He anonymously guns down some of his victims in the street, but he actually gets to meet and know a few of them before he kills them. Over lunch with one of his intended victims, they discuss the rash of layoffs that have hit their industry. The victim says:

> You know, I been thinking about it. I haven't had much to do, the last couple of years, except think about it, and I think this society's gone nuts. . . . You know, there's been societies like primitive people in Asia and the like that, they expose newborn babies on hillsides to kill them off, so they won't have to feed them and take care of them. And there's been societies, like the early Eskimos, that put their real old folks out on icebergs to float away and die, because they couldn't take care of them any more. But this is the first society ever that takes its most productive people, at their prime, at the peak of their powers and throws them away. I call that crazy.[38]

The soon-to-be victim and his murderer argue that they both have skills, want to work, need to work but can't find work. As labor reformer and photographer Lewis Wickes Hine has suggested in a more scholarly, less dramatic way, human capital is our only true capital as well as our one basic resource. "Cities do not build themselves . . . machines cannot make machines—unless, back of them all, are the brains and the toil of men."[39]

Jobs are disposable; workers are not. There is no viable alternative to work. To eliminate work is to eliminate the principal means by which we come to know and identify ourselves, and one of the primary sources of our sense of dependence upon and need of others. The worker is the key ingredient and purpose of all work. To be stripped of work is to be denied access to our full humanity. Jeremy Rifkin illustrates this with the story of George Wilkinson, a laid-off manager of a small tool company, who put it this way in a clinical session with his psychologist: "There's only two worlds: either you work every day in a normal nine-to-five job with a couple of weeks vacation, or you're dead! There's no in between. . . . Working is breathing. It's something you don't think about: you just do it and it keeps you alive. When you stop you die." A year after making these remarks and still without work, Mr. Wilkinson killed himself with a shotgun.[40]

The Future of Work

> I am a true laborer: I earn what I eat, get what I wear, owe no man hate, envy no man's happiness, glad of other men's good.
>
> —William Shakespeare

EVEN WITH ALL OF ITS FAILINGS, WORK MUST BE saved. Work cannot go away, because it underlies all that we are as human beings. Work is the foundation, the precondition, for all that we do, acquire, and become. Neither the basic needs and necessities nor the highest intellectual and artistic achievements can be fulfilled without work. But, if Jeremy Rifkin is right that the information age is re-creating the nature of work and the marketplace, then we must revise, redefine, and reformulate what we mean by work. In other words, if work is the way we are molded and made, we must remake the work that makes us. The future of work will require new models, new metaphors, and a new sense of motivation. A large part of the task of redefining work will be political, social, and economic. The marketplace can no longer be seen as the only or even the primary catalyst for work. Valuable work can no longer be measured by money alone, and jobs traditionally far down the social and economic scales must be reinfused with dignity and meaning. Work must be recast to fit the needs of both individuals and the communities of which they are a part. Work must recapture its true purpose: To produce products people need and to help produce better people.

Short-Term Options

Arguing that work is the backbone of social integration, economist Edmund S. Phelps, in his important book *Rewarding Work,* maintains that as a society we must immediately address the pressing problems of the underclass and the growing proportion of the workforce that earns one-third or less of the median wage. Phelps lists the central economic and social problems facing us today as increasing structural unemployment, the decline in the market value of work, and the minimal adequacy of the welfare system to maintain the lives and well-being of those enrolled in it. Collectively, Phelps argues, these factors prohibit millions of workers and families from participating in "the mainstream way of life, with its bourgeois values."[1] Moreover, he claims that these individuals represent a serious social threat as well as a debilitating economic drain on the system.

Like William Julius Wilson, Phelps believes that poverty perpetuates poverty and that the cycle of poverty "fuels feelings of powerlessness and desperation, leading to idleness and dependency, and possibly drugs, crime, and violence."[2] Although Phelps maintains that some form of a minimal welfare system will always be necessary, the present melange of available programs and benefits have worsened rather than helped to relieve the problems of poverty and unemployment. In his view it simply makes no economic sense to work at a near-minimum-wage job for $10,000 per year when the possible benefits from various welfare programs can equal $13,000 per year. Again like Wilson, Phelps believes that the real problem of joblessness is not merely economic, but rather social-psychological—the loss of self-reliance and self-respect, disenfranchisement from the system, and the danger that long-term unemployment hardens into the condition of permanent "unemployability."[3]

The solution to the problems of unemployment, civil and political unrest, and the erosion of mainstream standards, says Phelps, is direct and cost-efficient. Rather than welfare entitlements—payments for doing nothing—employers should be given subsidies to hire low-skilled but competent workers and augment their base pay. These subsidies would have many effects: reduce the unemployment rate of low-skilled workers; put the paychecks of low-wage workers closer to the median scale; decrease the unemployed worker's feelings of exclusion, dependency, and powerlessness; inculcate the habits of self-efficacy and self-sufficiency; and increase employees' incentive to better themselves.

In brief, Phelps says that a graduated subsidy should be given to those in the lowest paying jobs until their promotions and pay increases bring them closer to the median wage, which he sets at $25,000 per year. For example an employer willing to hire someone for $5.00 per hour ($10,000 per year) will be given a subsidy of $3.00 per hour in order to bring the taxable wage up to $8.00 an hour ($16,000 per year). Phelps argues that bad pay, like welfare, creates a deterrent to work. Although $16,000 per year is by no means a sumptuous wage, it does represent $3,000 more than the maximum welfare benefits. Phelps maintains that the real economic costs per year of this subsidy program are less than the current cost of welfare benefits. He claims that as a nation we presently spend between $150 billion and $185 billion a year on welfare, whereas he estimates that his program would cost between $110 billion and $125 billion in 1997 dollars. More important, at the social and moral level, Phelps claims that low-wage employment subsidies will reestablish traditional norms within communities that accept not working as the norm, renew economic vitality to the inner cities, decrease the economic temptation and necessity of criminal activity and drug dealing, reduce the costs of achieving public safety (via police) and justice (via court systems), and reduce the costs of AACS, food stamp programs, and Medicaid payments. Low-wage employment subsidies, says Phelps, "are the most effective instrument we have available to re-create lost opportunities for work and self-support, to restore inclusion and cohesion and to reclaim responsibility for yourself and others."[4]

Phelps's plan appears to offer many benefits, and it warrants careful consideration. However, even if Phelps's proposal has real merit in the short run, it fails to take into account the futuristic scenario of an increasingly automated and jobless society. Phelps, as a market economist, is locked into much of the conventional wisdom of his craft, that is to say the market system, which sometimes with a little extra prodding, operates to produce the greatest good for the greatest number. His credo is an age-old one: High employment and direct wages means people are working, producing, and generating sufficient wealth to afford the products and services of others which in turn allows them to continue working, producing, generating wealth, and consuming. Supposedly the "cycle of prosperity" will be unending—jobs engendering jobs, and wages stimulating wages. Phelps believes that "with the productive population back at work and able to support themselves and meet basic responsibilities, families will flourish again and children will do well." Or, so goes the theory. But as Phelps himself pointed out, "Theory, like wishing, does not make a proposition so."[5]

Although Jeremy Rifkin is convinced that in the long run "the emerging knowledge sector will not be able to create enough new jobs to absorb the millions of workers displaced by re-engineering and automation," in the short run, he too offers a few proposals to temporarily stabilize the shrinking job market.[6] Ironically, in the face of his own projections regarding the diminishing job pool, Rifkin argues for a policy of full employment in order to ensure an equitable distribution of the fruits and benefits of technological progress. However, full employment for Rifkin does not mean that people will work a forty-plus-hour, five- to six-day schedule. Building on the Italian unionist slogan—*lavorare meno, lavorare tutti* (work less, and everyone works)—Rifkin is convinced that governments and industries must recognize their obligation "to maintain and create jobs through the reduction of working time in order to achieve greater equity at a time of very high and rising unemployment."[7] As machines increasingly replace workers in every industry and occupation, the choice will be between a few people being employed for longer hours while large numbers of workers (an estimated 20 million to 30 million additional people) are jobless and on the public dole, or spreading the available work out and giving more workers the opportunity to share shorter weekly work schedules.[8]

Rifkin points out that there are a number of successful examples already in place, and Volkswagen, Europe's largest automaker, is perhaps the best example to date. In 1992 Ferdinand Piëch, grandson of the original designer of the Beetle, became chairman of VW. Piëch inherited a company hobbled by high labor costs and lackluster models and sales. In 1993 VW adopted, with worker support and approval, a thirty-hour, four-day workweek in order to cut costs and save 31,000 jobs that might have been lost to competition and new technologies. The results were immediate and, Piëch claims, "the key to our survival." The four-day workweek cut $800 million in expenses. That, combined with other cost-cutting measures and the introduction of new models including the "new Beetle" in 1997–98, has reestablished VW as a major player in the world auto industry.[9]

There are, of course, problems to overcome with Rifkin's proposal for a reduced workweek for all. To begin with, many companies prefer to employ a smaller workforce at longer hours rather than a larger one at shorter hours, to save the costs of providing additional benefits. Second, although many workers desire more time off, few want to cut their take-home pay. Workers must be willing to embrace the idea of a shorter workweek as an acceptable alternative to large-scale permanent layoffs. Management analyst Michael Hammer points out yet another weakness in Rifkin's idea: You can reduce the workweek only "if everybody does it." Hammer contends that even "if you're going to pay people the same amount for less hours of work, then you're basically raising the cost of your products, and you can only do that if everyone is willing to go along with it."[10] Finally, Rifkin believes that corporate resistance to the shorter workweek will soften only when companies become more aware of the "need to bridge the gap between greater productive capacity and falling consumer purchasing power."[11] Rifkin urges that corporations and CEOs must recognize that it makes good business sense to keep people employed. The shorter workweek isn't just an issue of social equity, but a short-term tactic for economic survival. Inevitably, says Rifkin, we're going to need fewer and fewer workers, and, in a postmarket economy, we are going to have to develop a more comprehensive strategy to cope with a time when most formal work will have passed from human beings to machines.

Long-Term Options

William Julius Wilson argues that the old economic orthodoxy (technical innovation and rising productivity will guarantee a full-employment economy) is being discredited with every labor-saving machine that is installed on a work site. It is a naive and bankrupt notion, suggests Wilson, to believe that an unfettered marketplace will produce the greatest good for the greatest number. The conventional belief that an upturn in the business cycle will automatically solve most of our social and economic problems has been debunked by the ability of the system to increase productivity while reducing the number of jobs and thus widening the divide between the haves and the have-nots.[12]

Wilson insists that we are morally obligated to fight joblessness and the problems of social inequality that threaten the very fabric of our society. Welfare was a well-intended idea that has not worked. We cannot afford, financially or ethically, to keep paying people to stay unemployed indefinitely.[13] We need, says Wilson, to address the simultaneous problems of economic growth, joblessness, and wage inequities. No matter what the structural restraints imposed by the information age, Wilson argues that work remains the only way out. We must create programs that create work, so that people can create themselves.

The primary function of government, suggests Wilson, is to do those things that the people cannot do for themselves or that the private sector is unwilling or no longer able to do. If labor market changes have permanently reduced private-sector demand for low-skilled workers, then the government must become the employer of last resort and provide social safety nets for those unable to work. Simply put, if private-sector jobs are not available, then public-sector jobs must be created. "It's quite clear," says Wilson, "that we're going to have to revive discussion of the need for WPA-style jobs."[14]

It can be argued that Roosevelt's Works Progress Administration, Truman's GI Bill, and Eisenhower's National Defense Highway Act are the most successful government programs ever enacted because of the projects they produced and the numbers of people they employed and educated. The WPA was announced by Roosevelt in his State of the Union address in 1935 and was proposed as a public works program to create jobs for millions of Americans trapped in the unemployment cycle of the Depression. According to Mickey Kaus in *The New Republic*:

> In its eight-year existence . . . the WPA built or improved 651,000 miles of roads, 953 airports, 124,000 bridges and viaducts, 1,178,000 culverts, 8,000 parks, 10,000 playgrounds and athletic fields, and 2,000 swimming pools. It constructed 40,000 buildings (including 8,000 schools) and repaired 85,000 more. Much of New York City—including LaGuardia Airport, FDR Drive, plus hundreds of parks and libraries—was built by the WPA. . . . Lester Thurow has suggested that New York's infrastructure is now decaying because no WPA has existed to replace these public works in the half-century since.[15]

The GI Bill has been called "the law that changed America" because it sent 8 million returning World War II veterans to college or trade school.[16] Most of these young men were children of the Depression, and many of them went from the Civil Conservation Core to the WPA to the army without finishing their educations or fully preparing themselves for a career or a trade. The formula for government-subsidized betterment was simple and effective: one day of tuition for every day of military time served. Colleges and universities were overrun with twenty-five-year-old freshmen, and trade and technical schools couldn't keep up with the demand for admissions. From the government's point of view, the Depression and the war had created a generation of unprepared workers. From the veteran's point of view, education equaled employability. The GI Bill was a perfect symbiotic relationship, and it set the stage for the postwar boom in goods, services, salaries, and lifestyles.

Dwight D. Eisenhower was the father of the interstate highway program because of his experiences in the military. As a young officer on a training exercise, it had once taken him sixty-two days to lead an Army convoy across America. World War II also taught him the immediate combat benefits of broad, well-maintained highways for troop movement and deployment. Although Eisenhower's motives for building 43,000 miles of stoplight-free roads linking every major city in America may have been primarily based on military logistics, its civilian benefits far exceeded the costs of this forty-year project. The car culture became king, the trucking industry thrived, hotels and motels popped up across the land, suburbia flourished, the fast-food burger became a national staple, and state and local communities created patronage fiefdoms building and maintaining access roads and inner-city expressways that feed into the interstate system.[17]

Wilson argues that although the costs of contemporary versions of the WPA, GI Bill, and interstate system will be high, the costs of not priming the system will be incalculably higher in terms of joblessness, social instability, and the worsening economic life of urban families and neighborhoods. Too many workers will simply not be able to find jobs, says Wilson, unless the government becomes both the employer and social service provider of last resort.[18] What we need today, he says, is a combination of jobs, education, child care, and universal health care that is "race neutral" and open to anyone and everyone in order to close the growing gap between the haves and the have-nots in our society.[19] We need "public service infrastructure maintenance jobs" that include road repair, and painting bridges. We need "public service jobs" such as playground, gymnasium, and library assistants, nurse's aides, clerks, cooks, and child-care helpers. Finally, says Wilson, we need a massive neo-WPA program for the construction of new highways, stadiums, schools, hospitals, playgrounds, and subways.[20]

Jeremy Rifkin also believes that we must begin making long-term plans to harness the unused energy and labor of the growing numbers of people who will be unemployed in the postmarket era. The commodity value of labor in the production and distribution of goods and services will dwindle, and new approaches to provide personal identity, social status, income, and purchasing power will need to be implemented.[21]

A large part of Rifkin's solution, like Wilson's, is dependent upon the government's recognition of its responsibility to be the employer of last resort as well as its ability to extend tax credits and provide a living social wage to those who can no longer find work in a rapidly diminishing private-market sector. However, Rifkin believes that the government must do much more than just finance and set up model economic Empowerment Zones in a select number of inner cities. Furthermore, he does not believe that a massive public-works programs to fix the country's bridges and tunnels, mend highways, and create high-speed rail and mass transit will be enough to sustain our long-term social and economic needs.

For Rifkin, neither the marketplace nor government spending in the public sector will be enough to address our social and economic problems of the near future. We must now turn to the third sector—the social economy, the sector of community organizations and independent or voluntary groups—if we hope to sustain political stability and the allied concepts of self-worth and self-sufficiency.

In the 1830s Alexis de Tocqueville, French statesman and philosopher, claimed that the single most important characteristic of American life was our propensity, even compulsion, to create and join associations (groups of like-minded individuals coming together for a common purpose) for any and every issue. Rifkin agrees: "The independent sector is the bonding force, the social glue that helps unite the diverse interests of the American people into a cohesive social identity. If there is a single defining characteristic that sums up the unique qualities of being an American, it would be our capacity to join together in voluntary associations to serve one another."[22] Many of the institutions that define and describe the American way of life were created by the third sector; these include the nation's first schools, colleges, and universities; hospitals, social service organizations; theaters, libraries, museums; civic associations; and volunteer fire departments.[23] Anthropologist Margaret Mead once remarked, "If you look closely you will see that almost anything that really matters to us, anything that embodies our deepest commitment to the way human life should be lived and cared for depends on some form—often many forms—of volunteerism."[24] Like de Tocqueville, Rifkin is convinced that volunteerism is a catalyst for community, and a critical ingredient in the maintenance of a democratic way of life.

According to Rifkin, the business sector presently makes up 80 percent of the gross national product (GNP), the government sector accounts for 14 percent, and the independent sector contributes approximately 6 percent of the GNP and is responsible for 9 percent of the total national employment. In fewer than fifty years, suggests Rifkin, these figures could and perhaps should be turned on their head, until approximately 80 percent of the workforce is involved in the social-sector effectively rebuilding thousands of local communities and creating a way of life that flourishes independent of the marketplace and the public sector. As fewer people are needed in the formal market economy, says Rifkin, legislation will need to be enacted to provide millions of permanently unemployed Americans with meaningful work in community services.[25] He warns that the options facing the government are stark: Either finance additional police protection and build more jails to incarcerate a growing and desperate workless class who turn to crime as their only economic option, or finance alternative forms of work in the third sector that ties a guaranteed wage to community service.[26]

According to George Bush's "Thousand Points of Light" speech in 1988, in which he praised the volunteer sector as the spiritual backbone of the American democratic spirit, and Colin Powell's 1997 "call to action, service, and voluteerism" to save our children and our communities, Rifkin suggests that seed money and self-help are the only realistic ways to rebuild our local infrastructures. He wants to find a way to harness and fund community-based volunteer programs that will give people something to do, support community needs, and afford people recognition and self-worth. Rifkin advocates not a massive, federally directed Marshall Plan, but a *marshaling* of talent and energy to produce an immediate effect on both local communities and society as a whole.[27]

Rifkin warns that the transition from a society based on mass employment in the private sector to one based on nonmarket criteria for organizing social life will require a rethinking of our current economic worldview, as well as a fundamental restructuring of our present understanding of the social contract as it exists between the market, government, and the social economies:

> Community service is a revolutionary alternative to traditional forms of labor. Unlike slavery, serfdom, and wage labor, it is neither coerced nor reduced to a fiduciary relationship. Community service is a helping action, a reaching out to others. It is an act entered into willingly and often without expectation of material gain. In this sense, it is more akin to the ancient economics of gift giving. Community service stems from a deep understanding of the interconnectedness of all things and is motivated by a personal sense of indebtedness. It is, first and foremost, a social exchange, although often with economic consequences to both the beneficiary and the benefactor. In this regard, community activity is substantially different from market activity, in which the exchange is always material and financial and where the social consequences are less important than the economic gains and losses.[28]

No matter how difficult the transition will be, we must as a nation address the question raised by Robert Reich, "What do we owe one another as members of the same society who no longer inhabit the same economy?"[29]

Philosophical Options

The large-scale remedies and alternatives offered by Phelps, Wilson, and Rifkin, are as yet untried and untested. None of them stands out as intuitively correct or clearly preferable. and all of them are dependent upon a complex calculus of economic strategizing, political will, and policy manipulation. There is no one perfect formula to achieve a balanced economy, meaningful employment, and a stable infrastructure. Nevertheless, as Charles Handy argues in *The Hungry Spirit,* "We have today the opportunity, which is also the challenge, to shape ourselves, even to reinvent ourselves."[30] Part of this reinvention is, I think, directly dependent upon reanalyzing how we look at work and reinfusing all work with dignity.

Theodore Roosevelt was undoubtedly right when he suggested that the best prize that life can offer us is the chance to work hard at work worth doing. The problem is, of course, that not all jobs are intrinsically meaningful, obviously purposeful, interesting, or engaging. Although we cannot always change the nature of the work, we can, however, affect the morale of the workers and the attitudes of society.

No work that needs doing should be considered demeaning, and all work that must be done deserves praise, recognition, and just compensation. The workbench and the plough are the bases of civilization and human solidarity. Even those with the most highly regarded positions today, such as doctor, lawyer, business executive, or academic, are, most likely, in the not too distant past directly related to someone who dug a ditch, reefed a sail, drove a truck, or toiled in a factory to help us get to where we are today. Surely Thomas Carlyle was guilty of romantic idealism when he said, "Work is the grand cure of all the maladies and miseries that ever beset mankind." And surely he was correct when he suggested that work that must be done is noble and in the doing we are ennobled. Biblical injunctions aside, work is not a curse—but drudgery without dignity, betterment, and respect is!

My Uncle Mike worked construction most of his adult life. Uncle Mike both loved and hated his job. Being a construction worker wasn't his idea of perfect work, but he took pride in being able to do the job:

> You do what you gotta do. You think I wanted to spend my life bustin' my ass pushin' cement and hauling bricks up two flights of scaffolding? Don't be stupid. But, it was honest work. I got treated good and I made a decent living. During the Depression I had to quit school to help out my old man. Like everybody else, I took what I could get. I did anything that came my way. I did janitor work, worked down on the docks, and even worked for a junk collector for a while. Believe me, I felt really lucky when I got hired by this construction crew to dig ditches and do whatever other scut work there was. I was making eighty-five cents an hour before I got drafted in 1942.
>
> When I got out of the service I had a wife and a kid, but no education. The GI Bill was for guys who wanted to go to college or get a trade—I couldn't do that, I had to find a job right away. There was a building boom goin' on and my old boss took me back. I wanted to lay bricks, but the union was tight and I didn't have the boost [bribe] to buy my way in. So, anyway, I settled for [concrete] finishing and general yard work. It wasn't so bad—at least till I

> turned about forty-five—then everything hurt all the time. But you gotta expect that. Anyway, I can't complain. I got a nice house, three good kids, and the wife never really had to work—except for a long layoff or she wanted something really special.

Uncle Mike died at the age of fifty-eight of a massive heart attack on the job pushing a wheelbarrow. He was tan, slim but muscular, stoop-shouldered, and all gray. He looked closer to seventy-five than his actual age. It wan't just the job that killed him (four packs of Camels a day and a steady diet of homemade Chianti also contributed to his demise). At the funeral I remember people saying to Aunt Annie, "He was a good man and a hard worker." I think Uncle Mike would have agreed with them.

In 1988 George Bush told a Los Angeles high school graduating class, "You don't have to go to college to be a success. . . . We need the people who run the offices, the people who do the hard physical work of our society." Liberal pundits were appalled and thought Bush's comments patronizing. Jesse Jackson denounced Bush for "gross insensitivity," telling a cheering university crowd: "Let *him* shine shoes! *You* keep going to college!" Although both men were guilty of dramatic overstatement, both statements contain an element of truth. Our society will always need both blue- and white-collar workers to survive and thrive. As former Xerox CEO David Kearns put it, "We can't have a world-class economy without a world-class workforce, from senior scientists to stockroom clerks."[31]

Respect in this country is based on class, and class is directly dependent on education, job status, and pay. Syndicated columnist William Raspberry once said that although work is our most common link, it also divides us, keeps as separate, and makes us afraid of each other. He argued that we are doing something awful to our young people: we are teaching them contempt for manual labor. Manual labor is not something we want our kids to do. We want our kids to go to college and become professionals, and we are alarmed if our kids tell us that they are thinking of a career as an electrician or a carpenter or a transmission specialist. It's not because the jobs don't pay enough, but because they lack prestige. Such a mentality, Raspberry suggests, races us faster toward a two-tiered society and impossibly widens the gulf between the knowledge-elite and the worker-drones.[32]

Capitalism, as it is presently structured, makes the goal of a perfectly classless society, at best, a utopia. Nevertheless, we must develop a new vision of work, a vision that neither demeans nor denigrades necessary toil. A vision of work, to quote Theodore Roszak, in which "the doing is as important as what gets done, the making as valuable as the made."[33] A vision of work under which devotion to useful and necessary tasks confers a special dignity and worth on the worker. A vision of work that maintains that every job must offer respect, independence, and hope. A vision of work that understands the subtleties and nuances of John Gardner's famous admonition:

> The society that scorns excellence in plumbing because it is a humble activity, yet accepts shoddiness in philosophy because it is an exalted activity, will have neither good plumbing nor good philosophy, and as a result neither its pipes nor its theories will hold water.[34]

We need a vision that recognizes and honors the precept that, minimally, work must do two things—maintain life and add to it.

Epilogue

> If I enjoy my work, if it is "play" or "fun" or "creative," then work is not only an "economic activity."
>
> —Raymond Benton

TOO MANY OF US COME HOME AT THE END OF the day feeling like the "working wounded." If we were lucky, we made some money and managed to maintain our self-respect. Only a few of us feel that our work is worth doing, and fewer still feel that they like what they do and work well at doing it. Too many of us feel that we are caught in unavoidable, low-prestige tasks. Most of us have jobs or careers, but few of us can claim to have a vocation that makes a contribution and really counts. To paraphrase psychologist Otto Rank, work is for most of us a livelihood and not a living. Only a few of us feel engaged, energized, or ennobled by what we do. Most of us feel used rather than useful.[1] Sadly, most of us settle for the standard compromise—a salary that we hope will offer us some solace off the job. As poet Donald Hall suggests: "When work is utterly disagreeable and week awaits weekend, our delight in recreation reveals our misery."[2] Too many of us intuitively understand why the basic term for work, job, is spelled the same way as the name of the long-suffering and patient character in the Bible, Job.

Of course, some people are happy in their work. My longtime collaborator Terry Sullivan has said that "some people are lucky, others are artists—defined by John Dewey as people who get paid to do what they would do anyway. Some others are artists of their own psyches—folks who can manage to make the best of any situation and wring a measure of satisfaction from the humblest, most back- and spirit-breaking occupations. For at least as many, however, work's a chain gang—from the modern stoop-laborers hunkered in the glow of a million cathode ray tubes to untold legions asking us if we'd like fries with that."[3]

But whether we are happy or numbed by what we do, work we must, and, like it or not, our work is the mark of our humanity. Work will never be completely free of disappointment, drudgery, and toil, but all work should, at least, offer the possibility of purpose and hope. In the words of Joseph Conrad: "I don't like work—no man does—but I like what is in work—the chance to find yourself. Your own reality . . . "[4]

Arthur Dobrin offers the following definition:

WORK

> A labor of love is the work we do not because we are paid but because of the satisfactions it provides. A labor of love cannot be indifferent work, for love cancels out indifference. It is done to the best of our ability because we want to give our best for its own sake. We care so much for what we do that we take the care to do it properly.
>
> When labor is not that of love, then how can we talk about it? Is it a labor of hate, is it work without care, is it something done without feeling? It is utopian to think that we can love all our work. We cannot always find the perfect fit; sometimes the fit is fractured. But it is demeaning to think that we must separate labor and love. For work without love is servitude.
>
> Work and love together define our humanness. A humane world creates a place for both to exist, to make room for both, even to have the two together.
>
> To hate our work is to breed hatefulness, it is to fragment our lives so that we may never fit the pieces together again.
>
> Work we must, but what work we do, the way we use our time, the manner in which we labor is more than a statement about our values: they are the values themselves.[5]

Notes

Preface

1. Jeffrey K. Salkin, *Being God's Partner* (Woodstock, VT: Jewish Lights Press, 1994), 156.

Chapter I

1. Arthur Miller, *Death of a Salesman* (New York: Penguin Books, n.d.), 138–39.

2. Everett C. Hughes, "Work and the Self," in John H. Rohrer and Muzafer Sherif, eds., *Social Psychology at the Crossroads* (New York: Harper, 1951), 313–23.

3. Gregory Baum, *The Priority of Labor* (New York: Paulist Press, 1982), 10.

4. Matthew Fox, *The Reinvention of Work* (San Francisco: Harper San Francisco, 1994), 32–33.

5. Pope John Paul II, "Laborem Exercens," in Gregory Baum, *The Priority of Labor* (New York: Paulist Press, 1982), 104–6, 112.

6. E. F. Schumacher, *Good Work* (New York: Harper Colophon Books, 1979), 3.

7. Baum, *The Priority of Labor*, 15.

8. Karl Marx, "The German Ideology," in Lloyd Eastern and Kurt Guddat, eds. and trans., *Writings of the Younger Marx on Philosophy and Society* (New York: Doubleday, 1967), 409.

9. Schumacher, *Good Work,* 41–42.

10. Pope John Paul II, "Laborem Exercens," 112.

11. Sigmund Freud, *Civilization and Its Discontents*, trans. James Strachey (New York: W. W. Norton, 1962), 48.

12. Ibid.

13. Nathan Hale, "Freud's Reflections on Work and Love," in Neil J. Smelser and Erik A. Erickson, eds., *Themes of Work and Love in Adulthood*

(Cambridge, Mass.: Harvard University Press, 1980), 30.

14. *Work in America: Report of a Special Task Force to the Secretary of Health, Education and Welfare* (Cambridge: MIT Press, 1980), 8.

15. Martin Heidegger, *Being and Time,* trans. John Macquarrie and Edward Robinson (New York: Harper and Row, 1962), 102–86. Also, Martin Heidegger, *The Basic Problems and Phenomenology*, trans. Albert Hofstadter (Bloomington: University of Indiana Press, 1982), 168–71.

16. Erik H. Erikson, "Themes of Adulthood in the Freud-Jung Correspondence," in Neil J. Smelser and Erik H. Erikson, eds., *Themes of Work and Love in Adulthood* (Cambridge: Harvard University Press, 1980). 43–74.

17. Douglas La Bier, *Modern Madness: The Emotional Fallout of Success* (Reading, Mass.: Addison Publications, 1986), 37.

18. Connie Fletcher, *What Cops Know* (New York: Villard Books, 1991), ix.

19. Bernard Lefkowitz, *Breaktime* (New York: Hawthorn Books, 1979), 16–17.

20. Erickson, "Themes of Adulthood in the Freud-Jung Correspondence," 55–58.

21. Robert L. Kahn, *Work and Health* (New York: Wiley, 1981), 11.

22. Leonard Fagin, "Psychiatry (and Work)," in Sandra Wallman, ed., *Social Anthropology of Work* (London: Academic Press, 1979), 31–36.

23. Robert Bly, "Backtalk: Reinventing Iron John," *Mother Jones,* May–June 1993, 5.

24. Fagin, "Psychiatry (and Work)," 31–36.

25. Kahn, *Work and Health,* 11, 12.

26. *Work in America,* 6.

27. Schumacher, *Good Work,* 112–23.

28. Adina Schwartz, "Meaningful Work," in A. R. Gini and T. J. Sullivan, eds., *It Comes with the Territory* (New York: Random House, 1989), 153–63.

29. Robert J. Lifton, *Home from the War* (New York: Simon and Schuster, 1973).

30. Bob Black, *The Abolition of Work* (self-published, 1996), 18.

31. Walter Tubbs, "Karoushi: Stress-death and the Meaning of Work," *Journal of Business Ethics* 12 (1993), 869–77.

Chapter 2

1. Pope Pius XI, "Quadragesimo Anno," in D. M. Byers, ed., *Justice in the Marketplace: A Collection of the Vatican and U.S. Catholic Bishops on Economic*

Policy, 1891–1984, (Washington, D.C.: U.S. Catholic Conference, 1985).

2. Peter Berger, "What Is the Point of Working?" *Time,* May 11, 1981, 93–94.

3. Matthew Fox, *The Reinvention of Work* (San Francisco: Harper, 1994), 5.

4. Terry Sullivan and Al Gini, *Heigh-Ho! Heigh-Ho!* (Chicago: ACTA Publications, 1994), 19.

5. T. J. Sullivan, "What Do We Mean when We Talk about Work?" in A. R. Gini and T. J. Sullivan, eds., *It Comes with the Territory* (New York: Random House, 1989), 115.

6. Ibid., 116.

7. Ibid., 117.

8. Joseph Epstein, "Work and Its Contents," *American Scholar*, summer 1983, 306–7.

9. Mike Royko, "Silver Spoon Fits, Why Not Wear It?" *Chicago Tribune,* November 11, 1985, section 1, 3.

10. Frank Tannenbaum, *A Philosophy of Labor* (New York: Knopf, 1951), 9.

11. Studs Terkel, *Working* (New York: Pantheon Books, 1974), xi.

12. Hannah Arendt, *The Human Condition* (Chicago: University of Chicago Press, 1958), chapter 2, nn. 39 and 81; chapter 3, n. 3.

13. Fox, *The Reinvention of Work*, 6.

14. Witold Rybczynski, *Waiting for the Weekend* (New York: Viking, 1991), 33.

15. Leonard Fagin, "Psychiatry (and Work)," in Sandra Wallman, ed., *Social Anthropology of Work* (London: Academic Press, 1979), 33.

16. *The New Oxford Annotated Bible* (New York: Oxford University Press), Gen. 3:17.

17. Adriand Tilgher, *Homo Faber: Work through the Ages*, trans. Dorothy Canfield Fisher (Chicago: Henry Regnery, 1965), 11–12.

18. *Plutarch's Lives* (New York: Modern Library, 1932), 183.

19. Sar A. Levitan and Wm. B. Johnston, *Work Is Here to Stay, Alas* (Salt Lake City: Olympian Publishing, 1973), 28.

20. Ibid.

21. Tilgher, *Homo Faber,* 49.

22. Michael Cherrington, *The Work Ethic: Working Values and Values that Work* (New York: AMACOM, 1980), 20–33.

23. Michael Argle, *The Social Psychology of Work* (New York: Taplinger Publishing, 1972), 22–23.

24. Cherrington, *The Work Ethic,* 20.

25. Gerhard E. Lewski, *The Religious Factor: A Sociological Study of Religious Impact on Politics, Economics, and Family Life* (New York: Doubleday, 1961), 4–5.

26. Michael Maccoby and Katherine A. Terzi, "What Happened to the Work Ethic?" in W. M. Hoffman and T. J. Wyly, eds., *The Work Ethic in Business* (Cambridge, Mass.: Oelgeschlager, Gunn and Hain, 1981), 22.

27. Cherrington, *The Work Ethic*, 35.

28. Jesse L. Lemisch, ed., *Benjamin Franklin: The Autobiography and Other Writings* (New York: New American Library, 1961), 35.

29. Cherrington, *The Work Ethic*, 35.

30. Daniel T. Rodgers, *The Work Ethic in Industrial America*, 1850–1920 (Chicago: University of Chicago Press, 1978), 14.

31. C. Wright Mills, "The Meaning of Work throughout History," in Fred Best, ed, *The Future of Work* (Inglewood Cliffs, N.J.: Prentice Hall, 1973), 6.

32. Levitan and Johnston, *Work Is Here to Stay, Alas,* 31.

33. Daniel Yankelovich, *New Rules: Searching for Self-Fulfillment in a World Turned Upside Down* (New York: Bantam Books, 1982), 7.

34. Stephen Countz, "On the Edge," *Chicago Tribune Magazine,* Oct. 11, 1992, 13–14.

35. Robert Wright, "Who's Really to Blame?" *Time,* November 6, 1995, 37–38.

36. R. C. Longworth, "The Dream, in Pieces," *Chicago Tribune Magazine*, April 28, 1996, 16.

37. Carol Kleiman, "Serve the Company, Be Loyal to Yourself," *Chicago Tribune,* June 14, 1998, Jobs section, 1.

38. "The New Faces of America: How Immigrants Are Shaping the World's First Multicultural Society," *Time* (special issue), Fall 1993.

39. Jack Barbash, "Which Work Ethic?" in *The Work Ethic—A Critical Analysis* (Madison, Wis.: Industrial Relations Research Association, 1983), 258.

40. Levitan and Johnston, *Work Is Here to Stay, Alas*, 31.

41. Rybczynski, *Waiting for the Weekend*, 226.

42. Herbert G. Gutman, *Work, Culture, and Society* (New York: Vintage Books, 1977), 3–5.

43. Gus Tyler, "The Work Ethic: A Universal View," in *The Work Ethic—A Critical Analysis* (Madison, Wis.: Industrial Relations Research Association, 1983), 197–98.

44. Elmore Leonard, *Split Images* (New York: Avon, 1981), 13.

45. Epstein, "Work and Its Contents," 307.

46. Michael Harrington, "Time to Kill: Automation, Leisure, and Jobs," in A. V. Guthrie, ed. *Psychology in the World Today* (Reading, Mass.: Addison-Wesley, 1968), 312.

47. Sigmund Freud, *Civilization and Its Discontents*, trans. J. Strachey (New York: W. W. Norton, 1961 [1930]), 27.

Chapter 3

1. "Dave Barry: An Interview," *Metropolis*, WBEZ-FM, NPR, Chicago, October 19, 1996.

2. "New Breed of Workers," *U.S. News & World Report*, September 3, 1979, 35.

3. Daniel Bell, *Work and Its Discontents* (Boston: Beacon Street, 1956).

4. Jeremy Rifkin, *The End of Work: The Decline of the Global Labor Force and the Dawn of the Post-Market Era* (New York: Putnam, 1995), 59–61.

5. Ibid., 8.

6. *Work in America: Report of a Special Task Force to the Secretary of Health, Education and Welfare* (Cambridge: MIT Press, 1980), 15–17.

7. *Working Women Count! A Report to the Nation,* U.S. Department of Labor Women's Bureau (1994), 4.

8. "Tony Mazzochi: An Interview," *Terry Gross Show,* WBEZ-FM, NPR, Chicago, July 26, 1995.

9. K. T. Walsh et al., "The New-Collar Class," *U.S. News & World Report,* September 16, 1985.

10. Marc Levinson, "Hey, You're Doing Great," *Newsweek*, January 30, 1995, 42, 42A, 42B.

11. K. T. Walsh et al., "The New-Collar Class," 97.

12. Studs Terkel, *Working* (New York: Pantheon Books, 1974), xxvi.

13. Stanley E. Seashore and J. Thad Barnowe, "Collar Color Doesn't Count," *Psychology Today,* August 1972, 80.

14. One of the most important surveys to directly deny this contention is M. R. Cooper et al., "Changing Employee Values: Deepening Discontent? *Harvard Business Review*, January–February 1979, 117–25.

Chapter 4

1. Michael Maccoby, *Why Work?* (New York: Simon and Schuster, 1988), 51.

2. Abraham H. Maslow, *Eupsychain Management* (Homewood, Ill.: Irwin-Dorsey Press, 1965), 6–13.

3. Lance Morrow, "What Is the Point of Working?" *Time,* May 11, 1981, 93–94.

4. Alex C. Michalos, "Job Satisfaction, Marital Satisfaction and the Quality of Life: A Review and a Preview," in Frank M. Andrews, ed., *Research on the Quality of Life* (Ann Arbor: University of Michigan Institute for Social Research, 1986), 62–63.

5. Ibid., 57–83.

6. John Shack, "Toward a Dynamic-Interactionalist Taxonomy of Work Style," in A. R. Gini and T. J. Sullivan, *It Comes with the Territory* (New York: Random House, 1989), 219–22.

7. Ibid., 228–29.

8. William James, "The Will to Believe," in John J. McDermott, ed., *The Writings of William James* (New York: Random House, 1967 [1897]), 731–35. Also see James, "Faith and the Right to Believe," in the same volume.

9. Daniel Yankelovich, "The Meaning of Work," in Jerome M. Roson, ed., *The Worker and the Job: Coping with Change* (Englewood Cliffs, N.J.: Prentice Hall, 1974), 44–45.

10. "New Breed of Workers," *U.S. News & World Report,* September 3, 1979, 35–36.

11. Carol Kleiman, "Hate Your Job? Welcome to the Club," *Chicago Tribune,* October, 18, 1987, Jobs section, 1.

12. Carol Kleiman, "Workers Only Part of Productivity Woes," *Chicago Tribune,* March 24, 1991, Jobs section, 1.

13. Paul Ray Berndison, *Why Executives Look for New Jobs* (Ithaca, N.Y.: Cornell University Center for Advanced Human Resources Studies, 1992.)

14. "A Special Report about Life on the Job," *Wall Street Journal,* November 29, 1994, 1.

15. Tom Welch, "Job Dissatisfaction Can Kill You" *Career Dimensions,* October 17, 1995.

16. Alan Deutschman, "Men at Work," *GQ,* January 1997, 100–7.

17. E. F. Schumacher, *Good Work* (New York: Harper Colophon Books, 1980), 27.

18. Studs Terkel, *Working* (New York: Pantheon Books, 1974), xxxiv.

19. Karl Marx, "Estranged Labor," in Dirk Struik, ed., *The Economic and Philosophic Manuscripts of 1844,* trans. Martin Milligan (New York: International Publishers, 1964), 110–11.

20. George Strauss, "Workers: Attitudes and Adjustments," in Jerome M. Roson, ed., *The Worker and The Job: Coping with Change* (Englewood Cliffs, N.J.: Prentice Hall, 1974), 86–87.

21. Robert L. Kahn, "The Meaning of Work: Interpretations and Proposals for Measurement," in A. Campbell and Converse, eds., *The Human Meaning of Social Change* (New York: Basic Books, 1972), 49.

22. Strauss, "Workers: Attitudes and Adjustments," 83.

23. Pope John Paul II, "Laborem Exercens," in David M. Byers, ed., *Justice in the Marketplace: A Collection of the Vatican and the U.S. Catholic Bishops in Economic Policy 1891–1984.* (Washington, D.C.: U.S. Catholic Conference, 1985), 305.

24. Schumacher, *Good Work,* 118–19, 129.

25. W. H. Auden, *A Certain World: A Commonplace Book* (Englewood Cliffs, N.J.: Prentice Hall, 1985), 134.

26. Yankelovich, "The Meaning of Work" 35–36.

27. Robert L. Kahn, "The Work Module: A Proposal for the Humanization of Work," in J. O'Toole, ed., *Work and the Quality of Life* (Cambridge: MIT Press, 1989), 4–5.

28. *Work in America: Report of a Special Task Force to the Secretary of Health, Education and Welfare* (Cambridge: MIT Press, 1980), 4–5.

29. Patricia H. Werhane, *Persons, Rights and Corporations* (Englewood Cliffs, N.J.: Prentice Hall, 1985), 134.

30. Norman E. Bowie, "Empowering People as an End to Business," in G. Enderle, B. Almond, and A. Aragandona, eds., *People in Corporations* (The Netherlands: Kluwer Academic Publishers, 1990), 107–8.

31. Ibid., 111.

32. Joanne B. Ciulla, "On the Demand for Meaningful Work," in G. Enderle, B. Almond, and A. Aragandona, eds., *People in Corporations* (The Netherlands: Kluwer Academic Publishers, 1990), 117.

33. Albert Camus, *The Myth of Sisyphus* (New York: Alfred A. Knopf, 1942), 119.

34. Adina Schwartz, "Meaningful Work," *Ethics* 92, 2 (July 1982), 302–3.

35. Arthur Kornhauser, *Mental Health of the Industrial Worker: A Detroit Study* (New York: Wiley, 1964), 252–70.

36. Ibid., 263.

37. F. B. Herzberg, *Work and the Nature of Man* (Cleveland, Ohio: World Publishing Co., 1966). Also F. B. Hertzberg, B. Mausner, and B. Synderman, *The Motivation to Work* (New York: Wiley, 1959).

38. Strauss, "Workers: Attitudes and Adjustments," 86.

39. Robert Kahn, *Work and Health* (New York: Wiley, 1981), 48.

40. C. W. Mills, *White Collar* (New York: Oxford University Press, 1951), 220.

41. Karl Marx, "The German Ideology," in Lloyd Easten and Kurt Guddat, eds. and trans., *Writings of the Young Marx on Philosophy and Society* (New York: Doubleday, 1967), 409.

42. Joseph Epstein, "Work and Its Contents," *American Scholar,* summer 1983, 308.

Chapter 5

1. Theodore Roszak, *Person/Planet* (New York: Doubleday, 1979), 227.

2. Richard McKnight, "Spirituality in the Workplace," in J. D. Adams, ed., *Transforming Work* (Alexandria, Va.: Miles River Press, 1989), 142.

3. Matthew Fox, *The Reinvention of Work* (San Francisco: Harper, 1994), 122.

4. E. F. Schumacher, *Good Work* (New York: Harper Colophon Books, 1980), 3, 119–20.

5. Studs Terkel, *Working* (New York: Pantheon Books, 1974), xiii.

6. Schumacher, *Good Work,* 118.

7. Keith A. Breclaw, "*Homo Faber* Reconsidered: Two Thomastic Reflections on Work," *Thomast* 37, 3 (July 1994), 591.

8. Fox, *The Reinvention of Work,* 34.

9. Adam Smith, *The Wealth of Nations* (New York: Modern Library, 1937 [1776]), 4–5, 7.

10. Ibid., 9.

11. Robert A. Russell, "Retrospective Comment" in L. E. Boone and D. D. Bowen, eds., *The Great Writings in Management and Organizational Behavior* (Tulsa, Okla: Penn Well Books, 1980), 52.

12. Michael Hammer and James Champy, *Reengineering the Corporation* (New York: Harper Business, 1994), 12.

13. Smith, *The Wealth of Nations,* 734–35.

14. Theodore Roszak, *The Voice of the Earth* (New York: Simon and Schuster, 1992), 316–17.

15. Fox, *The Reinvention of Work,* 84.

16. Ibid., 32.

17. Ibid., 23.

18. Nancy Morse and Robert Weiss, "The Function and Meaning of Work," *American Sociological Review* 20 (April 1966), 191–98.

19. Michael Maccoby and Katherine A. Terzi, "What Happened to the Work Ethic?" in Michael Hoffman and T. J. Wyly, eds., *The Work Ethic in Business* (Cambridge, Mass: Oelgeschlager, Gunn and Hain Publishers, 1981), 33.

20. W. B. Lacy, J. L. Bokemeier, and J. M. Shepard, "Job Attribute Preferences and Work Commitment of Men and Women in the United States," *Personnel Psychology* 3 (1983): 315–29.

21. Meaning of Work International Research Team, *The Meaning of Work* (London: Academic Press, 1987), 251–52.

22. Alan Deutschman, "Men at Work," *GQ*, January 1997, 100–7.

23. *Work in America: Report of a Special Task Force to the Secretary of Health, Education and Welfare* (Cambridge: MIT Press, 1980), 15–16.

24. Maccoby and Terzi, "What Happened to the Work Ethic?" 34.

25. Deutschman, "Men at Work."

26. Barbara Ehrenreich, *Fear of Falling: The Inner Life of the Middle Class* (New York: Pantheon Books, 1989), 75–78.

27. Fox, *The Reinvention of Work,* 107.

28. Anastasia Toufesis, "Workers Who Fight Firing with Fire," *Time,* April 25, 1994, 36–38.

29. Andrew Guy, Jr., "Taxi Drivers Don't Fare Well in Danger Tally," *Chicago Tribune,* July 9, 1996, Business section, 1.

30. Toufesis, "Workers Who Fight Firing with Fire," 36.

31. Ibid.

32. Guy, "Taxi Drivers Don't Fare Well in Danger Tally," 1.

33. Marjorie Kelly, "Was 1996 the Year without Employees?" *Business Ethics,* March–April 1997, 5.

34. Fox, *The Reinvention of Work,* 92ff.

35. Ibid., 9.

36. George Gilder, *Wealth and Poverty* (New York: Bantam Books, 1982); George Gilder, *The Spirit of Enterprise* (New York: Simon and Schuster, 1989).

37. Fox, *The Reinvention of Work,* 107.

38. Ibid., 14.

39. Ibid., 50.

40. Ibid., 61–64.

41. Ibid., 244.

42. Terry Sullivan and Al Gini, *Heigh-Ho! Heigh-Ho!* (Chicago: ACTA Publications, 1994), 162.

Chapter 6

1. Juliet B. Schor, *The Overworked American* (New York: Basic Books, 1991), 10.
2. Witold Rybczynski, *Waiting for the Weekend* (New York: Viking, 1991), 52.
3. Schor, *The Overworked American,* 6.
4. Rybczynski, *Waiting for the Weekend,* 215.
5. Schor, *The Overworked American,* 46–47.
6. Ibid., 6–7.
7. Ibid., 43–48.
8. David Ewing, *Freedom inside the Organization* (New York: McGraw-Hill, 1977), 12.
9. Judith Rossner, *Emmeline* (New York: Simon and Schuster, 1980).
10. Upton Sinclair, *The Jungle* (New York: Signet Classics, n.d.[1906]), 109.
11. Schor, *The Overworked American,* 50–51.
12. Ibid., 73.
13. Louis B. Wright et al., *The Democratic Experience* (Chicago, Ill: Scott, Foresman, 1963), 251.
14. Pope Leo XIII, "Rerum Novarum," in David M. Byers, ed., *Justice in the Marketplace: A Collection of the Vatican and the U.S. Catholic Bishops on Economic Policy, 1891–1984* (Washington, D.C.: U.S. Catholic Conference, 1985), 19–20.
15. Ibid., 28. Also see Gregory Baum, *The Priority of Labor* (New York: Paulist Press, 1982), 5.
16. Pope Pius XI, "Quadragesimo Anno," in David M. Byers, ed., *Justice in the Marketplace* (Washington, D.C.: U.S. Catholic Conference), 55.
17. Samuel Eliot Morison, *The Oxford History of the American People* (New York: Oxford University Press, 1965), 770–71.
18. Wright et al., *The Democratic Experience,* 243.
19. Ibid., 244.
20. Daniel J. Boorstin, *The Democratic Experience* (New York: Random House, 1973), 504.
21. Schor, *The Overworked American,* 7.
22. Rybczynski, *Waiting for the Weekend,* 132.
23. Ibid., 142–47.
24. Schor, *The Overworked American,* 61–62.
25. Rybczynski, *Waiting for the Weekend,* 142.
26. Ibid., 143–44.

27. Ibid., 216.

28. Ibid., 144.

29. Ibid., 53.

30. Arlie Russell Hochschild, *The Time Bind* (New York: Metropolitan Books, 1997), 26.

31. Charles Handy, *The Age of Paradox* (Boston: Harvard Business School Press, 1994), 29–30.

32. "Periscope," *Newsweek Magazine,* Sept. 4, 1989, 8.

33. Schor, *The Overworked American,* 30–31.

34. Sunni DeNicola, "Class Time," *College News,* April 1995, 1, 6.

35. Thomas Geoghegan, "The Role of Labor," Baumhart Business Ethics Lectures, Loyola University Chicago, May 4, 1996.

36. "Multiple Jobholders," U.S. Bureau of Labor Statistics, *Employment and Earnings,* January 1996, in *Statistical Abstract of the United States, 1996* (Lantham, Md.: Bernan Press, 1996), 403.

37. *Working Women Count! A Report to the Nation,* U.S. Department of Labor, Women's Bureau (1994), 13.

38. "Workforce Trends," *Spotlight: Journal of Career Planning and Employment,* 16, 11, January 18, 1994, 1.

Chapter 7

1. "Changing Profile of the U.S. Labor Force." *U.S. News & World Report,* September 2, 1985, 46–47.

2. Bradley K. Googins, *Work/Family Conflicts* (New York: Auburn House, 1991), 1, 286.

3. Barbara Ehrenreich, "Strategies of Corporate Women." *New Republic,* January 27, 1987, 28.

4. Carol Kleiman, "On the Job," *Chicago Tribune,* November 1, 1998, Jobs section, 1.

5. Kathryn M. Borman, "Fathers, Mothers, and Child Care in the 1980s," in K. M. Borman et al., eds., *Women in the Workplace: Effects on Families* (Trenton, N.J.: Ablex Publishing, 1984), 73.

6. Stephanie Coontz, *The Way We Never Were: American Families and the Nostalgia Trap* (New York: Basic Books, 1992), 31–41.

7. Ibid., 31.

8. Ibid., 32.

9. Ralph E. Smith, ed., *The Subtle Revolution: Women at Work* (Washington,

D.C.: Urban Institute, 1979), 1.

10. "Are Men Becoming the Second Sex?" *Chicago Tribune,* February 9, 1997, Women's News secton, 6.

11. "Sixth Annual Salary Survey," *Working Woman,* January 5, 1985, 65.

12. *Statistical Abstract of the United States,* 116th ed., no. 626, "Employment Status of Women" (Latham, Md.: Bernan Press, 1996), 400.

13. Borman, "Fathers, Mothers, and Child Care in the 1980s," 73.

14. John Schmeltzer, "Daughters Will Face Many of Mom's Barriers at Work," *Chicago Tribune*, April 28, 1994, Business section, 1.

15. *Statistical Abstract of the United States,* 116th ed., no. 626.

16. Arlie Russell Hochschild, *The Second Shift* (New York: Viking, 1989), 2.

17. Ibid., 93–94; Daniel Evan Weiss, *The Great Divide: How Females and Males Really Differ* (Crofton, Md.: Poseidon Press, 1991), 32.

18. Carol Kleiman, "Women's Voices Poll Speaks of Solutions as Well as Questions," *Chicago Tribune,* November 12, 1996, Business section, 3.

19. John W. Wright, *The American Almanac of Jobs and Salaries* (New York: Avon, 1997), 650–51.

20. *Working Woman,* January 1985, 65.

21. *Working Women Count! A Report to the Nation,* U.S. Department of Labor Women's Bureau, 1994, 13; Lisa Anderson, "Women Escape Affirmative Action Feud," *Chicago Tribune,* May 16, 1995, 1.

22. *Working Women Count,* 10.

23. Coontz, *The Way We Never Were,* 23.

24. Googins, *Work/Family Conflicts,* 95.

25. Ibid., 4.

26. Ibid., 5.

27. Sara Ann Friedman, *Work Matters* (New York: Viking, 1996), xii.

28. Hochschild, *The Second Shift,* 263.

29. Maureen Brendan, Director, Career Center and Placement, Loyola University, Chicago, 1996.

30. Friedman, *Work Matters,* xii.

31. Gloria Emerson, *Some American Men* (New York: Simon and Schuster, 1985), 32.

32. Daniel Yankelovich, "The New Psychological Contracts at Work." *Psychology Today,* May 1978.

33. Roper Starch Worldwide survey, quoted in *Working Woman,* October 1995, 22.

34. Ibid.

35. Coontz, *The Way We Never Were,* 266.

36. David R. Koller, president, Cornerstone Realty Advisors, Inc., Chicago, 1996.

37. Coontz, *The Way We Never Were,* 22.

38. Googins, *Work/Family Conflict,* 22.

39. Coontz, *The Way We Never Were,* 3, 15.

40. Hochschild, *The Second Shift,* 249.

41. Schmeltzer, "Daughters Will Face Many of Mom's Barriers at Work," 2.

42. Judith Rosener, "Coping with Sexual Static," *New York Times Magazine,* December 7, 1986, 89ff.

43. Patricia H. Werhane, "Sexual Static and the Ideal of Professional Objectivity," in A. R. Gini and T. J. Sullivan, eds., *It Comes with the Territory* (New York: Random House, 1989), 170.

44. Rosener, "Coping with Sexual Static."

45. Werhane, "Sexual Static and the Ideal of Professional Objectivity," 173.

46. Ibid., 171.

47. *Working Women Count,* 36.

48. Amanda T. Segal and Wendy Zeller, "Corporate Women," *Business Week,* June 8, 1992, 76.

49. "Breaking Through," *Business Week,* February 17, 1997, 64. Survey by Catalyst, Inc., a New York research firm that focuses on women in business.

50. Barbara Sullivan, "Women Cross 10% Barrier in Presence on Boards," *Chicago Tribune,* Dec. 12, 1996, Business section, 1–2.

51. "The State of the States for Women and Politics" (Washington, D.C.: Center for Policy Alternatives, n.d.), 2–3.

52. Segal and Zeller, "Corporate Women," 74.

53. Mike Dorning, "Poll Details Global Role of Gender Bias," *Chicago Tribune,* March 27, 1996, 1.

54. *Working Women Count,* 20.

55. Carol Kleiman, "Equal Pay for Work of Equal Value: A Gender-Free Gain," *Chicago Tribune,* September 17, 1996, Business section, 3.

56. *Working Women Count,* 13.

57. Ibid., 31–32.

58. Hochschild, *The Second Shift,* 96.

59. Felice N. Schwartz, "Management Women and the New Facts of Life," *Harvard Business Review,* January–February 1989, 65–76.

60. Betsy Morris, "Is Your Family Wrecking Your Career?" *Fortune,* March 17, 1998, 71–72.

61. Ibid., 72.
62. Ibid., 26.
63. Ibid., 3–4, 260.
64. Ibid., 259.
65. Ibid., 12.
66. Arlie Russell Hochschild, *The Time Bind* (New York: Metropolitan Books, 1997), 249.
67. Laura Shapiro, "The Myth of Quality Time," *Newsweek*, May 12, 1997, 64.
68. Arlie Russell Hochschild, "There's No Place Like Work," *New York Times Magazine,* April 20, 1997, 53.
69. Ibid., 53.
70. Ibid., 84.
71. Al Gini, "Work, Time, and Hochschild," *Metropolis,* WBEZ, Chicago, May 21, 1997.
72. Schwartz, "Management Women and the New Facts of Life," 66.
73. Morris, "Is Your Family Wrecking Your Career?" 72.
74. Friedman, *Work Matters,* 231.

Chapter 8

1. Deborah Baldwin, "As Busy as We Wanna Be," *Utne Reader,* 61, January–February 1994, 54.
2. Ibid.
3. Ibid., 56.
4. Ibid., 55.
5. Charles Handy, *The Age of Paradox* (Boston: Harvard Business School Press, 1994), 27–32.
6. Nancy Gibbs, "How America Has Run Out of Time," *Time,* April 24, 1989, 59.
7. Baldwin, "As Busy as We Wanna Be," 52.
8. Juliet B. Schor, *The Overworked American* (New York: Basic Books, 1991), 17.
9. Gibbs, "How America Has Run Out of Time," 58.
10. Baldwin, "As Busy as We Wanna Be," 52.
11. Jerome McDonald, "World View: The Mid-Day Show," WBEZ, Chicago, July 17, 1996.
12. Neil Postman, *Amusing Ourselves to Death* (New York: Viking, 1985).

13. Lance Morrow, "Hooray for Bill Gates . . . I Guess," *Time,* January 13, 1997, 84.

14. Maxine Chernoff, *American Heaven* (Minneapolis: Coffee House Press, 1996), 158.

15. Witold Rybczynski, *City Life* (New York: Scribner, 1995), 173ff.

16. Stephanie Coontz, *The Way We Never Were: American Families and the Nostalgia Trap* (New York: Basic Books, 1992), 265–66.

17. Gibbs, "How America Has Run Out of Time," 60.

18. Coontz, *The Way We Never Were,* 264–65.

19. J. G. Hoppe, MAI, CRE, Real Estate Consultants, Oak Park, Ill., and David R. Koller, MAI, Cornerstone Realty Advisors, Inc., Chicago, Ill.

20. Schor, *The Overworked American*, 80–81.

21. Coontz, *The Way We Never Were,* 261–66.

22. Carol Kleiman, "Will Downsizing's Ultimate Loser Be the Company?" *Chicago Tribune,* July 21, 1996, Jobs section, 1.

23. Gibbs, "How America Has Run Out of Time," 60.

24. William McDonnell, *SRA*, MAI, McDonnell and Associates, Elmhurst, Ill.

25. Coontz, *The Way We Never Were,* 265.

26. Ibid., 29.

27. Ibid., 8ff.

28. Bradley K. Googins, *Work/Family Conflicts* (Westport, Conn.: Auburn House, 1991), 4–5.

29. Ibid., 3.

30. Arlie Russell Hochschild, *The Second Shift* (New York: Viking, 1989), 8.

31. Googins, *Work/Family Conflicts,* 169.

32. J. B. Schor, *The Overworked American,* 21.

33. Ibid., 20–21.

34. Baldwin, "As Busy as We Wanna Be," 53.

Chapter 9

1. Josef Pieper, *Leisure: The Basis of Culture* (New York: Mentor-Omega Books, 1963), 50.

2. Daniel R. Rodgers, *The Work Ethic in Industrial America, 1850–1920* (Chicago: University of Chicago Press, 1978), 7.

3. Nancy Gibbs, "How America Has Run Out of Time," *Time,* April 24, 1989, 58.

4. Diane Fassel, *Working Ourselves to Death* (San Francisco: Harper, 1990), 28–30.

5. Fassel, *Working Ourselves to Death,* 3.

6. Harold I. Kaplan, Benjamin J. Sadock, and Jack A. Grebb, *Synopsis of Psychiatry, 7th Edition* (Baltimore: Williams and Wilkins, 1994), 383–93.

7. Ibid., 796ff.

8. Fassel, *Working Ourselves to Death,* 2–3.

9. Jeffrey K. Salkin, *Being God's Partner: How to Find the Hidden Link between Spirituality and Your Work* (New York: Jewish Lights, 1994), 147.

10. Fassel, *Working Ourselves to Death,* 81, 18.

11. Ibid., 10, 49.

12. Martin C. Helldorfer, *Work Trap* (Mystic, Conn.: Twenty-Third Publications, 1995), 14.

13. Fassel, *Working Ourselves to Death,* 72.

14. Ibid., 4.

15. Ibid., 123.

16. Ibid., 109.

17. Robert Bly, *Iron John* (Reading, Mass.: Addison-Wesley Publishing, 1990), 233–37.

18. Fassel, *Working Ourselves to Death,* 54.

19. Bernard Baumohl, "When Downsizing Becomes Dumbsizing," *Time,* March 15, 1993, 55.

20. Carol Kleiman, "Will Downsizing's Ultimate Loser Be the Company?" *Chicago Tribune,* July 21, 1996, Jobs section, 1.

21. Ralph Nader, *Morning Edition,* National Public Radio, August 15, 1996.

22. Mary Scott, "An Interview with Scott Adams," *Business Ethics,* July–August 1996, 27.

23. Scott Adams, *The Dilbert Principle* (New York: Harper Business, 1996), 53.

24. Arlie Russell Hochschild, *The Time Bind* (New York: Metropolitan Books, 1997), 53.

25. Ibid., 56.

26. Juliet B. Schor, *The Overworked American* (New York: Basic Books, 1991), 69.

27. Marilyn Macholowitz, "Workaholism: What It Is," in A. R. Gini and T. J. Sullivan, eds., *It Comes with the Territory* (New York: Random House, 1989), 261.

28. Hochschild, *The Time Bind,* 56–57.

29. Fassel, *Working Ourselves to Death,* 30–33.

30. Hannah Arendt, *The Human Condition* (New York: Anchor Books, 1959), 10.

31. Ernest Becker, *The Denial of Death* (New York: Free Press, 1973).

32. Connie Lauerman, "The Duress of Success," *Chicago Tribune Magazine,* July 12, 1992, 12, 14.

33. Bob Condor, "Beating the Clock," *Chicago Tribune,* August 28, 1996, Tempo section, 1.

34. Lauerman, "The Duress of Success," 12.

35. Bob Condor, "Life Is a Stress Test," *Chicago Tribune,* November 6, 1996, Tempo section, 1, 9.

36. "Breaking Point," *Newsweek,* November 6, 1995, 56–62.

37. Arlie Russell Hochschild, *The Second Shift* (New York: Viking, 1989), 9.

38. "Breaking Point."

39. Charles R. Figley, "Compassion Fatigue as Secondary Traumatic Stress Disorder," in Charles F. Figley, ed., *Compassion Fatigue* (New York: Brunner Mazel, 1995), 1, 12.

40. Ronald E. Yates, "Japan Facing Its 'Work to Death' Syndrome," *Journal of Business Ethics* 12 (1993), 875.

41. Walter Tubbs, "Karoshi: Stress-Death and the Meaning of Work," *Journal of Business Ethics* 12 (1993), 875.

42. Ibid., 871.

43. Ibid., 870.

44. Jeffrey K. Salkin, *Being God's Partner* (Woodstock, Vt.: Jewish Lights Press, 1994), 155.

45. John Robinson and Geoffry Godbey, *Time for Life: The Surprising Way Americans Use Their Time* (University Park: Pennsylvania State Press, 1997); Richard Wronski, "Time Warped," *Chicago Tribune,* June 15, 1997, Perspective section, 1, 4.

46. Marc Peyser, "Time Bind? What Time Bind?" *Newsweek,* May 12, 1997, 69.

47. Workaholics Anonymous, P.O. Box 289, Menlo, CA 94026-0289.

Chapter 10

1. Terry Sullivan and Al Gini, *Heigh-Ho! Heigh-Ho!* (Chicago: ACTA Publications, 1984, 237), 48.

2. Deborah Baldwin, "As Busy as We Wanna Be," *Utne Reader,* January–February 1994, 51ff.

3. Juliet B. Schor, *The Overworked American* (New York: Basic Books, 1991), 4.

4. Michael Elliot, *The Day before Yesterday: Reconsidering America's Past, Rediscovering the Future* (New York: Simon and Schuster, 1996), 17.

5. Ibid., 21ff.

6. Schor, *The Overworked American,* 2.

7. Daniel Bell, "Work and Its Discontents," in A. R. Gini and T. J. Sullivan, *It Comes with the Territory* (New York: Random House, 1989), 117.

8. Ibid., 126.

9. Mark Sagoff, "The Ethics of Consumption," *Philosophy and Public Policy,* 15, 4 (fall 1995), 2.

10. David A. Crocker, "Consumption and Well-Being," *Philosophy and Public Policy,* 15, 4 (fall 1995), 13.

11. Adam Smith, *The Wealth of Nations* (New York: Modern Library, 1937 [1776]), 625.

12. Gregory Baum, *The Priority of Labor* (New York: Paulist Press, 1982), 5.

13. Erich Fromm, *To Have or To Be?* (New York: Harper and Row, 1976), 19.

14. Ibid., 15–16.

15. Ibid., 26.

16. Tibor Scitovsky, *The Joyless Economy* (New York: Oxford University Press, 1978), 59ff.

17. Herbert Marcuse, *One-Dimensional Man* (Boston: Beacon Press, 1964), 9, 79.

18. Ibid., xii, 56, 158.

19. Ibid., 18.

20. Ibid., ix.

21. W. H. Auden, "The Unknown Citizen" in Edward Mendelson, ed., *W. H. Auden: Selected Poems* (New York: Vintage International, 1989), 85–86.

22. Schor, *The Overworked American,* 107–9.

23. Jon Anderson, "Shop till You Drop," *Chicago Tribune,* July 15, 1994, Tempo section, 1.

24. Schor, *The Overworked American,* 107–8.

25. Amanda Vogt, "It's a Mall, Mall World," *Chicago Tribune,* April 8, 1997, Kids news section, 1.

26. James Coates, "Expectations Ease for Business On-Line," *Chicago Tribune,* July 21, 1997, Business section, 2.

27. Matthew Fox, *The Reinvention of Work* (San Francisco: Harper, 1994), 41.

28. Theodore Roszak, *Person/Planet* (Garden City, N.Y.: Anchor Press, 1979), 229ff.

29. Christopher Lasch, *The Minimal Self: Psychic Survival in Troubled Times* (New York: W.W. Norton, 1984), 27.

30. Peter F. Drucker, *Concept of the Corporation* (New York: John Day, 1946), 179.

31. Thomas H. Naylor, William H. Willmon, and Rolf Osterberg, *The Search for Meaning in the Workplace* (Nashville, Tenn.: Abingdon Press, 1996), 69.

32. Anderson, "Shop till you Drop."

33. Schor, *The Overworked American,* 64, 112ff.

34. Fox, *The Reinvention of Work,* 7–8.

35. Al Gini, *Working Ourselves to Death: A Play of Sorts* (Chicago: Chicago-Works-Production, 1997).

Chapter 11

1. Steven Levy, "Working in Dilbert's World," *Newsweek*, August 12, 1996, 52–57. Also, Mary Scott, "Dilbert's Scott Adams," *Business Ethics,* 10, 4, July–August 1996, 26–29.

2. Scott Adams, *The Dilbert Principle* (New York: Harper Business, 1996), 11–17.

3. Charles Handy, *The Age of Paradox (*Boston: Harvard Business School Press, 1994), 11–27, 158–59.

4. Carol Kleiman, "Morale Dilemma," *Chicago Tribune,* March 10, 1996, Jobs section, 1.

5. *Sources and Consequences of Workplace Pressure: Increasing the Risk of Unethical and Illegal Business Practices* (Bryn Mawr, Pa.: American Society of CLU and ChFC, 1997), 2–6.

6. Maynard M. Dolecheck and Carolyn C. Dolecheck, "Ethics: Take It from the Top," *Business,* January–March 1989, 13.

7. James Patterson and Peter Kim, *The Day America Told the Truth* (New York: Prentice Hall, 1991), 1, 20–22.

8. "Quotable Quotes," *Chicago Tribune Magazine*, January 1, 1996, 17.

9. B. F. Skinner, *Beyond Freedom and Dignity (*New York: Knopf, 1971), 107–8, 150, 214–15.

10. Stephen R. Covey, *The Seven Habits of Highly Effective People* (New York: Fireside, 1990), 42–43.

11. John Dewey, *Theory of the Moral Life* (New York: Holt, Rinehart and Winston, 1960), 3–28.

12. Jean-Paul Sartre, *Existentialism and Human Emotions* (New York: Wisdom Library, n.d.), 23–44.

13. John Rawls, "Justice as Fairness: Political not Metaphysical," *Philosophy and Public Affairs* 14 (1985), 223–51.

14. The academic issue of which system of ethics best answers the question of what we ought to do is a moot point and may in fact be artificial. However, the reality is, whichever way one decides to answer the question, what we ought to do is an endemic requirement of the human condition.

15. Matthew Fox, *The Reinvention of Work* (San Francisco: Harper, 1994), 29–99.

16. Mike Cowklin, "Book Tour," *Chicago Tribune,* February 1, 1995, Tempo section, 2.

17. Norman E. Bowie, "Challenging the Egoistic Paradigm," *Business Ethics Quarterly* (1991), 1–21.

18. R. Edward Freeman, "The Problem of the Two Realms," Loyola University, Chicago, The Center for Ethics, spring 1992.

19. Henry Ford, Sr., quoted in Thomas Donaldson, *Corporations and Morality* (Englewood Cliffs, N.J.: Prentice Hall, 1982), 57.

20. Donaldson, *Corporation and Morality,* 14.

21. Freeman, "The Problem of the Two Realms."

22. General Robert Wood Johnson, quoted in Frederick G. Harmon and Gary Jocobs, "Company Personality: The Heart of the Matter," *Management Review* (October 1985), 74.

23. Georges Enderle, "Some Perspectives of Managerial Ethical Leadership," *Journal of Business Ethics* 6 (1987), 657.

24. Joseph C. Rost, *Leadership for the Twenty-First Century* (Westport, Conn.: Praeger, 1993).

25. Garry Wills, *Certain Trumpets* (New York: Simon and Schuster, 1994), 13.

26. Ibid., 17.

27. E. Hollander, *Leadership Dynamics* (New York: Free Press, 1978), 4–6, 12.

28. In a recent article Joseph Rost made a change in his use of the word *followers:* "I now use the word followers when I write about leadership in the industrial paradigm. I use the word collaborators when I write about leadership in the postindustrial paradigm. This is a change from *Leadership in the Twenty-*

First Century—in which I use the word followers all the time. The reason for the change is the unanimous feedback received from numerous professionals throughout the nation. . . . After trying several alternative words, I settled on the word collaborators because it seemed to have the right denotation and connotative meanings. In other words, collaborators as a concept fits the language and values of the postindustrial paradigm and so its usage should not be a problem to those who want to articulate a new paradigm of leadership." Joseph C. Rost, "Leadership Development in the New Millennium," *Journal of Leadership Studies* (1993), 109–10.

29. James MacGregor Burns, *Leadership* (New York: Harper Torchbooks, 1979), 426.

30. Al Gini, "Moral Leadership: An Overview," *Journal of Business Ethics* 16 (1997), 323–30.

31. James O'Toole, *Leading Change* (San Francisco: Jossey-Bass, 1994). Lynn Sharp-Paine, "Managing for Organizational Integrity," *Harvard Business Review* (March–April 1994), 106–17.

32. Peter M. Senge, *The Fifth Discipline* (New York: Double/Currency Books, 1990), 345–52.

33. Christina Hoff Sommers, "Teaching the Virtues," *Chicago Tribune Magazine*, September 12, 1993, 16.

34. Tom Peters and Bob Waterman, *In Search of Excellence* (New York: Harper and Row, 1982), 245.

35. Burns, *On Leadership*, chaps. 2 and 5.

36. Ibid., xi.

37. William James, *The Will to Believe* (New York: Dover Publications, 1956), 1–31, 184–215.

38. John W. Gardner, *On Leadership* (New York: Free Press, 1990), 8.

39. Gail Sheehy, *Character: America's Search for Leadership* (New York: Bantam Books, 1990), 311.

40. Ibid., 66.

41. Burns, *Leadership*, 36.

42. Ibid., 439.

43. For Senge, the three primary tasks of leadership are leader as designer, leader as steward, and leader as teacher.

44. Senge, *The Fifth Discipline*, 353.

45. Abraham Zaleznik, "The Leadership Gap," *Academy of Management Executive* 4, 1 (1990), 12.

46. Rost, *Leadership for the Twenty-First Century*, 124.

47. Howard S. Schwartz, *Narcissistic Process and Corporate Decay* (New York: New York University Press, 1990).

48. Howard S. Schwartz, "Narcissism Project and Corporate Decay: The Case of General Motors," *Business Ethics Quarterly* 1, 3 (July 1991), 250.

49. Thomas W. Norton, "The Narcissism and Moral Mazes of Corporate Life: A Commentary on the Writings of H. Schwartz and R. Jackall," *Business Ethics Quarterly* 2, 1 (January 1992), 76.

50. Robert Jackall, *Moral Mazes* (New York: Oxford University Press, 1988), 6.

51. Adams, *The Dilbert Principle*, 6–7.

52. Ibid., 51–52.

53. Robert Jackall, "Moral Mazes: Bureaucracy and Managerial Work," *Harvard Business Review* (September–October 1983), 130. Also Jackall, *Moral Mazes,* 202–4.

54. Kathleen McCourt, "College Students in a Changing Society," *Discourse and Leadership: In Service to Others in Jesuit Higher Education* (The Proceedings of Heartland Conference, 1994), 5–22.

55. Michael Novak, *Business as a Calling: Work and the Examined Life* (New York: Free Press, 1996), 10–11.

56. Dolecheck and Dolecheck, "Ethics: Take It from the Top," 14.

Chapter 12

1. William Greider, *One World Ready or Not* (New York: Simon and Schuster, 1997).

2. Michael Hirsh, "The Evils of Markets," *Newsweek,* February 10, 1997, 67.

3. Jeremy Rifkin, *The End of Work* (New York: Putnam, 1995), 5.

4. Ibid., 60.

5. Ibid., 61.

6. Ibid., 61–69.

7. Keith H. Hammonds, Kevin Kelly, and Karen Thurston, "The New World of Work," *Business Week,* October 17, 1994, 80.

8. Ibid., 81.

9. Rifkin, *The End of Work,* 7.

10. Ibid., 235.

11. E. F. Schumacher, *Small Is Beautiful* (New York: Harper Colophon Books, 1973), 95ff.

12. Lewis Mumford, *Technics and Civilization* (New York: Harcourt Brace &

World, 1963), 3–4,10–12, 109.

13. Rifkin, *The End of Work,* 59–60.

14. Ibid., 60.

15. Ibid., 61.

16. Mumford, *Technics and Civilization,* 45, 185ff.

17. Rifkin, *The End of Work,* xi.

18. Ibid., 15.

19. Ibid., 21, 15–16.

20. Ibid., 17.

21. Ibid., 24.

22. Ibid., 29.

23. Ibid., 15.

24. Ibid., 110.

25. Ibid., xii.

26. Ibid., 8.

27. "Jeremy Rifkin: An Interview," *Metropolis,* WBEZ Chicago, July 20, 1996.

28. Rifkin, *The End of Work,* xii–xiii.

29. Ibid., 64–65.

30. Ibid., 35.

31. Ibid., 174–175. Also A. J. Vogel, "A Future without Jobs," *Across the Board: The Conference Board Magazine,* July–August 1995, 43.

32. "Jeremy Rifkin: An Interview," *Metropolis.*

33. Rifkin, *The End of Work,* 5.

34. Edward E. Gordon, Ronald R. Morgan, and Judith A. Ponticell, *Future Work: The Revolution Reshaping American Business* (Westport, Conn.: Praeger Books, 1994), 42.

35. Rifkin, *The End of Work,* 36.

36. Ibid., 3–4.

37. Ibid., 25.

38. Ibid., 11.

39. "All Things Considered," WBEZ, Chicago, September 1, 1997.

40. Matthew Fox, *The Reinvention of Work* (San Francisco: Harper 1994), 2.

41. Rifkin, *The End of Work,* xv.

42. R. C. Longworth, "The World of Work," *Chicago Tribune,* September 4, 1994, Perspective section, 1.

43. Richard J. Barnet and John Cavanagh, *Global Dreams* (New York: Simon and Schuster, 1994), 213.

44. Rifkin, *The End of Work,* xv, 12.

45. Ibid., 88, 131.

46. "All Things Considered," WBEZ, Chicago, July 24, 1997. Also see Stephen Franklin, "Fast Track: Unions Do Slow Burn," *Chicago Tribune,* July 25, 1997, 1.

47. "Downsizing Leaves Survivors Watchful," *Chicago Tribune,* December 16, 1996, Business section, 3.

48. "Bulletin Board: Guru Watch," *Inc.,* February 5, 1995, 11.

49. Rifkin, *The End of Work,* 68.

50. Ibid., 84.

51. Charles Handy, *The Age of Paradox* (Boston: Harvard Business School Press, 1994), 29, 218–19.

52. Brad Edmondson, "Workers with Attitudes," *American Demographics,* April 1995, 2.

53. R. C. Longworth, "The World of Work," 4.

54. Rifkin, *The End of Work,* 134, 166.

55. "All Things Considered," WBEZ, Chicago, June 19, 1996.

56. Rifkin, *The End of Work,* 129–30.

57. Ibid., 148–49.

58. David Young, "Secretary Layoffs: Automation, Cost-Cutting Cited," *Chicago Tribune,* April 29, 1996, Business section, 3.

59. Deborah Baldwin, "As Busy as We Wanna Be," *Utne Reader,* January–February 1994, 55.

60. Rifkin, *The End of Work,* 153.

61. Hammonds, Kelly, and Thurston, "The New World of Work," 80.

62. Rifkin, *The End of Work,* 5–6.

63. "Bulletin Board: Guru Watch," *Inc.*

64. Rifkin, *The End of Work,* 12.

65. Ibid., 236.

66. Ibid., 12.

67. Ibid., 70ff.

68. David Remnick, "Dr. Wilson's Neighborhood," *The New Yorker,* April 29–May 6, 1996, 97.

69. William Julius Wilson, *When Work Disappears: The World of the New Urban Poor* (New York: Knopf, 1996), 52–55, 164.

70. Laura S. Washington, "In Search of a Full-Time Job," *Chicago Tribune,* July 7, 1997, Section I, 13.

71. Jack E. White, "Let Them Eat Birthday Cake," *Time,* September 2, 1996, 45.

72. Wilson, *When Work Disappears*, xiii, 52.

73. Ibid., 72.

74. Ibid., 20.

75. Robert D. Putnam, "Bowling Alone: America's Declining Social Capital," *Journal of Democracy,* January 1995, 65–78.

76. Wilson, *When Work Disappears*, 52–53.

77. Ibid., 75–78.

78. Rifkin, *The End of Work,* 221.

79. "Bulletin Board: Guru Watch," *Inc.*

80. Vogel, "A Future without Jobs," 42–43.

Chapter 13

1. Douglas W. Kmiec, "Overworked in America," *Chicago Tribune,* November 17, 1997, 17.

2. Benjamin Kline Hunnicutt, "The Way We Work," *Chicago Tribune*, May 18, 1997, Books, 1.

3. Richard Todd, "All Work, No Ethic," *Worth,* December–January 1996, 78.

4. *Initiatives: A Publication of the National Center for the Laity,* no. 78, January 1997, 5.

5. Ibid., 5.

6. Robert Wuthnow, *Poor Richard's Principle: Rediscovering the American Dream Through the Moral Dimensions of Work, Business, and Money* (Princeton, N.J.: Princeton University Press, 1996). Also Alan Wolfe, "The Moral Meanings of Work," *The American Prospect,* September–October 1997, 82–83.

7. Studs Terkel, *Working* (New York: Pantheon Books, 1974), 222.

8. Neil Postman, *Amusing Ourselves to Death* (New York: Penguin Books, 1985).

9. John Paul II, *Centesimus Annus* (Boston: St. Paul Books, n.d.), 62.

10. Richard T. DeGeorge, "The Right to Work: Law and Ideology," *Valparaiso University Law Review* 19 (Fall 1984), 15–16.

11. Alan Gerwirth, *The Community of Rights* (Chicago: University of Chicago Press, 1996), 214–29. Also Vincent J. Samar, "Positive Rights and the Problems of Social Justice," *Business Ethics Quarterly* 9, 2, April 1999, 361ff.

12. "The Economy: Human Dimensions: A Statement Issued by the Catholic Bishops of the United States," November 20, 1975, in David M. Byers, ed., *Justice in the Marketplace: A Collection of the Vatican and the U.S. Catholic Bishops on Economic Policy, 1891–1984* (Washington, D.C.: U.S. Catholic Conference, 1985), 470–71.

13. Kmiec, "Overworked in America," 17.

14. Theodore Roszak, *Person/Planet* (Garden City, N.Y.: Anchor Books, 1979), 222ff.

15. Arlie Russell Hochschild, *The Second Shift* (New York: Viking, 1989), 62–63.

16. *Initiatives: A Publication of the National Center for the Laity,* no. 80, March 1997, 5.

17. Matthew Fox, *The Reinvention of Work* (San Francisco: Harper, 1994), 26, 50.

18. Alan Wolfe, "The Moral Meanings of Work," *American Prospect,* September–October 1997, 82.

19. Robert Bellah et al., *Habits of the Heart* (New York: Harper and Row, 1986), 84.

20. Ibid., 56.

21. Ibid., 66.

22. John Raines and Donna C. Day-Lower, *Modern Work and Human Meaning* (Philadelphia: Westminster Press, 1986), 112.

23. Hunnicutt, "The Way We Work," 1, 9.

24. Robert Kanigel, *The One Best Way* (New York: Viking, 1997), 10.

25. Ibid., 8.

26. Ibid., 8.

27. Ibid., 16.

28. Hunnicutt, "The Way We Work," 9.

29. Judy Peres, "Laying Off Older Workers, Legally," *Chicago Tribune,* December 8, 1997, 1, 13.

30. Hunnicutt, "The Way We Work," 9.

31. Eric Pooley, "The Great Escape," *Time*, December 8, 1997, 52–65.

32. Witold Rybzynski, *City Life* (New York: Scribner, 1995), 110ff.

33. Ibid., 225.

34. Ibid., 219ff.

35. Charles Handy, *The Age of Paradox* (Boston: Harvard Business School Press, 1994), 259.

36. Robert Schmuhl, "So Long Civility," *Chicago Tribune,* October 26, 1997, Book section, 4.

37. Frederick Pohl, *Midas World* (New York: TOR Book, 1983), 65.

38. Donald E. Westlake, *The Ax* (New York: Mysterious Press, 1997), 82–83.

39. Larry Thall, "In Making Pictures with a Purpose, Lewis Hine Created Art," *Chicago Tribune,* September 7 and 15, 1989, 53.

40. Jeremy Rifkin, *The End of Work* (New York: Putnam, 1995), 195.

Chapter 14

1. Edmund S. Phelps, *Rewarding Work* (Cambridge, Mass.: Harvard University Press, 1997), 154.

2. Ibid., 138.

3. Ibid., 93, 105, 154.

4 Ibid., 7, 52, 93–113.

5. Ibid., 172, 93.

6. Jeremy Rifkin, *The End of Work* (New York: Putnam, 1995), 229.

7. Ibid., 226.

8. Ibid., 233.

9. Daniel McGinn, "New Legs for a Bug," *Newsweek,* January 12, 1998, 48.

10. Rifkin, *The End of Work,* 232.

11. Ibid., 229.

12. William Julius Wilson, *When Work Disappears* (New York: Knopf, 1996), 153–60.

13. Ibid., 209, 221.

14. "A Special Report: America's 25 Most Influential People," *Time,* June 17, 1996, 57.

15. Wilson, *When Work Disappears,* 229.

16. Steve Johnson, "Post-War Makeover," *Chicago Tribune,* October 22, 1997, Tempo section, 3.

17. Ibid.

18. Wilson, *When Work Disappears,* 225.

19. "A Special Report: America's 25 Most Influential People."

20. Wilson, *When Work Disappears,* 226–29.

21. Rifkin, *The End of Work,* 216.

22. Ibid., 245.

23. Ibid., 244.
24. Ibid., 245.
25. Ibid., 256.
26. Ibid., 249.
27. Jonathan Alter, "Powell's New War," *Newsweek,* April 28, 1997, 30.
28. Rifkin, *The End of Work*, 242.
29. Ibid., 180.
30. Charles Handy, *The Hungry Spirit* (New York: Broadway Books, 1998), 113.
31. David Whitman et al., "The Forgotten Half," *U.S. News & World Report,* June 26, 1989, 45–48.
32. William Raspberry, "School Daze," *Chicago Tribune*, May 12, 1998, 13.
33. Theodore Roszak, *Person/Planet* (Garden City, N.Y.: Anchor Books, 1979), 227.
34. Terry Sullivan and Al Gini, *Heigh-Ho! Heigh-Ho!* (Chicago: ACTA Publications, 1994), 122.

Epilogue

1. Matthew Fox, *The Reinvention of Work* (San Francisco: Harper, 1994), 120.
2. Donald Hall, *Life Work* (Boston: Beacon Press, 1993), 37.
3. Terry Sullivan and Al Gini, *Heigh-Ho! Heigh-Ho!* (Chicago: ACTA Publications, 1994), 2–3.
4. Joseph Conrad, *Heart of Darkness* (New York: Dover Publications, n.d.), 25.
5. Arthur Dobrin, *Spelling God with Two O's* (New York: Columbia Publishing, 1993), 152.

Index

Absenteeism, 56, 68, 132
Achievement, 44
Adams, John, 74
Adams, Scott, 127–28, 151–52, 160, 165, 167–68
Addiction, 51, 123
The Affluent Society (Galbraith), 117
AFL-CIO, 182, 194
African-American workers, 187–90
The Age of Paradox (Handy), 110
Alcoholism, 55
Alger, Horatio, 23
Alienation, 51
Amateur, 19
"American Beauty rose," 81
American Dream, 24, 115–16
  middle-class squeeze, 116–17
  prototypical U.S. family, 118
  two paycheck families and, 117–18
American Institute of Stress, 130
Americans' Use of Time project, 121
Andersen Consulting Company, 185
Anderson, Sherwood, 147
Arendt, Hannah, 17, 129
Aristotle, 19–20, 28, 73, 143, 154, 162
Armstrong, Neil, 113
Asceticism, 22, 141
Attali, Jacques, 173
Auden, W. H., 52, 144
Autobiography (Franklin), 22–23
Auto workers, 50
  mental health of, 55
  production line, 94
The Ax (Westlake), 206

Bacon, Roger, 144
Bad work; *see also* Good work/bad work
  alienation and, 51
  defined, 49–50
Baldwin, James, 43, 164
Barnet, Richard J., 182
Barnowe, J. Thad, 41
Barry, Dave, 33
Baum, Gregory, 2
Becker, Ernest, 130
Being and Time (Heidegger), 145
Bellah, Robert, 199–200
Bell, Daniel, 29, 33–34, 141, 199
Ben-Gurion, David, 31
Benton, Raymond, 223
Berger, Peter, 13
Berry, Wendell, 64
The Bible, 19
"Bionic grinds," 129
Black, Bob, 12
Bleak House (Dickens), 77
Blue-collar blues, 41
Blue-collar workers, 31–42
  class distinctions and, 36
  elite laborers, 40
  income statistics for, 40
  in information age, 34

job satisfaction, 40–41
stereotypes of, 32, 35
Blumenfeld, Samuel, 161
Bly, Robert, 9, 106, 127
Book of Genesis, 19
Boredom, 140
Boutique labor sector, 180–81
Bowie, Norman E., 53–54, 157
"Bowling Alone" (Putnam), 189
Braverman, Harry, 139
Brenner, Belinda, 150
Bridges, William, 184
Brooks, Van Wyck, 139
Buffington, Megan, 99–100
Bureau of Labor Statistics, 85, 92
Burnout, 67, 131
Maslach Burnout Inventory, 131
symptoms of, 131–32
Burns, James MacGregor, 160–61, 163
Bush, Barbara, 94
Bush, George, 217, 220
Business
management lies, 167–68
as patrimonial bureaucracies, 165
Business as a Calling (Novak), 168
Business ethics, 151–55
as communal enterprise, 156–58
leadership and, 151, 154
Business leadership, 159
character and, 162–63
followership and, 159–60
mutual purposes and goals, 163–64
stewardship and, 160–61
teaching, 164
values and ethics, 161–63
Business Week, 98
Butler, Samuel, 6, 8
Byrne, Jane, 99

Calvin, John, 21–22, 28
Camus, Albert, 10, 54, 190
Capitalism, 3, 21, 60
citizen and consumer, 143
Communism's failure and, 111–12, 172
continuous production and consumption, 84–85
culture of consumers and, 141
labor movement and, 82–83
need to work and, 76–77
new vision of work, 71
owners vs. laborers, 35
patriarchy and, 90
predatory capitalism, 83
as secular religion, 172
unfreedom and, 144
worker exploitation and, 77–81
Capra, Frank, 203
Careerists, 99, 128
"Career primary" track, 101
Carlyle, Thomas, 219
Carter administration, 116
Carver, Raymond, 50
Catalyst, Inc., 98
Cathy, 148
Cavanagh, John, 182
CBS News Poll, 153
Center for Policy Alternatives, 92, 99
Centesimus Annus (Pope John Paul II), 197
Champy, James, 62
Character: America's Search for Leadership (Sheehy), 162
Character, 162–63
Cherrington, Michael, 21
Chesterton, C. K., 18
Chicago Haymarket Square bombing, 81–82
Chicago Tribune, 16
Chicago Tribune Magazine, 24
Child care, 101

China, 112
Chronic fatigue syndrome, 131
Churchill, Winston, 2
City Life, 202
Ciulla, Joanne B., 54
Civilization and Its Discontents (Freud), 5
Clerk, etymology of word, 33
Clinton, Bill, 89, 182–83
Commodity fetishism, 143, 148
Community, 60, 164, 200
  individuals and, 71–73
  networking as social capital, 189
Company man, 25
Competition, 200–202
Compulsive behavior, workaholism and, 129
Computer technology, 172–73
  machines as new proletariat, 173
"Conditions of production" (industralization), 4
Conrad, Joseph, 224
Consumerism, 139, 142, 149–50
  culture of hedonism and, 141
  debt and dependency syndrome, 149
  having and being, 143–44
Consumption, 141–43
Coontz, Stephanie, 90, 117
Corporate reengineering, 62
Cozzens, James Gould, 75
Craftsmanship, 34
Cromwell, Oliver, 142
Cultural Pluralism Research Center, University of Chicago, 39
Culture of work, 109

Daley, Richard J., 99
Darwin, Charles, 83
David Copperfield (Dickens), 77
The Day before Yesterday (Elliot), 140
Death of a Salesman (Miller), 1
Debt syndrome, 139, 149
Decision-making, 45, 52–53
The Declining Significance of Race (Wilson), 187
De Gaulle, Charles, 159
Deitz, Park, 68
Delayed stress, 11
Democracy in America (Tocqueville), 142
Deng Xiapong, 112
The Denial of Death (Becker), 130
Department of Labor, 93, 100, 181
  Women's Bureau, 101
Dependency, 123
Depersonalization, 131
Depression, 51, 68, 130
Dershowitz, Alan, 157
Descartes, René, 12
Dewey, John, 155, 223
Dickens, Charles, 23, 77
Dignity of work, 82
Dilbert, 127–28, 151–52
DINKS (Double-Income-No Kids), 93
Disillusionment/disappointment, 67–68
DISKS (Double Income Some Kids), 93
A Distant Mirror (Tuchman), 27
Diversion, 19
Division of labor, 60–61, 117
Divorce, 95–96, 105–6
Dobrin, Arthur, 224
Downsizing, 10, 25, 70, 127–28, 183
Drucker, Peter, 148, 186
Drug addiction, 55
Dual-career/income families, 104–5
Durant, Will, 109

Eckhart, Meister, 60
Edison, Thomas, 109

"The Education of Youth" (Smith), 62
Edwards, Jonathan, 28, 81, 142
Ego boundaries, 8
Ehrenreich, Barbara, 68, 90, 134
Einstein, Albert, 193
Eisenhower, Dwight D., 214–15
Elite laborers, 40
Elliot, Michael, 140
Emerson, Gloria, 94, 106
Emmeline (Rossner), 78
Emotional exhaustion, 131
Employee rights, 78
Empowerment, 59
Empowerment Zones, 216
Enderle, George, 159
The End of Ideology (Bell), 199
The End of Work (Rifkin), 172, 191
Enfranchisement, 59
ENIAC computer, 179
Epstein-Barr syndrome, 131
Epstein, Joseph, 10, 16, 29, 57
Equal Pay Act, 100
Eros and Civilization (Marcuse), 191
Esquire magazine, 91
Ethics, and values, 75, 161; *see also* Business ethics
Ethics of sequential loyalty, 26
Etzioni, Amitai, 73
European Common Market, 112, 181
Ewing, David, 78
Exhaustion, 67, 131

Factory system, 3
Fagin, Leonard, 9–10, 18
Fair Labor Standards Act, 80, 85
Families and Work Institute, 86
Family, work and, 89–90
Fassel, Diane, 122–27, 129
Fast-track careerists, 128
Fatigue, 121, 131, 135
Fatigue disease, *karoshi*, 132
Faulkner, William, 13
Fear of Falling (Ehrenreich), 68
Federal Express, 68
"Female" jobs, 90
Feminism, 94, 99
The Fifth Discipline (Senge), 160
Figley, Charles R., 131
Fletcher, Connie, 6
Flextime, 45, 101
Followership, 159–60
Ford, Henry, 84, 112, 158, 201
Ford Motor Company, 84
Ford, Tennessee Ernie, 32
Fortune, 102
Fox, Matthew, 14, 18, 59, 71–72, 74, 147, 157, 181, 199
Franklin, Benjamin, 22–23, 28–29
Frankl, Victor, 73
Fraser, Douglas, 25
Fredkin, Edward, 172
Freedom, 200
Freeman, R. Edward, 157–58
Freud, Sigmund, 5, 30, 89
Friedan, Betty, 94
Fromm, Erich, 143, 148
Frugality, 22
Früm, Carlos M., 171
Fund for the Feminist Majority, 99
Future Shock (Toffler and Toffler), 113

Galbraith, John Kenneth, 117
Gallop poll, 100
Gardner, John, 162, 221
Gender roles, 127
General Motors, 184–85
The General Theory of Employment, Interest and Money (Keynes), 177
Generation X, 24
Geoghegan, Thomas, 86
"The German Ideology" (Marx), 4
Gerwirth, Alan, 198

GI Bill, 214–15
Gilbreth, Frank, 62
Gilbreth, Lillian, 62
Gilder, George, 71, 72
Gingrich, Newt, 194
Giving-getting compact, 24
Glasbergen, Randy, 121
Glass ceiling, 97–100
Glass floor, 98
Global Dreams (Barnet and Cavanagh), 182
Global economy, 111–13
Goal setting, 45
Godbey, Geoffrey, 135
Gompers, Samuel, 35, 194
Good-old-boy network, 107
Good work; *see also* Job satisfaction
  defined, 56
  as ennobling, 52
  as fun, 129
  as "humanistic work," 53
  meaningful work, 52–55, 60
  vision and, 59–74
  well-balanced personality and, 57
  workers health and, 55
  workers' needs and, 59–60
  as your perk, 127
Good work/bad work, 12, 43–57, 74
  attitudes towards, 65–66
  job satisfaction and, 48–49
  Newtonian operational model, 63–64, 71
Googins, Bradley, 118
Gorbachev, Mikhail, 111–12
Gordon, Edward, 180
GQ magazine, 49, 65–66
Great Depression, 85, 110
Great Expectations (Jones), 25
Greider, William, 172
Guisewite, Cathy, 148
Gurney, Kathleen, 149
Gutman, Herbert, 28
Hall, Donald, 223
Hamilton, Alexander, 28–29
Hammer, Michael, 62, 185, 213
Hamper, Ben, 50
Handy, Charles, 86, 110, 152, 184, 204, 218
Happiness and satisfaction, 16, 45
Hard Times (Dickens), 77
Harrington, Michael, 29
Harvard Business Review, 140
Harvard University, 179, 186
  Technology, Public Policy and Human Development Program, 43
Hauptmann, Gerhart, 23
Havel, Vaclav, 149
Heidegger, Martin, 5, 145
Heilbroner, Robert L., 175, 178–79
Helldorfer, Martin, 124
Herzberg, Fredrick, 55
Hewlett Packard, 164
Hierarchial gap, 41
Hine, Lewis Wickes, 206
Hobbes, Thomas, 71
Hochschild, Arlie Russell, 86, 94, 103–5, 128, 131
Holmes-Rahe List of Stress-Rated Life Issues and Events, 132–34
Homo faber, man the doer, 60
Hughes, Everett C., 2
"Humanistic work," 53
The Hungry Spirit (Handy), 218
Hunnicutt, Benjamin K., 109, 193, 200
Hygienic measures, 56

Identity
  careers and, 5
  occupations and, 8–9, 12
Idleness, 18
Immigrants, work ethic, 23, 26–27
Individual, as worker, 4
Industrial revolution, 34, 76, 173

economy of scale, 142
Industrial sabotage, 68
Information age, 34, 113–14, 202, 209
human capital and, 205–7
job displacement and, 191
move to rural communities, 202
In Search of Excellence (Peters and Waterman), 54
International Association of Machinists, 178
International Labor Organization, 100
International Metalworkers Federation, 178
International Survey Research Corporation, 183
Interstate Child Labor Act, 80
Invisible hand of the marketplace, 71

Jackall, Robert, 165–66, 168
Jackson, Jesse, 193, 220
Jacques, Elliot, 10
James, William, 7, 47, 162
Job enrichment, 45
Job fit, 46, 52
Joblessness, 213
self-efficacy, 190
Job loss, self-esteem and, 10
Job performance, 68
Job prestige, 47
Job requirements, workaholism as, 128–29
Job satisfaction, 40–41, 55–56, 66–67
burnout and, 67
as career goal, 49
disillusionment/disappointment and, 67–68
exhaustion and, 67
factors for, 46–47
hygienic measures, 56
job fit and, 46–47
self-esteem and, 43–44
Job Shift: How to Prosper in a Workplace without Jobs (Bridges), 184
Jobwork, 18
Johnson, Robert Wood, 158
Johnson, Samuel, 18
Jones, Landon, 25
Journal of Business Ethics, 45
The Joyless Economy (Scitovsky), 143
Jung, Carl, 46
The Jungle (Sinclair), 79–80
Just-in-time workforce, 184

Kahn, Robert, 8, 52, 56
Kanigel, Robert, 200–1
Kanter, Donald L., 48
Karoshi (Japanese sudden death from overwork), 132
Kaus, Mickey, 214
Kazan, Elia, 5
Kearns, David, 220
Keillor, Garrison, 70, 147, 203
Kerr, Clark, 29
Keynes, John Maynard, 177
Kinney, Joseph, 69
Kleiman, Carol, 90
Knowledge workers, 34, 114–15, 179–82
job displacement and, 185, 212
Kornhauser, Arthur, 55

LaBier, Douglas, 2, 5
Labor, self-making and, 2
"Laborem Exercens" (On human work) (Pope John Paul II), 4
Labor movement, European Catholic labor movement and, 82
Laissez-faire dogma, 72, 83
Lasch, Christopher, 148

Leadership, 169
Leisure, 18–19, 134, 143, 194
crisis of, 140
decline of, 75
Leisure scare, 140
Leonard, Elmore, 29
Leontief, Wassail, 186
Lerner, Michael, 73
Lewis, John, 35
Life magazine, 50
Lifestyle occupations, 35
Lifton, Robert J., 11
Lindbergh, Charles, 113
Lombardi, Vince, 134
Los Angeles Times, 193
Loyalty, 165–66
Loyola University, Institute of Human Resources and Industrial Relations, 86
Luddites, 182
Ludd, Ned, 182, 191
Lundin, William, 152
Luther, Martin, 21, 23

Maccoby, Michael, 43
McCourt, Kathleen, 168
McCready, William, 39
Malls, as main street, 146–47
Manichaeanism, 141–42
Marcuse, Herbert, 144, 191
Marx, Karl, 3–4, 51, 57, 74, 143, 147, 148, 176–76
Masculinity, work and, 9
Maslach Burnout Inventory, 131
Maslow, Abraham, 43–44
Mass production, 142
Masuda, Yoneji, 179
Materialism, 142
May, Rollo, 10
Mazzochi, Tony, 35–36, 38
Mead, Margaret, 216
Meaningful work, 52–55, 199, 204
motivation and, 55–56
workers health and, 55
The Meaning of Work, 65
Means of production, technology innovation and, 187
"Men's movement," 9
Mental Health of the Industrial Worker (Kornhauser), 55
Mentoring, 154
Metaphysical angst, workaholism and, 129–30
Michalos, Alex C., 45
Midas World (Pohl), 205
Middle class
income statistics and, 38
traditional definition of, 39
Middle-class squeeze, 116–17
Miller, Arthur, 1
Miller, Sheldon, 131
Mills, C. Wright, 23
Milton, John, 19
Mirvis, Philip, 48
"Mitchum Report on Stress in the 1990s," 130
Mode of production, 63
"Mommy track," 102
Morale, 56
Moral leadership, 151–54
Moral legalism, 158
Moral life cycle, 115
Moral Mazes (Jackall), 165
Moral person, 154
Morgan, Ronald, 180
Morison, Samuel Eliot, 83
Morris, Betsy, 102, 106
Morrow, Lance, 115
Morse, Nancy, 64
Motivation, extrinsic and intrinsic factors for, 55–56
Multinational corporations, 112

Mumford, Lewis, 174–75
Murder 9 to 5 (Deitz), 68
The Myth of Sisyphus (Camus), 54

Nader, Ralph, 127
Narcissistic Process and Corporate Decay (Schwartz), 164
Nash, Ogden, 14
National Defense Highway Act, 214–15
National Institute for Occupational Safety and Health, 69–70
National Safe Workplace Institute, 70
Navistar International, 184
Neff, Jane, 99–100
"New-collar class," 36–37
New Deal, 85, 198
The New Republic, 214
New Rules: Searching for Self-Fulfillment in a World Turned Upside Down, 24
Newsweek, 38, 86, 131
Newtonian model, 64, 71
Newton, Isaac, 63
New York Times, 153
Nichomachean Ethics (Aristotle), 154
Nixon, Richard, 162
Nobility of work, 28
North American Free Trade Agreement, 183
Northwestern National Life Insurance, 69
Norton, Thomas W., 165
Novak, Michael, 168–69
Nussbaum, Karen, 96

Occupation, 18
Oil, Chemical and Atomic Workers Union, 35
Oliver Twist (Dickens), 77
Olson, Ken, 173
Olsten Corporation, 185
"On the Condition of the Working Class" (Pope Leo XIII), 82
The One Best Way (Kanigel), 201
One-Dimensional Man (Marcuse), 144
One World Ready or Not (Greider), 172
"On Human Work" (John Paul II), 52
Organizational totalitarianism, 165
Oswald, Lee Harvey, 113
O'Toole, James, 160
Our Town (Wilder), 203
The Overspent American (Schor), 139

Palmeri, Josephine Sally, 89
Patriarchy, 90
Patterning, 154
Penn State University, 86, 121, 135
Penn, William, 22
Perestroika, 111
Personal career satisfaction, 49
Personal development, 45
Personality development, 2
Personality typology, 46
Personal pleasure, work and, 15–16
Peter Principle, 151–52
Peters, Thomas, 54, 161
"Ph.D. syndrome," 7
Phelps, Edmund S., 209–11, 218
A Philosophy of Labor (Tannenbaum), 16
Piëch, Ferdinand, 212
Pink-collar workers, 31
Plutarch, 20
Pohl, Frederick, 205
The Politics of Meaning (Lerner), 73
Ponticell, Judith, 180
Poor Richard's Principle (Wuthnow), 195
Pope John Paul II, 4, 74, 197–99
Pope Leo XIII, 82

Pope Pius XI, 13
Porsche, Ferdinand, 84
Postindustrial society, 33
Postman, Neil, 114, 196, 201
Post-stress syndrome, 11
Powell, Colin, 217
Power, 107
Powershift (Toffler and Toffler), 113
A Prairie Home Companion (Keillor), 203
Predatory capitalism, 83
Prentice Hall, 153
Primitive societies, work and, 16
Product-driven economy, 34
Product idolatry, 143, 148
Professional occupations, 35
Profit, 53
The Protestant Ethic and the Spirit of Capitalism (Weber), 21
Protestantism, 21–23
Protestant work ethic, 23–24, 122, 126–27, 141
  changing attitude towards, 22–26, 29
  as management tool, 28–29
Pure Food and Drug Bill, 80
Puritan ethic, 22–23
Putnam, Robert D., 189

Quakers, 22

Radical individualism, 200
Rank, Otto, 68, 223
Raspberry, William, 220
Rawls, John, 156
Rayman, Paula, 115
Reduced personal accomplishment, 131
Reengineering, 10
Re-engineering the Corporation (Hammer), 185
Reformation, 20–22
Reich, Robert, 26, 115, 180, 218
The Reinvention of Work (Fox), 14
Reluctant workaholics, 127
Republic (Socrates), 160
Rewarding Work (Phelps), 209
Rifkin, Jeremy, 34–35, 111, 172–80, 182–84, 186–87, 190–91, 193, 201–2, 204–5, 207, 209, 212–13, 216–18
Right-sizing, 25
Right to work, 197–98
"Rinso-blue" workers, 36
Ripkin, Cal, Jr., 193
Rivethead (Hamper), 50
Robinson, John P., 121, 135
Rockefeller, John D., 81
Rodgers, Daniel, 23, 121
Role conflict, 45
Role modeling, 127, 154–55
Roosevelt, Franklin D., 161, 177, 198, 214
Roosevelt, Theodore, 218
Roper Organization, 25
Rosch, Paul J., 130
Rosener, Judy, 96–97
"Rosie the Riveter," 90–91
Rossner, Judith, 78
Rost, Joseph C., 159, 164
Roszak, Theodore, 64, 148, 199, 221
Rousch, J. Dwayne, 195
Routine jobs, 51–52
Royko, Mike, 16
Ruby, Jack, 113
Rural migration, 202–3
Russell, Bertrand, 14, 28
Russell, Robert A., 61
Rybczynski, Witold, 18, 202–3

Sahlins, Marshall, 76
St. Augustine, 141, 159

St. Francis of Assisi, 142
St. Thomas Aquinas, 12, 20, 28
Salary gap, 70
Sanative device, workaholism as, 129
Sartre, Jean-Paul, 155
Satisfaction, work and, 16
Saturday Evening Post, 140
Savory, Thomas, 174
Say, Jean Baptiste, 176
Say's Law, 177–78
Schlesinger, Arthur, Jr., 140
Schor, Juliet, 29, 75–76, 83, 86, 116, 119, 139, 141, 145–47, 149
Schumacher, E. F., 3, 11, 49, 51–52, 59–60, 62, 174
Schwartz, Adina, 11, 55
Schwartz, Felice, 101–2
Schwartz, Howard S., 68, 164–66
Schweitzer, Albert, 48
Scientific management, 61, 200
  basic ideas of, 61
  time-and-motion studies, 62
Scientific Management (Taylor), 61
Scitovsky, Tibor, 143
Sears, 185
Seashore, Stanley, 41
The Second Shift (Hochschild), 103
Sekaran, Uma, 93
Self-actualization, 44
Self-creation in work, 2
Self-definition, 195
Self-efficacy, joblessness and, 190
Self-esteem
  achievement and, 44
  job satisfaction and, 43–44
  workaholism and, 129
Self-identity, 2–5
  work and, 8–10
Self-image, money and, 149
Self-indulgence, 142
Self-realization, forms of work and, 59
Self-worth, 44
  business and overworked as, 110
Senge, Peter, 160, 164
Sequential loyalty, 26
Sexual harassment, 97
"Sexual static," 96–97
Shack, John, 46, 48
Sharp-Paine, Lynn, 160
Sheehy, Gail, 162–63
Shopping; *see also* Consumerism
  as cultural activity, 146–47
  as new opiate/religion, 147–48
Sinclair, Upton, 79–80
"Sixteen Tons" (Ford), 32
Skinner, B. F., 154–55
Smith, Adam, 60, 62–63, 71, 142
Smith, John F., Jr., 184
Social capital, community networking and, 189
Socialism, 79–80, 82
Social justice, 83
Social malaise, 68
Social morality, 82
Social organization, 189
Social Readjustment Rating Scale, 133–34
Social status, 31, 47; *see also* Underclass
  blue- and white-collar workers, 33
Socrates, 48, 141, 160
Sontoku, 134
Sorel, George, 27
Spencer, Herbert, 83
Spillar, Katherine, 99
Standard of living, 115–16
Stanek, John R., 183
Statistical Abstract of the United States, 86
Steinem, Gloria, 94
Stewardship, 71, 160–61
"Stockholm effect," 195

Strauss, George, 51–52
Strauss, Robert, 29
Streisand, Barbra, 107
Stress, 121–37; *see also* Burnout
  karoshi (sudden death from overwork), 132
  Social Readjustment Rating Scale, 133–34
  workaholism and, 130
Substance abuse, 68
Sullivan, Terry, 14–15, 223
Sweeney, John, 194
Synopsis of Psychiatry, 123

Tannenbaum, Frank, 16
Tardiness, 132
Taylor, Frederick Winslow, 61–63, 94, 200–1
Technology innovations, 205–6
  job displacement and, 172–78, 183–85
  workplace changes and, 175–81
Telecommunications technology, 113–14
Terkel, Studs, 12, 17, 41, 59, 195–96
Textile industry, 78
Theory of Social Darwinism, 83
Third industrial revolution, 173, 175
The Third Wave (Toffler and Toffler), 113
Thoreau, Henry David, 139
Thucydides, 151
Thurber, James, 105
Time, 115, 202
Time; *see also* Leisure
  crisis factors, 111
  pace of life and, 109–10
  poverty of time, 111
Time-and-motion studies, 62, 201
The Time Bind (Hochschild), 104–5
Time for Life: The Surprising Ways Americans Use Their Time (Robinson and Godby), 135
Tocqueville, Alexis de, 142, 216–17
Todd, Richard, 193
Toffler, Alvin, 113
Toffler, Heidi, 113
To Renew America (Gingrich), 194
Tradesmen, 37
Triangle Shirtwaist Factory fire, 77
Trickle-down economics, 72, 175–76
The Truly Disadvantaged (Wilson), 187
Truman, Harry S., 214
Tubbs, Walter, 12, 132, 134
Tuchman, Barbara, 27
Turnover rates, 45
Two-income families, 95, 117–18
Tyler, Gus, 29

Underclass, 186, 205
  culture of poverty, 188
  segregated neighborhoods, 189
  as social threat, 210
Unemployment, 181
  invisible unemployed, 188
  mental and emotional crisis, 10
  structural-technology unemployment, 190, 210
Union movement, 81
  Chicago Haymarket Square bombing, 81–82
  Ford's reforms, 94–95
United Auto Workers, 25
United Nations' Declaration of Human Rights, 198
United Nations Human Development Study, 184
U.S. Census Bureau, 36, 92
  household income statistics, 38
U.S. Department of Labor, Women's Bureau, 96
U.S. News & World Report, 33

United States Steel, 184
University of Michigan, 48, 66
  Survey Research Center, 64–65
"The Unknown Citizen" (Auden), 144–45

Virtual corporation, 183
Virtual workforce, 183
Vogel, A. J., 191
Volkeswagen, 84, 212
Voltaire, 14

Wage subsidies, 210–11
Waiting for the Weekend (Rybczynski), 18
Walesa, Lech, 111
Wallace, Chris, 193
Wall Street Journal, 130, 153, 181
Watergate affair, 162–63
Waterman, Robert, 54, 161
Watson, Tom, 173
Watt, James, 174
The Wealth of Nations (Smith), 60, 62
The Weavers (Hauptmann), 23
Weber, Max, 21–22, 29
Weiner, Norbert, 184
Weiss, Robert, 64
Welch, Tom, 48–49
Welfare, 210
Wellington, Sheila, 98
Weltanschauung (world view), 11
Werhane, Patricia, 53, 96–97
Westlake, Donald F., 206
What Cops Know (Fletcher), 6
When Work Disappears: The World of the New Urban Poor (Wilson), 186–87
White-collar workers, 31–42
  computer revolution and, 185
  hierarchical gap, 41
  human services and knowledge work, 34
  income statistics for, 40
  in information age, 34
  job satisfaction, 40–41
  in postindustrial society, 33
  stereotypes of, 35
"White flight," 202
Whitehead, Ralph, 36–37
Wilder, Thorton, 203
Willis, Garry, 159–60
The Will to Believe (James), 47
Wilson Learning Corporation, 70
Wilson, William Julius, 186–90, 204, 210, 213–15, 218
Winpisinger, William, 178
"Witness of others," 164, 166, 168
Wolfe, Alan, 115
Women in Film Hall of Fame, 107
Women's suffrage movement, 99
Women's Voice Project, 92
Women in workforce, 31–32, 89–107, 118–19
  as bosses, 100
  careerists, 99–100
  "career primary" track, 101
  children as impediments to advancement, 101
  "cultural permission" for, 90–92, 95
  family life and, 95
  glass ceiling and, 97–100
  incomes of, 95
  job satisfaction, 46
  justice at home, 103–7
  justice on the job, 96–102
  as menace, 91
  "mommy track," 102
  salaries of, 100–1
  self-definition and work, 94
  sexual harassment, 97
  "sexual static," 96–97
  as "stalled revolution," 104
  stereotype of, 90
  "women's" jobs, 93

work as form of "home," 104–6
Work
as center of our lives, 2
compulsion and desire and, 14–16
defined, 13–30, 224
as downtime, 50
as drudgery, 70–71
end of, 171–91
etymologies of the word, 17–19
failure of, 193–96, 204
family and, 89–90
as form of "home" and "neighborhood," 104–5
future of, 209–21
long-term options, 213–18
philosophical options, 218–21
short-term options, 209–13
government's neo-WPA program, 214–15
history of, 75–79
impact on psyche and character, 3–6
industrial revolutions, 34
inner life and development, 2
lack of vision, 59–74
as law of life, 16
moral life and, 23
as necessity of nature, 20, 197–99
negative necessity of, 17–19
as nondiscretionary activity, 13
organization and rewards of, 200–1
psychopathology of, 10
regularity of life and, 5
right to work as human right, 197–98
self-definition and assessment by, 43
as self-portrait, 1–12
social purpose of, 168–69
standard of living and, 115–16
as status symbol, 135
as "Stockholm effect," 195
as structuring activity, 195–96
as university of life, 11, 52
women and, 89–107
workforce evolution, 31–34
Workaholics Anonymous, 121, 137
Workaholism, 121–22
as addiction, 123–24
as enslaving, 123–24
rewards of, 125–26
self test, 136–36
types of work addiction, 126
command and control, 129
fast-track careerists, 128
job as perk, 127
job requirements, 128–29
low self-esteem, 129
metaphysical angst, 129–30
Protestant work ethic, 126–27
role models, 127
sanative device, 129
work as fun, 129
Work in America (HEW), 53, 65
Work day
forty-hour week, 83
Great Depression and, 85
history of, 75–77
length of, 193
post-World War II, 85–87
Work enrichment, as career goal, 49
Worker apathy, 52
Workers; *see also* Blue collar workers; White collar workers
division of labor and, 60–61, 63
labor exploitation of, 77–80
"new-collar class," 36–37
Workers health, meaningful work and, 55
Workers' needs, 59
Work ethic, 193–94; *see also* Protestant work ethic
beliefs of, 21–22
changing attitude towards, 24–26
myth vs. reality, 27–28

origin of, 20–21
post-WWII culture, 24
secularization by Franklin, 22
The Work Ethic in Industrial America (1850–1920) (Rodgers), 121
Work fixation, 124
Work and Health (Kahn), 8
Working class
blue- and white-collar workers, 35–38
money factors, 37–38
Working Ourselves to Death (Fassel), 122
Working (Terkel), 17
"Working Women Count," 86, 93, 98, 100–1
Workplace violence, 51, 68–70
"Work and the Self" (Hughes), 2
Works Progress Administration, 214
Work stress, 55
World Health Organization (WHO), 122
Worth, 193
Wright, John W., 92
Wuthnow, Robert, 195

Yankelovich, Daniel, 24, 29, 48, 52, 94
Yuppie's Disease, 131

Zeleznick, Abraham, 164